# My Real-Life Rom ♡ Com

# My Real-Life Rom♡Com

## HOW TO BUILD CONFIDENCE
## AND WRITE YOUR OWN RELATIONSHIP RULES

# CARRIE BERK

Post Hill
PRESS

A POST HILL PRESS BOOK
ISBN: 979-8-88845-052-9
ISBN (eBook): 979-8-88845-053-6

My Real-Life Rom-Com:
How to Build Confidence and Write Your Own Relationship Rules
© 2023 by Carrie Berk
All Rights Reserved

Cover design by Daniela Hritcu
Cover photo by Nigel Barker

Post Hill Press
New York • Nashville
posthillpress.com

Published in the United States of America
1  2  3  4  5  6  7  8  9  10

*To Mom. You are my everything.*
*Thank you for teaching me everything I know.*

*- Bootsie*

# Table of Contents

# Introduction

I HAD MY FIRST MAKE out when I was four years old. And yes, I made the first move. It went something like this: a 2 p.m. screening of *The Princess and the Frog* and after hours at my apartment, sealed with a smooch from my kindergarten crush.

He tended to be shy, so, of course, I had to initiate the kiss. Earlier that week, I handed a letter to him in school that read, "Can I kees you?" Clearly, spelling did not come naturally to me. The kid's mother found the Post-it hidden in the back of his English folder and later reported the note to my mom. "Carrie gave this to my son in class today," she explained when they were out to lunch, passing the paper across the table. Thankfully, the two of them laughed it off. We were just kids—we didn't even know how to kiss. Surely, nothing would happen. Right?

Wrong. After we saw *The Princess and the Frog*, we went back to my apartment. I shut the door to my room and plopped down on my bed. He sat "crisscross applesauce" at my side. "I'll be the princess, and you can be the frog," I instructed him. "I just have to kiss you, and you'll turn into my prince!" He glanced nervously around the room. We had already established that we were boyfriend and girlfriend and dated as much as two four-year-olds could. We spent several playdates in Central Park and grabbed ice cream together at a local candy shop after school. Kissing seemed like a logical next step to my kindergarten self. When I realized he wasn't keen on making a move, I took it upon myself to lean in and plant one on him. Neither of us knew what we were doing. The kiss was slimy, and he licked my face for lack of better knowledge. But even though it was wet and sloppy, I still maintained that it was special. And it was—you never forget your first kiss.

I've been boy crazy from the second my parents stuck me in elementary school. It's in my blood. I was named after Carrie Bradshaw, the unapologetically bold protagonist played by Sarah Jessica Parker in *Sex and the City*. Carrie writes about her past dating encounters in a sex column, with inspiration and support from her best friends. Whenever she's not shopping for shoes, having brunch with the girls, or going out on dates, she's typing away fearlessly at her window about her amorous adventures.

I had no idea who Carrie was until I was thirteen. All I knew was that my mom adored the character when she worked as a writer on the HBO website—so much so that a Hirschfeld caricature of the four leading ladies is displayed on our dining room wall. By coincidence, I hung out a few times with Sarah Jessica's son when I was twelve. My camp friend went to school with him, and she introduced us. Our friendship started with sharing a Lollipop Passion Goblet at The Sugar Factory, followed by a screening of the latest superhero film. I swam in Sarah Jessica's pool in the Hamptons, bounced around on her trampoline, and chilled until midnight in their cozy townhouse back in the city. She served me banana juice, lent me her sweatpants, and listened patiently as I spoke about my passion for writing. Yet as she walked through her home with wet hair and a robe, I never realized just how much she—or her on-screen character—would inspire me in years to come.

My birth certificate actually reads Caroline—it would have been too humiliating for my mom to name her daughter after the character she wrote about every day. But my nickname has been Carrie from the second I was born—and the shoe fits. Like Carrie Bradshaw, I'm a New York City native who has always been interested in love and relationships. I received my first dose of dating information from my school friend Tara, who introduced me to what she called "the real world" at our Long Island beach club in first grade. Tara took me by the hand and led me to the back of a cabana while my parents rested on lounge chairs outside. "You won't believe what I learned yesterday," she whispered. Tara had a twin brother and an older sister, so her span of knowledge was greater and more mature than mine. "Apparently, we have something called a vagina. And guys have a penis. It's also a wiener or a dick, and sometimes, they have wet dreams!" she dished. My jaw dropped to the floor. Every time I looked in the mirror, I dissected my hair, nails, and clothes. It never occurred to me that something else could be underneath. With no phone to Google my new vocabulary on, I innocently asked my dad. "Dad, do you have wet dreams?" I mumbled. His face turned red, and my mom gasped. "Carrie, where did you hear that from?" she asked. I glanced down at my feet. "Tara," I shrugged. I didn't see anything wrong about inquiring.

Sensing he was uncomfortable, I decided to discuss my new discoveries with another school friend instead. "We should get bras! Tara has one," I dished. Six-year-old Tara had not yet developed breasts, but buying the clothing item made her feel mature. I wanted to do the same. Unfortunately, my eagerness backfired. "Carrie is telling dirty stories," my friend's mom disclosed to mine one day in the school yard. My mom laughed. I was an innocent five-year-old with a passion for ballet and cupcakes. I wasn't being promiscuous. I was just curious, and I didn't know how to keep my mouth shut. She had nothing to worry about.

I didn't receive proper education on what Tara tried to teach me until sex-ed class in sixth grade. We learned about sex organs, sexual health, and the basics of reproduction. One of our assignments was to go to a drug store and buy condoms for the first time. Around the classroom, guys laughed and patted each other on the back while girls planned trips to CVS in large groups. I didn't consider anyone in my class a close enough friend to take along, so I dragged my mom to the store. The condoms happened to be situated directly above an employee behind the counter. I placed a bottle of water and cup of tuna salad in front of him first, then pointed to the top shelf. "Could I also get a box of Trojan condoms?" I asked. His eyes widened in disbelief. "It's for a homework assignment, I promise," I laughed uncomfortably. The world will never know whether he believed me.

All this goes to say, I've come a long way since kindergarten and middle school. Now in college, I've listened to friends, family, and professional resources to take in everything there is to know about love and relationships. Not to mention, I've binge-watched the entire *Sex and the City* series several times. The episodes are a safe space I frequent when I'm feeling lost in love.

Over the years, from FaceTime flirtations to quick hookups to prolonged connections, I've lived and learned a lot. I tend to romanticize my relationships, placing myself inside a rom-com over reality when it comes to love. It comes natural to me as a writer. I see myself as the main character in my story, and each of the boys who grace the pages of my life are featured players. My friend once told me not to go for a guy who's a ten but instead to pursue a seven or an eight. I can't help but set my expectations high—nothing's wrong with chasing the romance you deserve.

However, my tendency to romanticize does have a downside. After spending just a few hours with a guy, I envision what it would be like to date, despite the fact that I really know nothing about him. My eagerness to jump in and ignore potential red flags is not ideal (although without taking risks, I wouldn't have had as many adventures in dating). Reveling in my personal rom-com has left me heartbroken several times as a teenager. Every Google search told me that spending time with friends and family buffers the pain, but that tactic never worked for me. Talking through why I was hurting was not effective. It's impossible to fully depict the depth of my experiences in dialogue—which leads me here to this book.

Writing sometimes seems like the only way to capture what's going on inside my mind and heart. When I first started writing the book, I was in the middle of a mental health battle. Faced with anxiety amid the pandemic, I woke up quivering, shed lots of tears, and remained unproductive for an entire month. I was isolated from the rest of the world—there were no friends nor boys in sight. My parents, puppy, and grandparents were around me, but still, I felt helpless and alone. I wrote my way out.

The idea for *My Real-Life Rom-Com* came to me while I was riding my Peloton, where my creativity and inspiration always thrive. As I pushed cadence against high resistance, I considered how I could adopt a similar means of perseverance and courage off the bike. I have always been a writer, but I resisted writing about myself because I feared judgment. It's scary to put yourself out there. Yet as I watched my output soar on the bike, my attitude suddenly shifted. Writing would give me a sense of control amid chaos and confusion. It would help me synthesize my thoughts and make peace with my past. The pandemic may have placed my life on hold, but I wasn't about to let it put a damper on my memories, especially those related to romance.

These chapters capture my exploration of love over the past few years as well as the important lessons I have learned. You will find that I'm attracted to the unconventional, and I repeatedly wind up in situations where the odds are stacked against me. Think kissing your best friend's ex-boyfriend or having the love of your life dump you through his mother.

I present to you the unfiltered version of me: the teenager behind the children's books, cheesy TikTok voiceovers, and Instagram fashion posts. Behind the screen, I'm just like all of you, navigating the world of dating and trying to find my voice in love as a young adult. Perhaps your guy ghosted you, or your girl relegated the two of you to "situationship" status. Your worries about what could be or could have been end now. It's time to write your own rules for teenage dating.

Each of these chapters is dedicated to a different guy who crossed my life during my tween and teen years. With every dating encounter, I ultimately discovered more about myself and how to navigate the turbulent waters of relationships. I've made a lot of mistakes along the way, but I have no regrets. I hope my words resonate with you—and that you're encouraged to take the reins over your own romantic journey. I had the courage to grasp the pen and detail my intimate stories as if I were writing in my diary. I'm confident that after reading about my experiences, you can find similar self-confidence because you are most certainly not alone.

Dear boys who have done me wrong: thank you. If it weren't for you, I wouldn't be sitting here on my bed in my lucky purple hoodie as I write the introduction to this book. You've given me the platform to pour my heart onto the page and perhaps help others along the way. Here's to the ex who traveled with me across the country, the stranger who kissed me under the starry sky, and the one-timer who spun me around under strobe lights. This is my real-life rom-com—and I wouldn't have it any other way.

*Names in this book have been changed to protect the innocent (and not so innocent).* ♥

# Chapter 1

# The Bar Mitzvah Boy

WHEN I WAS THIRTEEN, I went to twenty-two bar and bat mitzvahs. The traditional rite of passage for a Jewish teen boy or girl featured a painfully long Torah reading, but the main attraction was the party that followed. Every Saturday, I wore a black Bebe bodycon dress, only to change into a duplicate of the look for a similar event on Sunday. There was an unspoken competition among celebrations in New York City. Each boy or girl wanted the best playlist, most elaborate décor, and expensive outfit. Some of the parties I attended even featured celebrity appearances. Consider Nick Jonas serenading the bat mitzvah girl after she entered on an indoor zipline. Or Becky G bopping alongside the DJ. Hundreds of thousands of dollars were spent on creating the perfect night for guests.

I myself contributed to the elaborate mitzvah scene: my family created a "Carriewood" themed celebration for me. The room was decked out in eight-foot, glistening gold Oscar statues, bright lights, and a virtual reality game. Each table was dedicated to one of my favorite films (*Clueless*; *The Devil Wears Prada*; *Bridget Jones's Diary*), and customized movie tickets directed guests to their seats. My video montage featured personalized messages from some of my favorite celebrities: Zendaya, Kris Jenner, Jimmy Fallon, Shay Mitchell, Isaac Mizrahi, and more.

Besides the dancing and décor, attendees brought another element to the table: hookups. Midnight make-out sessions from secluded hallways were characteristic of bar and bat mitzvahs. A celebration was not complete without a couple ducking behind the DJ booth to kiss. Very rarely did these interactions transform into romantic connections. People hooked up because they could, and because it was fun to do something "scandalous" at age thirteen. Not to mention, there was peer pressure to do so.

One instance in particular stands out. I was sitting in the lunchroom in seventh grade when a friend started divulging the details of her weekend. "Anthony and I hooked up this weekend. It was so hot," she dished. Everyone in the surrounding area gasped. "No way! How long did it last?" I asked. Her eyes widened. "Thirty minutes," she revealed. At the time, I only had given a boy a peck, with the exception of a longer kiss in a theater production. The details of her hookup made me feel inexperienced and embarrassed, so I quickly placed pressure on myself to scout out a potential suitor.

Luckily, I came across my very own mitzvah make-out expert. Caleb was a blonde-haired, blue-eyed stud in my grade at school. He was short and skinny, and his clear braces were almost always yellow. Yet his shaggy locks and smooth talk drew me in, as well as several other girls who pursued him. We took selfies together on Webcam Toy during class, and occasionally, our teacher grouped us together for a science lab. We were friendly, but we never hung out beyond the classroom. If he was going to be my first make out, that needed to change—fast.

After some prodding, Caleb offered up his house for the afternoon to hang out. Absolutely terrified, I forced my friend Leah into coming along as the third wheel. The three of us walked over after school, and she frequently sped ahead so that Caleb and I had the chance to flirt. "What are we going to do when we get there?" Caleb asked, inching closer so that his shoulder brushed mine. I glanced around the city streets anxiously. Was he expecting a hookup already? I nervously fiddled with the hem of my Brandy Melville t-shirt. All I wanted was to get to know him in an out-of-school setting so that I'd warm up to his company. I wasn't prepared for anything more just yet. "I guess we could…um…play a game?" I suggested. I had no idea what I proposed, but in the moment, that was the best reply I could come up with. Caleb scoffed. "Sure…a game," he declared with a wink. I could instantly tell that Monopoly wasn't on his mind.

When we arrived at Caleb's apartment, he placed chocolate chip cookies on paper plates. "Here. You can have one of mine," he said, setting down the dessert in front of me. I blushed. It was clear he was making an effort to connect, and I needed to reciprocate. "Wait, I just realized I don't have your number!" I exclaimed, sliding my phone across the dining room table. He quickly inserted himself in my contacts, then stopped to meet my eyes. "I'm going to add myself on Snap too," he said. Leah kicked my foot from under the table. Snapchat is a signature site of teen flirtation. When a guy gives you his Snap username, late-night messages and shirtless selfies are practically guaranteed to follow. I stared at his Bitmoji on the screen, then at his face in front of me: a single cookie crumb resided at the corner of his smile. Instead of telling him to take a napkin, I held my tongue. Speaking up would only demonstrate that my eyes were on his lips (and they were).

After devouring two cookies each, we made our way to Caleb's bedroom. A large mirrored closet was to our left, and I observed the order in which we were arranged. Caleb dangled his feet off the bed while fiddling with the phone in his jean pocket. I sat in the middle staring at the ceiling, and Leah laid on her stomach while scrolling through Instagram. There was an awkward silence. I tuned into the loud vibrations of the air conditioner. "So," Leah said, breaking the tension. I glanced around the room to gain inspiration for conversation. The space was relatively dull: the walls were white, the sheets were gray, and the windows overlooked the back of the apartment building. I couldn't help but compare his room to mine, a lilac purple-painted space packed with picture frames and pageant crowns. My peers tended to embrace a more minimalistic style at that age. Thus, I gazed judgmentally at my pale pink tee while Caleb stared out the window.

"Let's play Truth or Dare," I announced. A 6 p.m. dinner reservation with my family was quickly approaching. It was now or never. Caleb shifted his body so that he faced me. "Okay, Carrie. Truth or dare?" I knew exactly what to choose. "Dare." Caleb scratched his head. "I can't think of anything." Leah quickly searched something on her phone: it was a Truth or Dare app, "dirty party" edition. Caleb rubbed his hands together. "I'm down," he said. I suddenly feared the phone and what it had to say more than I feared Caleb. Yet I hid my concerns for the sake of impressing him. "Me too," I fibbed.

The app had several levels of intensity to select from. "Oh, we have to pick high intensity," Caleb claimed, grabbing Leah's phone to press the "red zone." I took a deep breath and tried to keep my composure. He chose first—naturally, he picked "dare." "Switch clothes with someone else in the room," Caleb read. He raised an eyebrow, then rested a hand on my thigh. My heart skipped a beat as soon as we came in physical contact. "Carrie?" he said. I shook my head. "There's no way I'm getting naked in front of you guys. I'll change in the closet, though," I suggested. Caleb lifted his shirt off in front of me, revealing a striking display of six-pack abs. Leah shot me a look, and I giggled under my breath. He knew exactly what he was doing.

He handed me his shirt, and I took it with me behind the mirrored doors. "I'll be fast," I said. I changed in the cramped closet from my bright tee into his white V-neck. I pushed open the door and did my best model strut over to Caleb, who still sat shirtless on the bed. "Nice!" he exclaimed as he pulled my pink top over his head. Somehow, the color made his blue eyes pop even more. "Cute!" I laughed, although internally, I cringed at my subtle attempt to flirt.

All three of us were uncomfortable with the rest of the Truth or Dare questions. One "truth" asked us to tell the story of our "first time," while another dare encouraged a player to give someone in the room a spanking. Snacks were a better option. Caleb packed two cookies in plastic bags for Leah and me to take home. On our way to the living room, he touched my shoulder to stop me. I glanced down at his fingertips. "I'll snap you," he said. I found myself grinning from ear to ear. Following our brief flirtation that afternoon, I had full faith that he would.

As soon as I left, I pondered what to text him that evening, or whether I should message him at all. Should I tell him that I had a good time? Too obvious. That I was looking forward to spending time with him soon at a bar mitzvah? Too forward. I wound up simply sending "Hey, it's Carrie," so that he could insert my contact information into his phone. The conversations that followed were surface level: he'd send a "Hey" or "What's up" along with a shirtless Snapchat selfie. It was clear he wasn't interested in getting to know me.

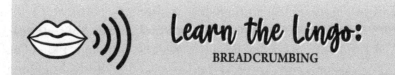

## Learn the Lingo:
### BREADCRUMBING

*Breadcrumbing* means he's dropping hints—and not in a good way. The guy very well knows he's single, but he'll send just the right (also known as breadcrumbs) to keep you interested. Leading you on is a game to him: he doesn't want to commit, but he'll flirt for the fun of it. Breadcrumbers often keep details about their life private, flake on plans, and don't spend time learning more about you.

One message stood out from the rest. I woke up and noticed a text he sent at 1:51 a.m. that read "Let's hu." At first, I was

thrilled. Beyond the subtle flirtations and casual snaps, he explicitly revealed that he wanted to hook up. But then I wondered
why he was up so late, so I did some digging. His Instagram
story showed that he was drinking in a basement with friends,
not cozied up in his bedroom as I first presumed. The message
most likely came out of a drunken state, which made it seem
less genuine. Nonetheless, I remembered something a friend told
me about post-alcohol messages: drunk texts are sober thoughts.
People need "liquid courage" to say how they're really feeling.
I got a glimpse inside of his brain, and even though I replied
"No," I secretly hoped we'd get together at some point.

One party offered the perfect opportunity: a b'nai mitzvah,
which celebrated the coming-of-age of twin girls. "Hey, are you
going this Saturday?" I snapped Caleb after school one day.
Although I told myself it was because I had homework, I didn't
speak to him in person because I was shy. "Yeah, are you?" he
answered a few hours later. I pondered waiting to text so that
he wouldn't think I eagerly anticipated his reply. But I couldn't
help myself. Within seconds, I told him that I was attending with
an inviting duck-face selfie. This time, Caleb was quick to reply.
"Can't wait," he wrote with a winking emoji. At this point, it was
obvious a hookup was in the cards, so I fostered my fate. "How
are you getting home from the party?" I asked. I flirtatiously
twirled my hair from behind the screen, even though I knew he
couldn't see me. Still, he picked up on my cues: "I was just going
to take an Uber. Wanna split a car back?" Obviously, I agreed.

All that was left to do was steam my bodycon dress, reserve
makeup at Sephora, and inform my parents of my plans. The
last thing I wanted was for my mom to blow up my messages
mid-make out. "Don't text me. I'll text you," I said. She sighed.
Sending her thirteen-year-old daughter in a car home with a boy
she never met wasn't ideal. Still, she agreed to trust me for the
evening—with one exception. "Send me his phone number. I'll
only use it in case of an emergency," she promised. I was morti-

fied—what if she actually called him? I had no choice. She was trusting me, so I had to trust her as well. "I'll only call him if you don't pick up your phone for an extended period of time," she said. Much to my discomfort, I gave in and shared his contact.

On Saturday night, I slipped into my black bandage dress. I stood in front of the mirror in my bedroom and sent him a selfie once I was in full glam—stick-straight hair, shimmery eyeshadow and all. I always lean toward being fashionably late, so I planned on departing my apartment fifteen minutes prior to the party's scheduled start time. I took a tad too long perfecting the black eyeliner on my waterline though, which delayed me another ten minutes. Caleb had arrived early. He snapped me a short video from the venue downtown, with his face illuminated by purple strobe lights. It motivated me to get moving. I packed my Coach wristlet with all the essentials: a portable charger, NARS lip gloss, oil-blotting wipes (in case the room got stuffy), a pack of spearmint gum, and Ice Breakers. I took one last look in the mirror before hopping in the Uber. I practiced my pout at least a dozen times before, but one last check couldn't hurt. What if he thought I was a bad kisser? Or that my breath smelled bad? I popped in a piece of gum, smoothed out my dress, and told myself to calm down. Moments of self-doubt would only take away from my time with Caleb. I grabbed my phone and left with my head held high. It was go time.

When I arrived at the event, I had my mom leave me at the door so that other attendees wouldn't see. "Mom, all the people from my school came together, not with their parents," I said, avoiding eye contact as if she were a stranger. Deep down, I knew I was being disrespectful in pushing her out the door, but in the moment, I didn't care. Caleb was the only person on my mind.

All alone, I entered a room filled with couples cuddling on couches and friend groups huddled at the bar ordering Shirley Temples. "Party Rock Anthem" pierced my eardrums. The room was marked by more black bodycon dresses, mere centimeters away from revealing too much. Sweaty bodies jumped up and down on the large dance floor in the center of the room. The space was lined with posters to accompany "mazel tov" speeches made by friends, although each person's words were highly predictable ("I can't believe you're a woman"; "We have so many memories"; "Party hard tonight"). As hora music played and people began to crowd in front of the DJ booth, I felt uncomfortable and out of place. But I forced myself to stay for the sake of fitting in—nobody wanted to be the first to leave, the "baby" who couldn't stay out past his/her bedtime.

I was already a regular when it came to early departures, most notably during a Halloween party hosted by one of my classmates in 2015. Upon entering the Soho townhouse, I noticed that the host replaced the Kit Kats in a candy jar—it was now filled to the top with condoms. Empty beer bottles were scattered across the floor, and the smell of weed wafted through the air. I bolted after ten minutes. The decision was difficult, as I worried about being judged by my peers, but I ultimately knew I was making the right choice. Why place myself in an uncomfortable situation that sacrificed my morals at age twelve? Besides, no hookups took flight for me that evening (even though I was dressed in a stewardess costume). This time, Caleb was on the table, and it was too late to chicken out.

It took me a while to find Caleb among the dozens of teens in the b'nai mitzvah venue. His whereabouts were unsurprising considering his player past: he was seated between two girls on the couch with his arms draped over their shoulders. How was I supposed to compete with two others? I engaged in several minutes of self-talk on the dance floor before mustering the courage to walk over to him. *He asked you to hook up, so he wants you*, I told myself. I strutted over to him just as confidently as I did that day while wearing his white tee.

"Hey," I said, towering above his position on the couch. He immediately took his hands off the girls and stood up to hug me. "Hey, where have you been?" he asked. He gently rubbed my back, a subtle hint that he wasn't keen on only receiving a casual embrace that evening. "Around," I vaguely replied. He decided to ditch the girls, placing his hand on my waist to guide me to the bar instead. "Two waters please," he ordered. When my drink arrived, I kept my mouth on the straw to avoid conversation, worried that I would say something wrong. Thankfully, the loud music encouraged more grooving and less gabbing.

Around 11:00, I realized that my midnight curfew was quickly approaching. The party wasn't over—the cake had not been served, and goody bags were not yet laid out. Nonetheless, my mom set a specific time for me to be home, and I wasn't about to turn into a pumpkin. "I think I have to get going," I announced, lightly tapping Caleb on the shoulder. "Wait! The party's just getting started!" he shouted over Jason Derulo's "Want to Want Me." I had little faith that Caleb would leave the celebration an hour early—but I most certainly "wanted" him. "You don't have to ride home with me. It's okay if you want to stay longer," I said. He shook his head. "No, it's okay. Let's go. I'll order the Uber," he insisted, guiding us towards the coat check.

I inserted my address into his phone, sent my mom a brief text that I was leaving and slipped my coat over my shoulders. "After you," Caleb offered, opening the door to the car. The sweaty soles of my feet slid in my high heels as I climbed inside. I may have only moved a few centimeters ahead, but I knew I was stepping into something more significant—a more mature version of myself. That evening, on the corner of 23rd Street and Hudson River Park, I felt pressured into embracing a calm, confident, and collected Carrie. Being relaxed and self-assured in the face of my first-ever hookup seemed like the only way to ensure the evening was a success. Once I got out of my head, I recognized that even though Caleb had more experience, he anticipated the kiss just as much as I did. There was a reason why he wiped a bead of sweat off his brow—and it wasn't due to the thirty-degree weather.

As we rode up the West Side Highway, I glanced out at the Hudson River, secretly hoping that Mother Nature would help calm my nerves. And she did: the way the wind advanced the water reminded me to go with the flow while several stop signs encouraged me to pause and breathe. I was squished to one side of the car while Caleb was pressed up against the other. I wanted him to make the first move, so I decided to play coy. Every time he glanced over, I shot him a sly smile and flirtatiously twirled my hair. After all, we only had thirty minutes before pulling up to my apartment. "That was fun," he finally stated, fiddling with the handle of the party favors he snagged for us. "Yeah, I had a good time," I said. Several cars honked amid a traffic jam. Drake's soaring vocals flooded the vehicle. The driver let out a loud cough. But Caleb remained relatively silent—until he suddenly wasn't. "So," he started, inching closer to my side of the car. I felt my heart rate quicken again, and I clenched the edge of the seat to calm myself. "Want to hook up?" he asked bluntly.

Looking back, his decision to ask me straight-up was strange and abrupt. Wasn't a kiss supposed to happen organically? Easing into the make out when the moment feels right allows positive tension to build. Not to mention, the element of surprise is romantic when coming from someone you like. Thirteen-year-old me, however, didn't care. I thought that a boy verbally requesting a hookup was completely fine—in fact, it was actually sought after according to my friends. So I played into Caleb's request. "Sure!" I replied enthusiastically.

When he finally leaned in, I was clueless. Where was I supposed to put my hands? Did I need to close my eyes? All my internal doubts were silenced as soon as we locked lips. Instead of hyper-focusing on technique, I found it best to let the boy lead the way and set the scene. I was surprised to find that make outs are a dance—they have a rhythm, and you work in harmony with the other person. If Caleb stroked my arm, I would mirror him by gently brushing his hair. Keeping my eyes open took me out of the moment, so I shut them and trusted myself to determine what make out moves were best. At one point, I felt his hand gently graze my thigh and reach underneath my skirt. I opened my eyes wide as I realized what was about to occur. I didn't want to be criticized for my inexperience, but it was more important to stay true to my morals. I didn't want to jump into something I wasn't ready for. I grasped his wrist and pushed it aside. Instead of insisting on under-the-pants action as I had feared, he merely laughed it off.

## Double-Tap This:

**WHAT TO KEEP IN MIND FOR YOUR FIRST HOOKUP**

- Pack gum, mints, or breath spray. Listerine strips used to be my favorite to stash in my purse at bar/bat mitzvahs.
- Keep low expectations. The hookup is not going to be perfect, so try not to worry about if you're "good" or not.
- Exude confidence, even if you're not sure of yourself. He may not know it's your first hookup (unless you told him). If you keep a smile on your face and seem confident, he could assume you're an experienced pro.
- Relax your body. Try not to tense up; surrender to the moment.
- Start slow, then follow his lead if you feel like you don't know what you're doing. Mirroring his body language can help you become more comfortable.
- Don't feel pressured into doing anything you're uncomfortable with. Stop him if he wants to take things too far. Your friends shouldn't pressure you either. Just because your bestie is exploring her sexuality doesn't mean you have to. Don't rush into something if you aren't ready.
- Avoid getting too attached. If you had feelings for the person to begin with, that's a different story. But if it was a casual kiss, don't trick yourself into believing you want a relationship just because you locked lips. A hookup shouldn't cause unnecessary emotional baggage.

Soon enough, we pulled up to my apartment building. "Shh. Don't tell," Caleb hushed the driver as we exited the vehicle. I gulped. His words made me feel like I had done something improper. I pulled my dress down an inch to preserve my integrity. As we walked a few feet up to my apartment, I overanalyzed the kiss. Was my breath minty enough? Was the make out too short? Too long? But then I remembered that first hookups aren't going to be perfect—and they don't have to be. In fact, it's unrealistic to believe every kiss kindles fireworks. Awkward experiences are the only way you learn, and no future kiss will seem as magical without an average make out to compare it to.

Before Caleb and I parted ways, he pushed me up against a white brick wall. I felt my doorman's eyes on us, yet Caleb didn't seem to mind. He snapped the straps of my bandage dress and leaned in for a final kiss. I was standing on the same street I had grown up on since the age of four, the sidewalk that took me to my first day of kindergarten, my elementary school graduation, and more important milestones. But this moment felt different—I felt like a stranger inside my body. Make outs in the middle of the night were out of character for me, and I didn't recognize the teenager who stood in sky-high heels on the sidewalk. As I watched Caleb wave goodbye with a yellow-tinted metal grin, I felt uneasy and unsatisfied. What had I just done? Neither of us had deep feelings for each other, nor were we expecting a relationship. I suddenly felt guilty as I acknowledged my reality: everyone else in my grade had already experienced their first hookup, and I utilized Caleb as if he were a mark on a checklist.

My experience with him came to mind years later. When my friend suggested we start a "Hot Girl Summer" point system on vacation, I was hesitant. She proposed ten points for pecks, twenty points for full-on make outs, thirty points for stripping, and an instant win if either of us had sex. It was a game to see who would rack up the most points over the summer. At first, the task seemed exciting, but I soon realized it was wrong. It objectified us and boys. Physical chemistry should happen organically. It should not be forced for the sake of winning a game. Caleb may not have had feelings for me, but I used him just so I could say I had my first hookup. I set the game rules in my mind: kiss Caleb, and you'll get bonus points and praise from your peers. As soon as I offered my friend this analysis, she shut down our summer point system for good.

If I learned anything from Caleb, it's that you don't need a boy to make you feel sexy or mature at age thirteen. Confidence comes from within. The self-esteem that emanates from a hookup is fleeting. Although it may feel exciting in the moment, happiness from a meaningless kiss is short-lived. I felt most confident when I eventually stood in the center of a bar mitzvah solo in a bright coral bodycon among dozens of black Bebes. It took a long time to garner the courage to become comfortable in my own skin, but once I did, I felt free. Boys are drawn to what makes you unique, not what makes you a carbon copy of everyone else. Your first hookup will be more meaningful if it happens naturally, not when you pursue it for the sake of fitting in.

I said goodbye to black bodycons as quickly as I unadded Caleb on Snapchat post-hookup. Staring at the pile of dresses in the donation bag, I smiled and gave myself a mental "mazel tov." Hopping on the mitzvah train was fun, but being myself and taking on romance at my own pace was a far more exciting ride. ♥

# Chapter 2

# The First Love

I FELL IN LOVE WHEN I was sixteen…and then his mom broke up with me.

I met Jack during a social media tour that took place over the summer. I expected a seasonal fling, but nothing could have prepared me for the emotions I developed. He was a kind, compassionate, and respectful Aussie—my very own Chris Hemsworth. For the entirety of July and August, we went on a whirlwind adventure across America together—and it all started at the back of a tour bus.

Throughout the first day of the tour in San Francisco, he dropped hints that he was into me. He casually draped his arm around my shoulder as we waited to walk on stage and followed me around like a puppy dog while I met with fans. Each tour stop was part-show, part-meet-and-greet. Unlike other influencers on the tour, we weren't singing, simply visiting cities to meet supporters of our social media channels. We got to introduce a friend's song set together, and people immediately recognized the chemistry between us. "You guys are so cute together!" an influencer said as Jack and I huddled in the corner chatting.

As I shoved my way through the crowded tour bus after the show, I searched for Jack. A slice of pizza waited patiently on his lap. "Here, I saved a spot for you!" he exclaimed, scooting aside to make room for me to sit down. It was difficult to get to know him when cameras were flashing in our faces all the time, and we were constantly asked to participate in TikTok videos. Nonetheless, I had a gut feeling that waiting for him was worth it, so I was patient.

For three hours on the bus, he and I cuddled. The meet and greet we participated in earlier that day was exhausting. I dozed off on his shoulder as he rested his head gently on top of mine. He slid his pinkie over on the seat so that he could subtly grasp my hand. Our fingers remained interlaced as we fell asleep, but I still waited for him to initiate our first kiss.

I suddenly realized why he wasn't making a move. I squinted slightly while lying on his shoulder and saw the issue: everyone was watching. "Maybe we should try the bathroom?" I suggested. He took me by the hand and led me to the back of the bus. Guys patted his shoulders while girls giggled at me—they all sensed what was about to occur. But instead of paying attention to the rowdy soundtrack of the tour bus, I focused on my budding romance.

The bathroom scene wasn't exactly romantic: the faint smell of urine emanated from the toilet, and I could still hear every word of Gunna's "Baby Birkin" blasting from the radio. Once we locked the door, it was dark, forcing me to let go and trust the guy I had met just hours prior. I leaned against the door and felt his soft lips press up against mine. The spark was immediate, but other influencers extinguished the flame as they banged on the door. "I have to pee! Hurry up!" someone shouted. The moment was rushed and tense. I found it difficult to enjoy myself with so much background noise. We had no choice but to return to our seats.

When we were back in our row, Jack kept lifting his head up off of mine to scan the tour bus. "How are we going to do this?" he asked in his charming Australian accent. Eventually, we looked at each other and shrugged. The bus was not going to get any less crowded or quiet, so we had to kiss in public. Rap music was booming, but our make out served as a stark contrast: it was slow, sweet, and gentle. Time stopped as soon as I surrendered to the moment, and I didn't want to return to reality.

After a few minutes, we opened our eyes and smiled at each other. Our connection was quickly interrupted. "Woo hoo!" I heard someone scream, and several influencers started applauding wildly. Still in Jack's arms, I turned my head to take in the commotion: at least half of the bus was hovering over us. They were framing our midnight make out session, but instead of resenting them for it, we simply laughed off the lack of personal space.

Later on that night, we switched seats with another couple so that we were further up on the bus, separate from the rest of the influencers. They left a blanket on the seat, so we draped it over our heads. Under the blanket, we were shielded from the rest of the bus. I took my AirPods out of my backpack and handed him one. "This is my chill playlist," I said, seeking to transport us somewhere beyond the noisy vehicle. Kacey Musgraves and Lewis Capaldi serenaded us as we kissed.

We arrived at a hotel halfway to Los Angeles at 1 a.m. and separated into different rooms. As we held our luggage in front of the lobby, we hesitated to kiss in front of the tour staff and parents. He placed his suitcase on the curb and pulled me into a tight hug before heading upstairs. I knew it wouldn't be the last time we tapped into our chemistry.

Just a few hours later, we woke up at 5 a.m. to drive to Los Angeles. Jack reserved a seat for me on the bus once again, and I relaxed my tired body onto his. "Good morning," I quietly croaked. I lost my voice from screaming over influencers on the bus the evening before. The car quickly sped through highways to deliver us to the venue on time. Jack and I watched the sun rise slowly over the western mountains. Occasionally, I stared at how the golden light struck his face. He'd give me a quick kiss each time our eyes locked. We once again shared my AirPods, although his artist suggestion—Metallica—wasn't the best choice for an easygoing, early-morning album.

Once we arrived at the show in L.A., we continued to get cozy with each other to the point where I even needed some space. Every time I walked out of the green room, whether to grab breakfast or watch the sound check, Jack followed close behind. I was caught off guard by how clingy he was at times. At first, I was irritated rather than flattered, as it prevented me from bonding with other friends. But my attraction to him was undeniable.

While the artists and bands rehearsed, I met Jack's mom and younger sister and introduced him to my mom as well. While our parents got to know each other, I retreated into my head. Jack and I were both ending our time on tour in Los Angeles, and I suddenly wondered what would happen to our emerging relationship afterwards. We lived in separate countries across the world from one another. I wasn't sure what the future held, but I wasn't ready to say goodbye. "He should come with me to Disneyland tomorrow!" I blurted. His mom and sister did not confirm he was available until they witnessed our chemistry. In the green room, Jack and I were so exhausted, we napped on the couch in each other's arms. "You guys are so cute," his sister said while seated in a folding chair across the room. His mother nodded in agreement: "We can definitely make Disney work for tomorrow."

Jack and I continued to cuddle for hours. In fact, we almost missed our cue to introduce an artist in the show because we were so immersed in each other's company. The loudspeaker called us to be on standby, and we giggled as we stumbled our way backstage. I smoothed my hair, and Jack adjusted his tee. There was nothing subtle about our connection. It was obvious to everyone that we were obsessed with each other, even to the fans, who stopped us several times on the meet-and-greet line to ask if we were dating.

Disneyland was the first time we went public about our relationship. Too soon? Definitely. But I was following my heart. The morning of our excursion, Jack waited for me on the hotel lobby couch. As soon as the elevator doors opened, I ran straight into his arms and raised onto my tiptoes to kiss him.

We strolled through the amusement park hand in hand, and when we reached the castle, we took photos together. He planted a peck, and I raised a leg off the ground. The music from Main Street blasted my eardrums, and the strong wind almost caused my skirt to fly up, but nothing could hinder our moment. The photo we posted looked like it was straight out of a fairytale—and our followers were privy to the magic as well. But it wasn't about the online engagement or reaction from social media supporters. My connection with Jack was my only focus.

We could never find any privacy with one another—first, the tour bus, then backstage, and now, a crowded tourist attraction. Finally, we found a bench to sit down. "Alone at last," I sighed with relief as I inched closer to him. The romance didn't stop there: he kissed me in the queue area for the Haunted Mansion, and I gripped his hand as we wound through the dark in Space Mountain. We couldn't keep our hands—or lips—off each other and remained unbothered by onlookers.

But it wasn't always about physical chemistry—Jack's manners were what really sold me. He wiped down the seat with the edge of his shirt before I sat down on each ride to ensure the spot was clean. He opened the doors to let me enter first, and he always let me decide which attractions we would visit. Jack was the textbook definition of a perfect gentleman. Who knew that existed in teen form? The guys at my school were generally snarky and short-tempered—no one ever held open a door for me or uttered "Please" and "Thank you." Jack was different. I didn't know how I got so lucky.

After hours of thrill rides, I hugged him goodbye in the parking lot. I had no idea when or if I would see him again, but we both wanted to make an effort. We kept up with daily FaceTime calls: he interrupted his video game sessions to hop on the phone, and I called him in between summer classes. "I miss you so much. It's torture here without you," I complained from the dorm room. "I miss you more," he said as he lounged on his couch.

One day, I swiped up on his Instagram Story with a subtle yet bold statement: "Falling," along with a shushing face emoji. "Wait, babe, what kind of falling are we talking about? x," he typed back. Although he never said it to my face, Jack almost always called me "babe" via text, and he signed his messages with "x" for a virtual kiss. I kept the conversation ambiguous and replied with a woman-shrugging emoji and dual pink hearts. "Well, that sounds like a good thing," he replied with a laughing face. Jack was thousands of miles away, but he managed to make my heart flutter from behind a screen. "Ofc. Hbu?" I asked with a winky-face emoji. His response was almost instantaneous: "I've definitely fallen for you." He always knew what to say to make me feel special.

Texts weren't enough for us. With a little convincing, Jack and I managed to finesse our way into touring one more city together a few weeks later—Washington, D.C. Plus, Jack's mom agreed to fly their family out to the Hamptons, so he could spend time with me beforehand. "You can stay in our guest room one day!" I exclaimed over the phone, dreaming of waking up just a few feet away from him. The effort he made to visit me was incredibly romantic. I was excited to be with him outside the bounds of the tour but also anxious to see how he would fit into my everyday life and get along with friends and family.

Three weeks after our goodbye in Los Angeles, Jack arrived in the Hamptons. I wasn't planning on seeing him until the day after he arrived. But once I saw a Snapchat of him relaxing on the pool deck of his hotel, I couldn't help myself. I convinced my parents to drive me to where he was staying, just two miles from my home, so I could surprise him. When my dad pulled up in his convertible, I immediately noticed Jack's mom and sister lounging by the pool. I ran up to the fence and squinted under the sun to scan the area. "He's in the room," his sister said. I kept our initial hello brief so that I could head to his room, but once I was on his doorstep, I hesitated. What if he forgot the connection we established in California? What if he found another girl he was interested in back home? Doubts raced through my mind, yet I gathered the courage to knock on the door.

Jack opened the door shirtless, and his eyes immediately lit up. "What are you doing here?!" he exclaimed, pulling me into a tight hug and kicking the door closed behind me. The blinds were shut, and our parents were busy chatting, so we were safe to lock lips in seclusion. I stroked Jack's blonde hair and smiled—we picked up exactly where we left off. I handed him a bag of Rice Krispie Treats, his favorite dessert, but he presented me with a more lavish gift: a designer bracelet. "Just a little thank you for letting me visit," he stated. I was shocked by the present, but Jack always treated me well. The gesture was extremely generous, and I snapped a photo for my Instagram Story to capture the special memory. I turned my phone around to make sure he agreed with the caption: "My boyfriend got me the sweetest gift." Why was I rushing to put a label on our relationship so fast? Jack got me excited, so it was easy to get ahead of myself. Besides, he didn't hesitate when I showed him the caption. I slipped the bracelet on my wrist and smiled. It wasn't Jack's monetary gesture that mattered most—simply seeing his face again after weeks of work at a pre-college program was enough.

We eased into each other's arms on the couch and began to get to know each other better. I learned a few facts about his life: he had one girlfriend in the past, he loved social media, and he could play video games all day long. In the moment, the minimal knowledge was satisfactory. But looking back, I realize that I really didn't know much about him. I had a basic understanding of who he was as a person, and that was suitable because our physical attraction overshadowed everything. I revealed information and stories about me as well. "This guy I dated on the internet bullied me on social media. I've had really toxic relationships in the past," I explained, although my online crush and I were never officially together. It felt like I was forcing myself to open up for the sake of speeding my connection with Jack along. Our relationship always had a time limit, and neither of us knew when the hours were going to run out.

I was kissing Jack on the couch when I had a sudden epiphany: if we had so little time together, and I really cared about him, then we needed to get serious…fast. "I'm falling in love with you," I whispered while staring deeply into his eyes, although I didn't fully comprehend the weight behind the words I was uttering. "I'm falling in love with you too," he replied with a gentle smile. I sensed that Jack felt the same way as I did, but hearing the words aloud validated my emotions. Every time he looked into my eyes, he didn't just see me—he saw through me. He made me feel valued and worthy of affection, an unexpected sensation considering how little time we spent together. Now that we were vulnerable, and our feelings were laid out on the table, we were all in. "Wait, are we dating?" I laughed. Jack sat up on the couch and raised an eyebrow. "Do you want to officially be my girlfriend?" he asked. My answer was obvious.

That evening, instead of letting Jack sleep over, I had my parents drop him off at his hotel. Waiting another twenty-four hours for him to stay with me overnight would build up positive tension and excitement. As we stood outside of his hotel door, I placed my hands on his shoulders. "I'll see you soon. Promise," I said. I secretly wished that we could continue our time together, but I had to restrain myself. I needed to practice patience instead of speeding along our relationship more than I had already done.

The following day, I picked Jack up at his hotel, and we drove to my house to get ready for a party. As we stood in front of the mirror together, I scanned his head-to-toe Gucci ensemble; he had expensive taste. We made ourselves late perfecting our looks—and looking at each other.

Most of the guests were in their mid-twenties and thirties, so Jack and I immediately stood out as we took photos in front of the step and repeat. Each person I brushed past possessed a faint aroma of alcohol, as a large bar was just a few feet away. Jack and I mingled with guests, and I even ran into an old friend. "I'm so happy for you guys!" she swooned. The statement made me surprisingly uneasy—it felt like she was wishing us well on a marriage instead of a new relationship. "I'm going to another party in Easthampton in a bit. We're happy to drive you!" she offered. Jack and I weren't on the list, but the uncertainty excited me. "Whatever you want to do," Jack said. Next thing I knew, we were squished in the back seat of her convertible, racing down highways. Our hands were interlaced, and our hair blew with the wind. Pop tunes blasted from the radio at an uncomfortably loud volume, but I managed to tune out the vocals. It felt like we were flying, and Jack was soaring by my side.

When we arrived, a woman confirmed that Jack and I were not on the guest list, but she let us enter regardless. After all, the event was almost over. The second party was not nearly as fun. It didn't take long for Jack and I to come to a mutual agreement: "Let's leave." We missed our dinner reservation by two hours, so I took it upon myself to call and secure another table. "After you," he said, opening the door to the Uber as I punched the restaurant's name into my phone. I looked up from the screen and smiled. Jack was there to be with *me*. The elite parties, fancy convertible, and expensive dinners were just fluff.

Thankfully, the restaurant held the reservation. It was dark outside, so the sidewalks were illuminated by store windows and streetlights. As soon as Jack and I took our seats curbside, the owner, whom my family is friendly with, came over to say hello. "My girlfriend! How are you doing?" he bellowed. I rolled my eyes. When I was a little girl, he assigned me the nickname, "girlfriend," and he has called me that ever since. He wrapped his arm around my shoulder and pulled me in so close, I could smell the mint gum he was chewing. But with Jack there, I didn't need to worry about being uncomfortable. "Hey, mate, that's *my* girlfriend!" Jack proudly stated. I beamed with pride as he shook his hand. For the rest of dinner, the owner did not utter a word, other than, "Enjoy," when he personally delivered Jack's steak and my grilled salmon.

When we arrived back at my house around 10 p.m., I noticed that several stars decorated the night sky. "Let's make a wish," I said, grabbing Jack's hand. We closed our eyes in unison. My mind wandered as I recounted the magical moments of our day, but I tried to focus on making a meaningful wish. *I wish this would last forever*, I thought to myself while picturing Jack's adoring gaze. I had never felt so happy, so special in the arms of a guy, and I prayed to the stars that our relationship would never end.

The late-evening activity was the main attraction of our day, perhaps even of our entire relationship. As I sat with my legs crossed at the edge of my bed, scrolling through movies on demand, Jack stopped me on one particular film. "Let's watch *Clueless*," he suggested, since he knew it was my favorite movie. I shut the door to my bedroom, and we cuddled under my Tiffany Blue comforter for thirty minutes or so as the scenes played out. It didn't take long for me to doze off. I started to fall asleep on Jack's chest but kept my eyes half open to watch what he was doing. If I felt myself going under, his intoxicatingly strong cologne would jolt me awake. I felt him breathing up against me. The tension between us sent shivers through my body, and I waited patiently for Jack to lean in.

Finally, he pressed his lips against mine. I allowed him to gently slip my wide-neck, white cotton tee off my shoulders, revealing the black lace bralette I bought in town earlier that week. The movie began to fade into the background. I could finally focus on exploring my physical connection with Jack in the privacy we craved. At times, I was afraid, but he assured me that he was on the same page, which put me at ease. New experiences were taking place in my own bed, and the familiarity with my sheets and pillows established a sense of comfort.

*Clueless* seemed to have quickly reached its end. "Aw, we missed the entire middle of the movie!" I complained as the credits rolled. In reality, I didn't mind. Our activity was far more exciting than Cher and Josh's first kiss (spoiler alert). We were young, reckless, and free—free to explore, to laugh, and to love. I sent him off to bed in the guest room at midnight, sealing the evening with a kiss goodbye. What would my parents think if his room was empty?

Even though we didn't have sex, when we woke up the next morning, the house had a "morning-after" air that reminded me of scenes I saw in movies. "Good morning!" I whispered, pushing open the door to his room. I planted a kiss on his forehead, and Jack smiled as he slowly opened his eyes. My family was out at my dad's 5K run, so Jack was able to roam as he pleased. He pulled back the sheets, revealing a semi-naked body dressed in solely boxers. "Good morning," he said, leaning in for a kiss. I placed a hand on his cheek to stop him. "Wait, can you brush your teeth first?" I laughed. I had already scrubbed with mint toothpaste before entering his room. I walked behind Jack as he made a beeline for the bathroom. After a quick rinse, Jack pulled me in: "Where were we?" Once the *Clueless* evening concluded, we pressed fast-forward on our relationship. It was expedited to a more mature level, and the transformation was especially evident as we moved throughout our morning.

Jack and I continued to explore our connection during his final day in the Hamptons. We held hands as we strolled through town in the blazing heat after brunch. After a few hours, we walked over to my aunt and uncle's house for a brief introduction (they lived a few doors down). I was eager to show off my new boyfriend, and he was well-mannered as can be. He sat on the couch next to me with perfect posture, answering every question my family threw at him: "Where are you from? When did you guys meet? How long are you here for?" He spoke comfortably with his hands and always kept his composure. As my uncle nodded approvingly, I was proud.

Later, Jack splashed around in my complex's shared swimming pool and lounged in the hot tub. I sat across the tub from him and watched as his eyes squinted behind his aviator sunglasses. I wanted to move closer, but I cautiously scanned the pool area: several elderly couples and other property owners lined the space. The last thing I wanted was for them to think that I—the "little girl" they had come to know over the years—was improper for cozying up to a boy. So I held back.

I made up for our lackluster water excursion as soon as we got back to the house. I was starting to strip down for the shower when I suddenly got an idea. I raised my bikini strap back onto my shoulder and confidently opened Jack's door. "Want to come shower with me?" I whispered, careful that my parents wouldn't hear in the other room. His eyes widened in surprise. "Sure!" he agreed, taking my hand and following me back into the bathroom. Jack rubbed body wash on my skin in slow, gentle circles. We traded places in the tiny shower to wash shampoo out of our hair, our wet bodies brushing past each other each time. Water dripped down our faces and into our eyes as we kissed. The moment was messy when our relationship was anything but. The spontaneity was exhilarating.

Jack left the Hamptons after spending two days with me. I rejoined the social media tour solo in Philadelphia, but I didn't enjoy myself. I took a quick look around the stage: the lights still shined, and the audience threw scrunchies at influencers in adoration. I stood alone, with the exception of a few friends watching from the wings. It didn't feel the same without Jack by my side. He was waiting for me in D.C., and I wasn't interested in taking the bus to another city without him. "Can you check if there are last-minute plane tickets?" I asked my mom after making my final appearance on stage. Two seats were available on a flight to Washington that departed in two hours—it had to be a sign. I raced out the door and didn't look back—not even to say goodbye to my friends.

As soon as the Uber pulled up to the hotel in Washington, Jack was waiting in front. I bolted out of the car, leaving the luggage to my mom, and ran into his arms. He took me by the hand, and we hid behind a corner in the hotel to kiss each other hello. It had only been a few days, but each city we visited allowed me to see Jack in a new and exciting light. He pushed the bellman cart upstairs for us, and once our bags were dropped in the room, my mom dismissed us for the evening. "Let's hang out in the lobby," Jack suggested as we rode down in the elevator. The restaurant area was closed, and the small hotel did not have any private seating areas. "We can just sit on the floor," I shrugged, leading him by the hand to a spot away from the main lobby. Seated on the ground, we chatted for over an hour. "The tour was boring without you. I was so lonely," I whined. Jack always came up with a reply straight out of a storybook: "Well, we're here together now. That's all that matters."

We had the whole next day to ourselves before the final show. The group of influencers planned to visit the Capitol, but Jack and I had arrangements of our own. "Good morning!" I chirped, greeting him in the lobby. We went out for brunch and took pictures—smiling, kissing, and laughing. Afterwards, both of us wanted what he considered a "foreign adventure." Although I ordered a car to the Lincoln Memorial, a row of Lime scooters was lined up just a few feet away from us. I promised my mom I wouldn't ride one, but this was Jack. She approved of our relationship, so she would surely agree to an electric scooter ride, right? I tend not to look before I leap (case in point: diving into our relationship after a mere twenty-four hours)—this situation was no different. Next thing I knew, we were whizzing through streets for miles, past several grass fields and monuments under a picture-perfect sunny sky. We sped through stop lights and frequently lost our sense of direction, but the danger made it all the more exciting.

Once we passed by the Capitol—sweat dripping, water bottles in hand—we decided to join the rest of the tour members. "There they are!" a friend exclaimed as Jack and I walked into the building hand in hand. He wasn't surprised we were still together. As we roamed the Capitol grounds, Jack and I quickly agreed that the meeting chambers didn't hold a candle to our scooter ride. We said our goodbyes, and even though we missed a group couples' photo, the experience to follow compensated for it.

We rode our scooters back to the hotel to swim. The pool area was empty, and we had the entire space to ourselves. Jack immediately dunked under the water while I stood static, shocked by a burst of cold from stepping on the first stair. I gripped the railing, but he quickly took my hands and pulled me into an embrace. I was pressed up against the edge of the pool, but I instead focused closely on the connection between our bodies. The smell of chlorine permeated the space, yet his cologne clouded my senses. I noticed a single drop of water fall from his forehead, and a soft smile spread across his face. Our chemistry continued to build, and my entire body began to tingle. The sensation started at my lips, as his pillowy pout locked with mine. Then, it progressed down to my chest and back, as his hands grazed my upper body. His fingertips imprinted on my skin with the perfect amount of pressure—his touch was sometimes tense, sometimes soft. I felt safe. I trusted Jack wholeheartedly.

After the pool, it only seemed natural to continue the action in his hotel room. "So," I started, shutting the door behind me. "So," Jack repeated, pulling me close. He began to kiss me while we were standing, but we quickly moved onto the bed. I was so distracted by Jack that I didn't notice the five missed calls from my mom—until she sounded an emergency Find My iPhone alarm. I jumped off the bed and quickly gave her my whereabouts via text. "It's getting late. I have to head back to my hotel room in a few minutes to get ready for dinner with my mom," I told Jack, who still laid comfortably on the pillow. "No!" Jack whined, leaping off the mattress to walk over to where I was standing. "It's okay! I'll see you tomorrow!" I said.

The following day was the last I saw him. Although it was unspoken, there was a mutual understanding that we didn't know when we'd see each other after the show concluded. He would return to Australia while I stayed in America. We soaked up every second at each other's side while we still were together—chatting, cuddling on the couch, and snapping selfies to memorialize the moments.

The three-hour show quickly passed, and it was time for us to part ways. A teddy bear that a fan gifted me was wedged between us as he held me in his arms, and a flood of tears showered down my cheeks. "I don't want to leave you," I cried. I couldn't manage to look him in the eye—seeing his loving gaze for a potential last time was too emotional to handle. "Maybe I'll come to New York Fashion Week next month with you," he said. "I'll see you soon! And we'll FaceTime every night." "Promise?" I asked, holding out my pinkie. He wrapped his finger around mine. My eyesight was blurry, but one thing was clear: when I finally managed to look at Jack, he was glancing towards the ground. The sense of passion disappeared from his eyes, and fear and uncertainty took its place. The pinkie swears served as a lifeline for our relationship: the one string of hope we held onto as our emotional connection suffered in the weeks to follow.

At first, he maintained the communication from afar. I would leave movie theaters in the middle of previews to FaceTime him, despite the extra cost to make an international call. He would ditch family dinners to hop on the phone, and he often sent a "good morning" text when it was early in America. To express our feelings, there would be endless "I miss you"s. He would reinforce how "amazing" he thought I was and even went as far as to call me "the best person on the planet." But he never declared, "I love you," even though in the silences on FaceTime, it felt like he was on the cusp of saying it. I was saving the sentiment for when he arrived in New York. Uttering those words for the first time is not to be taken lightly, and I wanted to make sure I confessed in person.

Slowly, however, I noticed he was growing distant. His flirtatious texts turned into excuses. When he didn't pick up the phone, he said he was doing homework or busy spending time with friends. I was always the first to reach out, and if I didn't, several days of silence would pass. "Thanks for calling," I texted one day after he broke one too many promises to ring. "Oh crap, babe, I'm so sorry. I've been so busy hanging out with the guys and resting after coming back from the States," he replied. I couldn't blame him. It was understandable that he wanted to catch up at home after traveling all summer, but the sudden distance caught me off guard, especially since we spent so many hours together. It felt like there was a void in my life, one that could not be filled by a text. Every time he disappeared for a few days, I feared that I said or did something wrong. I neurotically scrolled through our texts, scanning every word to see if there was any tension between us. But the messages were flooded with red hearts and photos of what we were up to in our respective countries.

He and his family waited to meet with his new manager before making the final decision to come to Fashion Week. It was up to her whether or not the trip was worth it for his career—seeing me was an afterthought. "What's the percent-chance you're coming?" I asked on FaceTime. "Ninety-one percent," he said, although I sensed he was unsure. Every time I doubted myself, I pictured our pinkie promise. There was no way he'd take back his pledge.

I was wrong. Instead of texting me himself, his mom messaged my mom to notify her that New York was out of the question. My heart sank. After several tries to reach Jack, he finally picked up the phone. "I was excited to see you. I miss you so much," I cried to him on FaceTime. "I know, me too," he agreed. He only showed half of his face on the screen, so it was difficult to tell exactly how he was feeling. "I have to go back to sleep," Jack continually said, sounding eager to hang up the phone. The conversation was rushed, but I assumed it was because he was too upset to speak. I, on the other hand, wanted to hold on for as long as I could. Jack was not visiting anytime soon, but another disappointment lingered: I hadn't yet told him I loved him. I couldn't wait a second longer, so admitting my feelings over the phone would have to do. "Call me when you're awake. I forgot to tell you something," I texted him. Jack never replied, but considering the events that followed, something tells me he knew exactly what I was going to say.

Just a few hours later, my mom got another long text from his mom as we were walking through town in the Hamptons. "What did she say?" I asked. My mom looked down at her feet. "Don't worry about it. I'll show you later," she responded. "No, show me now," I said, grabbing the phone out of her hand. When I saw the message, I realized there was no perfect moment to read what she wrote. No matter the time or place, her words stung. The message read, "Hi. Unfortunately, Jack can't be in a relationship at this time. Long distance is very hard, and he can't deal with the pressure right now. He just has to be a kid for the time being." The world froze. I sprinted away from my mom and down the sidewalks that Jack and I once strolled along together.

"Where's your boyfriend?" the owner of the restaurant we went to shouted as I sped by. It felt like I was running back in time, back to before I knew Jack. Before the social media tour. Before I knew what love was. The streets became blurry, but I found an alleyway to hide in so that I could be alone. It felt like my heart was ripped out of my chest—I was empty inside. I struggled to catch my breath, and I was disconnected from my surroundings. The sunny skies that sat above me didn't seem real, nor did the laughing couple that strolled by or the several cars that honked at the traffic light. I dropped to the ground and sobbed. I had only seen heartbreak in the movies, and I assumed that their reactions were dramatized for the sake of film. I never truly understood what it felt like to lose someone you love—until that moment. I wasn't ready to let go. Then, I noticed a single penny on the ground of the alley. I picked it up and stared intensely. I determined that it was a sign from God. I was in tremendous pain, but He assured me that everything was going to be okay.

As roads whirled by in a dizzying haze on the car ride home, Lewis Capaldi's "Someone You Loved" started playing on the radio. Although I could relate to the lyrics, no words could alleviate my heartache. I was utterly broken. When I arrived at my house, I ran straight upstairs, shut the door to my bedroom and sobbed into my pillow. I kept my eyes tightly shut—the darkness felt easier to deal with than a sun-stained reality. Every time I drifted off to sleep, I fell back into his arms. I still couldn't catch my breath, and I wanted to be left alone with my emotions. Not only was I blindsided, but I felt disrespected because he hadn't broken up with me himself. Communication is essential in a relationship, and Jack failed to communicate with me directly. Instead, he took an immature route, going through a third party—his mother—to make his feelings known. "Read what my mom sent yours. I still want to be friends," he simply sent via Snapchat. It was a shocking, cowardly move to place responsibility in his mother's hands. I felt like a fool. Not only had I publicized the relationship all over social media—I allowed myself to feel deep emotions for someone who just flung me out of his life. But if I'm a fool, I'm pretty positive I'm not the only one. So many of us dive and fall and often hit the ground headfirst, causing pangs of disappointment and shame…because boys just *suck* sometimes. Growing up, my mom always told me, "Boys are stupid." Placing that as a mask of sorts over Jack was nearly impossible.

I never realized how much love hurts until I lost him. Throughout the day, I couldn't bring myself to my feet, but I did FaceTime a few close friends to get their input. All I received was pity—none of their words really stuck or helped fix the pain. The one person I really needed to talk to was Jack. I asked him to call me since it would be too painful to look each other in the eyes via FaceTime. We wound up engaging in a quick video call. His camera faced the ceiling. I couldn't even have a civil conversation with his face. "I'm sorry. It's just…you're so far, and I need to focus on myself right now. I'm sixteen. I need to be a kid," he explained. My head pounded, and it felt like there were no more tears left to cry. Heartbreak reaches a point where the world falls silent—I was numb.

Jack's words possessed a striking resemblance to his mother's, as if the two of them had written and rehearsed what they were going to say. The genuine boy I came to know and love was now gone. We had gone from lovers to strangers in a matter of hours. But I needed closure, so I managed to speak through my emotions. I didn't want to leave anything unsaid. "Before you go, I just have to tell you that I love you," I confessed. "You probably knew I was going to tell you that today. It would be a disservice to our relationship not to say it." Loving him wasn't enough. He never said it back. "I wanted to tell you at one point, but it felt like it was too serious," he revealed. It may have been "serious" for me to say I loved him, but I was being sincere. Suddenly, I no longer wanted to stay on the phone. We were talking in circles, and hearing his voice was too painful to bear.

His actions during the rest of the day were equally distressing. Someone asked in his Instagram Story question box, "Do you have a girlfriend?" He didn't have to reply, but he deliberately chose to publish his response: "Not right now." Additionally, a person wrote, "You're cute!" Jack responded with kiss emojis and red hearts, the same signature emoji he would sign his texts to me with. I was puzzled. Jack was always so polite and respectful. He was aware that I'd been crying for hours, so why be so insensitive? "I don't appreciate you posting about our relationship the day of our breakup," I Snapchatted him. Jack's robotic response didn't sound like it came from him: "I'm sorry, but the time wasn't right." This couldn't be the guy I had fallen in love with over the previous two months.

I'd never felt more alone than after that breakup. I spent days inside my room with the shades closed, hiding from the world while drowning in tears. I was falling apart. All I wanted was for someone to hold me and tell me everything would be okay. One day, when I went downstairs to grab a snack, I broke down in my grandma Bobbi's arms on the couch, sobbing uncontrollably. "I don't know what to do. It just hurts...so...bad," I cried, struggling to get the words out. Everywhere I looked inside the house reminded me of him—the shower, the bed, the guest room. It felt like I was frozen in time, stuck in the memory of his presence with no escape. No matter how much I wanted to hate him for breaking up with me, I couldn't. I cared about him too much.

I blamed the universe for failing me. Every time I noticed an evening star, I cursed the sky. Why did the wish upon a star I made that evening with Jack not come true? Was I too vague in wishing for "this" to last forever? Too unfocused? A future with Jack wasn't in the stars, and it wasn't fair to assign blame when the universe knew better and had other plans for me. Still,

I struggled to move forward. Although I tried to convince myself I was okay, I knew I was lying. I had lost myself—I forgot who I was without him. I prayed that my heart would eventually repair, and I would take slow steps in moving past the short-lived yet meaningful relationship. I told myself that I would eventually love again—Jack was not the end all be all.

Leaving my Hamptons house and going back to the city was the only way to try to cope with the heartbreak. Yet in the weeks that followed, Jack made it difficult. He began to post neutral, bot-like comments on my Instagram photos, such as the "rock on" emoji or a green heart. I wasn't sure if he was leaving the comments or his mother was, and I wasn't about to reopen the wound by asking. His sister often reached out via Instagram DM, whether to wish me good luck at school or "quick-reply" applause at a career accomplishment. Any time I felt like I was starting to move on, they reminded me of just how much I was hurting.

Heartbreak scars. You never forget your first love. There were days when my heart hurt because I missed him so much. Now that he was gone, I realized just how much I loved having him around. I feared I would forget all the experiences we had, but more significantly, I worried that I wouldn't ever be able to find a guy who made me feel as special and loved as he did. How would I ever open my heart again?

I reached out to friends and family in hopes of talking my way out of the pain. Jack gave me no closure, so I considered many potential causes of the breakup. "Didn't he just get a new manager? Maybe she's telling him that he has to be single," a friend suggested. "It makes him seem like a teen heartthrob to fans." That would explain why he posted that he was available just hours after the breakup. Then, of course, there was the obvious to consider: the long distance. How did I ever believe it would be possible to date from over ten thousand miles away?

# Swipe Left:

**HOW TO COPE WITH YOUR FIRST BREAKUP**

Nothing can prepare you for your first heartbreak. It's not cured with a tub of ice cream and a Netflix binge like you see in the movies. It takes time, patience, and a whole lot of tears. Heartbreak is a form of grief—the loss swallows you whole. In the immediate aftermath, it may seem difficult to pick yourself back up again, but trust your hardships. They're not your enemy—they're specifically placed in your life to make you stronger. While you're in your feels, consider some of the tips below to ease the pain.

- Show yourself grace. It's okay to be upset. Owning your emotions, not pushing them aside, is a healthy first step in the healing process.
- Mute his Instagram. That way, he won't pop up on your feed, which makes it easier to move forward. He won't even know you hid his posts.
- Hold your family and friends close. In the absence of your significant other's affection, it's more important than ever to embrace physical connections. You can't fill the void, but you can recognize how loved you are.

- Practice self-love. Your family and friends can only provide so much reassurance. Take some alone time to reflect on your emotions, then treat yourself to a bubble bath, a walk outside, a favorite book—whatever brings you joy.
- Don't distract, but instead *direct* your energy into something productive. Get some homework done ahead of time. Try a new YouTube workout. Clean up your bedroom. This is the perfect time to check goals off your to-do list.
- Move around. Exercise will boost your endorphins and reduce stress. If you're not in the mood for heart-pumping cardio, light stretching or yoga can also provide a physical and mental release.
- Write down how you're feeling. Journaling is my favorite way to process my emotions. It makes the anxiety and confusion surrounding the breakup less loud in my brain.
- Avoid the instant rebound. Those who rebound act out of pain and desperation to feel love again. Let your heart heal before opening up to someone else. Although a no-strings-attached fling can feel good in the moment, the heartbreak will still be there afterwards.
- This is only your first breakup, and it probably won't be your last. The potential for a stronger love awaits, so try not to dwell on the past.

He wasn't willing to travel across the country often (nor was I, to be fair), so it would be difficult to keep up our connection. With how busy our lives were, consistent FaceTime calls were impossible. No matter what potential reasons my friends proposed, I would defend Jack's decision. "I mean, it makes sense. He lives so far away," I said, fighting back tears. Why are we always tempted to defend the ones we love, even when they hurt us?

I continued to follow Jack on Instagram after the summer ended, but I didn't message him directly until four months later. I was sending invites for my birthday party to several friends from the tour, so I asked him and his sister as an act of goodwill. "I'm hosting a party in New York...would love if you both could make it!" I typed. She responded first on behalf of the two of them: "Thank you so much for the invite. We would have loved to come, but unfortunately, I'm still at school. We have our exams so are unable to leave Australia. Hope you have an amazing birthday. We will be thinking of you!" Jack couldn't muster a heartfelt reply of his own. All he wrote was "what she said" with a thumbs-up emoji.

Curious about why he was being cold, I decided to spark a conversation on Snapchat. "Hi," I said. Feeling vulnerable, I told him I missed him, but I soon regretted the message when he replied: "Thanks?" I asked him what he meant, but he vaguely responded, "Idk tbh." Although I was frustrated, I wasn't ready to end the conversation. "I just wanted to say I missed you. That was an odd response," I typed. "Well, that was an odd comment," he quickly snapped back. It was as if nothing ever happened between us. "I don't even know who you are anymore. You don't sound like yourself," I stated. An "okie doke" was all I got for an answer, so I decided to leave him on open. Our interaction brought up the same anxious, helpless emotions that I dealt with the day of our breakup. Why would Jack dismiss all of our history? Did our summer romance mean nothing to him?

His nonchalance was a painful wake-up call: the guy I dated was not as perfect as I thought he was. Falling in love felt magical when I was in the relationship. But at that moment, looking back to a time when I was so enamored with him, I felt ignorant. Little did I know he could change into a different person in such a short amount of time. I don't think he was putting up a false front over the summer. I saw the way he looked at me, and I still believe his feelings were genuine. Returning to Australia to further his career most likely got to his head. He began to value himself far more than he ever valued me. That realization was an important step in my personal healing process. Before our painful text exchange, I was working my way through sadness, but his words left me feeling angry with him for the first time. I previously held a grudge against his mom and manager. Now, I resented Jack. My sadness started to shatter little by little. I was ready to pick myself up and move forward at last.

For months, I considered if I was to blame for the breakup. Was I putting too much pressure on him to commit? In the immediate aftermath, I felt guilty for expressing my emotions so soon, since that would encourage him to do so as well. I couldn't hold back from saying the "L" word any longer—and that was nothing to be ashamed of. It stung that he never reciprocated my words, but the way he caressed me was the closest to love I felt at the time. When I was with him, nothing else mattered. It was just us two, looking deeply into each other's eyes with our hearts open and full of love—at least, that was what I thought love felt like.

The breakup drove me to question the entire notion of love. Was it even possible to fall in love in only one month? Was love at as young as sixteen inevitably impossible to accomplish? All I knew was that the second he let me go, it felt like I had suffered a severe loss. I was washed over with emotions similar to those I had experienced after a close friend's death. The second he called off our relationship, my body went numb. I may have been young, but I know myself better than anyone—and I knew just how much I was hurting. It felt like my world was turned upside down, and that's when I knew what I was feeling was love.

However, there's a difference between loving someone and being in love. The way I see it, being *in* love with someone is infatuation to the point where you don't want to let go. Jack's constant kindness, praise, and dedication to our relationship made it easy to get attached. To love someone is to love who they are internally, to embrace the cracks within their soul. If you truly love your significant other, you can't imagine your life without them. I wasn't with Jack long enough to establish such a deep connection, even though at the moment, I thought I did. In reality, I hardly knew him. I loved the idea of Jack and everything he had to offer, but I wasn't familiar with the bits and pieces of his heart. We never argued—our time together always remained at surface-level magic. Although it was wonderful to revel in the romance for the time being, our relationship was never positioned to last. Love is never perfect, and I should have seen our much-too-easy affection for each other as a red flag from the start. My experience with Jack taught me to stay grounded to reality while immersing myself in a passionate relationship. I was so blinded by his blue eyes and blonde locks that I forgot to look around me. I didn't think about what would happen once the tour was over and he went back home. Instead, I held onto the present moment and never lost sight of how strongly I felt for him. My lack of pragmatism set me on a path to heartbreak.

Our relationship was my first brush with love, and I sincerely thank him for teaching me it was possible. Besides, once you hit the rock bottom of your first heartbreak, the only place to go is up from there. I have no regrets. I believe everything happens for a reason, and the reason he came into my life was to demonstrate what I deserve in a relationship: someone who makes me feel heard, special, and cared for. Jack showed me that it's okay to set your expectations high when pursuing a guy—you deserve to feel like royalty and nothing less. Having a fairytale complex and holding onto hope for an epic love can actually help you filter through boys. Just be sure to remember who you are and that your identity is not determined by your Prince Charming.

"Happily ever after" isn't entirely fictional as long as you define it on your own terms. A union of prince and princess isn't necessarily the perfect ending. Sometimes, a breakup is a smarter, more suitable conclusion to your storybook. Only your heart knows what's right. But remember Cinderella would never settle for a selfish guy who calls it quits via text message, and neither should you. ♥

## Swipe Left:

### MOVING ON

Memory is complicated. In the immediate aftermath of a breakup, the memories seem so close, it often feels like too much to bear. But a year later, when memories start to fade, the feeling of forgetting can be just as painful. I worried that as Jack drifted further into my past, so would all of my memories with him. I wouldn't be able to remember our time together and tap into the joy I felt when I was around him.

That doesn't mean I didn't try. For the longest time, I had feelings for a close guy friend I hooked up with once. I couldn't stop thinking about him, and I didn't know why. Turns out, I didn't really like him. I liked what he symbolized. This friend and I walked the same streets I walked with Jack. We took part in the same activities in the same places. We did what my ex and I did, as well as what I wish we could've done. I tried to relive my relationship through him. I wanted to rewrite the narrative. Hopefully, this time, I would get my happy ending. When the friend rejected me, it felt like I was experiencing heartbreak all over again, all because I saw him as a representation of Jack.

What helped me was remembering that time passes and progresses, and memories fade to make room for new ones. When I close my eyes, I can't feel myself in Jack's arms like I used to. But I can look back at pictures years later and become overwhelmed with emotions, both positive and negative. Nearly three years after Jack and I broke up, I found out that one of my friends took part in a project with him. She gave me no heads-up before promoting it on social media. I didn't know whether to be angry or upset. Seeing him with my friend felt like he was closer to me than he had been in a long time. He had reentered my world, and that was a scary feeling.

Letting go of an ex is like disposing of an old, sentimental pair of pants. No matter how much you stretch to make it work, it just doesn't fit the same. Just like you might outgrow your favorite skinny jeans, you can outgrow a person. But that doesn't mean they never existed. I no longer see Jack as my boyfriend—he's just somebody that I used to know, somebody who was very special to me.

I've banished the phrase "moving on" from my vocabulary. Those words make it seem like there's something I need to run away from—or in the case of the social media post, swipe away from. In reality, I just needed to make peace with my past. The heart has the ability to heal itself if you feed it patience, understanding, and acceptance. My breakup with Jack was one of the most difficult experiences I've ever gone through. I acknowledge the pain he put me through, but I also find beauty in the fact that he was my first love. Instead of moving on, I've moved forward—closer to the man who's meant for me.

# Chapter 3

# The Vampire

I'VE ALWAYS BEEN A FAN of *The Vampire Diaries*, so when I was with Justin, one thing was clear—he loved to bite. Literally. Just like Damon Salvatore, Justin would dig his teeth into my lips, chin, cheeks, and neck, perhaps more than he would kiss me. Not only was his fetish for biting unusual, but it was downright painful, which made it more difficult to adapt to his habit.

Ironically, it all began one lonely evening under a full moon. I arrived at a weekend influencer event in the late afternoon. Just three months after my breakup with Jack, I dreaded the inevitable déjà vu. "I'm never going to find anyone here as special as Jack was," I told Jordan, one of my best friends and fellow influencer. No one said I needed to find myself a guy at every social media event. It was a pressure I placed on myself. After all, the number of hotties was hard to ignore. *Just be confident. Talk to as many guys as possible*, I encouraged myself at the door of the welcome meeting.

Being bold in front of guys—albeit social media stars with millions of followers—is easier said than done. I quietly sat down on the couch to listen in on the meeting. Influencers piled into the event manager's hotel room, taking a seat on the windowsill, sofa, or bathroom sink. I noticed a pattern: most girls had an arm draped over a guy. Some made a much-too-obvious effort to brush his shoulder. I noticed someone sneak out of the room with an influencer I had my eye on. "They're definitely going to film together," I said to Jordan, watching as the girl pointed to a TikTok sound on her phone. Jordan scoffed. "They're going to do more than that."

As the manager laid down the law (no fooling around; no wrecking the property; no drugs or alcohol), I scanned the room for a potential suitor. There were tall blondes and muscular brunettes, most of whom had a perm. No one measured up to Jack. Part of me hoped he'd surprise me and walk through the door. I dreamed that he'd make a grand gesture and fly across the country to profess his love, to tell me he made a mistake in letting me go. But the reality of the situation was that he was gone. I thought I was over him, but being back at a social media event hit me harder than expected.

After the meeting, Jordan and I went to our friend Sophie's room with a group of girls. They were planning which TikTok trends to try that evening, but my brain was elsewhere. I tried to focus on learning new dances and making friends, but it seemed impossible. I was hung up on Jack, and eventually, I couldn't conceal my heartache any longer. I ran outside and into the dark, leaned over the edge of the balcony and started to sob. A bunch of boys were on the floor below me, but they were too busy fixing their hair to notice. I was alone, and all I wanted was for Jack to wrap his arms around me and make me feel whole again. I was used to having a guy in an influencer setting. Being there single felt strange and uncomfortable.

Jordan had a gut feeling that something was wrong, and within seconds, she came outside to hold me while I cried. "It's okay. Let it out," she said softly as I cried into her shoulder. "Trust me, you can do so much better." I didn't believe in "better." At the time, I thought Jack was the best it could get for me. I didn't know how to move on, nor did I want to. "You're okay.

We'll find guys, and if not, we have each other. Let's just walk around," Jordan said.

I wiped the mascara from under my eyes to finish filming a lip-sync video with the girls. "Are you okay?" Sophie asked. I nodded, although it was clear my heart was hurting, and I needed some space. Jordan and I ditched the group, so we could roam downstairs. As we descended down a large staircase to the lobby, Jordan spotted two guys walking through automatic doors. They weren't at the meeting, but the way they carried themselves (head high, phone in hand) indicated that they were influencers. The boys, both brunettes, wandered aimlessly, so Jordan sparked a conversation. "Hey, are you guys doing the influencer event too?" she asked. I rolled my eyes. Frankly, I wasn't in much of a mood for flirtation. "Yeah, are you guys?" the boy responded in a Australian accent. I gulped. His voice had a striking resemblance to Jack's. I did have a thing for Aussies. He ran a hand through his short brown hair. "I'm Justin, and this is my friend, Mark. He's singing tomorrow," he explained.

The four of us walked upstairs to a dining area so we could sit down and chat. "The Aussie is cute, Jordan," I whispered. "I told you so! Go for it!" she said a bit too loud, causing Justin to turn around and stare. Jordan walked ahead with Mark so that Justin and I could chat. "Have you done any social media tours before?" I asked. "Yeah, but I feel like my following's too big for that now," he said. His ego was as large as his social media following. But I was set on making a connection. I needed someone to make me believe there was hope for romance outside of my relationship with Jack.

In the dining hall, Justin and I exchanged Snapchats so we could talk privately. Jordan and Mark were always on our tails. "Where can we hang out?" I typed. Justin wrote back from across the table: "My room?" I looked up at him while he was anxiously typing away on his phone. I knew it wasn't smart to go to a guy's hotel room solo after I just met him. I worried he was only interested in a hookup—not getting to know me better. But I talked myself out of the risks: *He's an influencer too. You have mutual friends. Everything will be okay.*

Eventually, we came to a compromise: Jordan and Mark would come with us. "I'm scared to be alone with him. Please stay with us," I begged Jordan when the boys weren't looking. There was just one problem: they were staying in a single room, and there was no bathroom door. There was no way Justin and I could have privacy unless our friends left the room completely. Jordan said that in case of an emergency, she would be next door. "Have your phone on you at all times," I demanded.

"What are you up to?" I started, taking a seat several inches away from Justin on the couch. He fiddled with his phone. Whatever occupied his screen was his sole focus. I was of secondary importance. "Are you singing tomorrow?" I asked, prying for his attention. "Jordan and I are doing a duet." Justin rolled his eyes. "Social media tours don't really help your career," he laughed. "I sang in a band at these events for years. I'm just here to support Mark." His arrogance was a turn-off, and I glanced eagerly towards the door. But one particular comment drew me back: "You smell good." Jordan had lent me her signature scent, Bath and Body Works's Into the Night. It never fails.

Now that he seemed grounded to the present, I asked more about his career. "Show me a video of your singing!" I said, inching closer to his phone. A photo of him and another girl popped up as he tapped the lock screen. "Oh, is that your girlfriend?" I joked, slightly uncomfortable at the prospect that I might be the "other woman." Justin shook his head. "No. Just someone special to me from before my aunt died." A long silence shot through the room. I could tell from his solemn stare that the wound was fresh. "I'm so sorry. When did she pass?" I asked. "A year ago," he replied, dignified but with lingering disappointment. He proceeded to tell me how close the two of them were, how his aunt was his biggest supporter. I hovered over Justin's phone to watch one of his performances that his aunt attended. As we sat closer together, I felt his dark brown strands brush against my shoulder with every head turn. Once several inches away on the couch, we were now so close, I could hear his steady breathing. His Australian accent was evident in his singing voice. Admittedly, his vocals weren't the best, but I could tell how passionate he was about his talent and making his aunt proud.

"Sing for me live," I requested on a whim. Justin agreed without hesitation and sat up, so he could project his vocals. He chose to sing "This Town," a Niall Horan tune about being stuck on an ex-lover. I couldn't get Justin's lock screen out of my head, and I wondered if the song was a hint at his own life. Nonetheless, I smiled, despite my skepticism and his poor pitch. I felt forced into stroking his ego to keep the flame. "You're so talented!" I exclaimed, placing a hand on his shoulder.

As soon as we came in physical contact, I saw a shift in Justin's eyes, as if he saw me in a new, romantic light. He leaned in for a kiss, and we reclined on the couch. One particular move caught me off guard. After several minutes of a casual make out, he began to bite. Justin nipped at my chin to the point where it was actually painful. I wondered if this was typical foreplay or a unique fetish. It was unlike any hookup I'd experienced before. As he kissed me, I no longer envisioned the self-centered singer beside me. He was like a vampire, gnawing at every patch of skin he desired. The sensation was strange, slightly painful yet exhilarating. Why did I like and hate the biting at the same time? Just as a vampire compels his victims, Justin encouraged me to allow his "fangs" to dig in. I initially saw the biting as playful, but after a while, it was weird, and I wanted him to stop. I didn't stay in Justin's room too late because we didn't know each other well enough. Not to mention, I needed an ice pack for my face. Around 10 p.m., I texted Jordan that I was ready to leave, and Justin and I parted ways with a quick peck.

Jordan and I hung out in our friend's room for a while, but I kept thinking about Justin. The sharp pain on my chin made it hard to forget. The experience was spontaneous and shocking. Oddly enough, I found myself craving more of him. "Tonight was fun," I texted Justin with a winky face. He responded quickly: "Sure, it was an amazing night with you. Smash it tomorrow. Can't wait to watch." I crawled into bed on a high. Despite his distaste for social media tours, I appreciated that he was offering his support. Let's just say my dreams that night were... bloody good.

The following morning, as I washed my face in the mirror, I noticed a whopping hickey—on my chin. My makeup artist had to color-correct the purple, laughing as she dabbed the beauty blender along my complexion. How was I supposed to show up on stage looking like I fell on my face? The concealer covered the bruise as best as possible, but it wasn't perfect. As soon as I ran into Justin in the ballroom, I pointed at my chin. "Good job," I joked. He shrugged, unbothered by the bruise. It seemed like it wasn't the first time he gave a chin hickey.

We ate lunch together, and the conversation was awkward and strained. "Are you excited for today?" I asked. He shoved a cheeseburger into his mouth. The smell of grease made me want to gag. "Eh. I'm honestly kind of bored," he blurted. I glanced down at my metallic sweatsuit. Was I boring him? I was the one keeping the conversation alive. Every time the room fell quiet, I asked him something about himself. He didn't express much interest in my life. Not to mention...we split the bill (major red flag).

At least he didn't forget about our night together. On our way backstage, he gave me a quick kiss. He would also drape his arm around me, and we took pictures together in front of the stage (yes, the chin bruise was visible). We sang along to Mark's stage set, and Jordan videoed us swaying together on her phone. However, when it was my turn to take the stage, Justin was nowhere to be found. He blew hot and cold. I was waiting for him to place his ego aside and indicate whether or not he was into me. Constantly boosting his confidence was tiring when he didn't lift me up in return. Thankfully, he redeemed himself. "I have to go say hi to my dad," I said at the meet and greet. He clasped my arm to stop me from walking away. "Where is he? I want to meet him!" he exclaimed. Justin was friendly, so I wasn't too surprised. But still, I wondered why he was so eager to meet my family. Next thing I knew, they were shaking hands, and I was forced to leave them chatting, so I could return to the meet and greet line.

I was eager to see Justin after the meet and greet, but he seemed to be too busy for me. I'd try to spark a conversation, asking where he was or telling him to meet me by the game room. He would take hours to respond, and when I would follow up, all he would say was "hey." I blew up his phone, typing, "comeee," "where ru," or "let's find somewhere to chat." I was hanging out with my friends in the arcade around 9 p.m. when I finally spotted Justin outside: he was chatting up a group of adoring fans. I hid inside a driving simulator and pretended I hadn't seen him. As I closed the dark curtain, I shut out the high-pitched arcade machine noises along with it. I took a deep breath and reveled in the moment of silence I had with myself. The arcade was upbeat, filled with free prizes and foosball. But as tears welled in my eyes, I was anything but lively. It felt like I was just another girl in a crowd of fans to Justin. We had just met—who gave him the right to make me feel small?

Once Justin was done taking selfies with his followers, he came inside to entertain a special supporter: me. His greeting—a casual hug and "how are you"—made me feel like a fan rather than a fling. We filmed a quick couple's TikTok sound together, and I spontaneously kissed him on the cheek at the end. I was hoping the peck would reignite our connection, but Justin didn't budge. "I'm going back to my room to take a nap," he declared.

Clearly, he wasn't interested. In fact, within the hour, word got to me that he was hanging out with another girl. I clenched my arcade tickets in my hand and scrunched them into a ball. Not only was I livid, but deep down, I was in pain.

To prevent myself from getting too upset, I took a note from Justin: don't shy away from being self-confident. I strutted back inside the game room and pulled my guy friend aside. We sent Justin a selfie sticking our tongues out, captioned "what you're missing." Justin loved to joke around—the majority of the photos we took earlier, he was sticking his tongue out too. I hoped that once he saw my Snapchat, he would come downstairs to be with me instead. Justin took the picture a little too seriously—he assumed I was hooking up with someone else. He was supposed to tag along with Jordan and me to Disney World the following day, but an angry text I received the following morning disrupted our plans. "Why did you Snapchat me that?" he typed. "I don't want to play games. I'm heading out." My heart sank. Afraid of being rejected all over again, I needed to win Justin over. I anxiously tapped my acrylic nails on my screen until I figured out what to reply. "I'm not looking to play games!" I said, despite the fact that I was standing next to the arcade while waiting for a car. "We weren't alone in the game room! We were in a group! I only have eyes for you, I promise. I'm sorry!"

As I explored Disney World, I was glued to my cell phone, refreshing repeatedly to see if Justin replied. On It's a Small World, I noticed he unadded me on Snapchat. I wanted to scream against the high-pitched singing. When I got off the ride, I took a seat on a park bench, so I could text Justin and ask why he unadded me. "You would have done the same if I sent a photo of a girl," he replied bluntly. There was a double standard: he could hang out with other girls, yet I couldn't hang out with other guys. Still, I apologized several times, and our conversation eventually dwindled.

Once I left the event and had space from the site of the drama, I realized Justin was gaslighting me. He was trying to make me feel like I did something wrong when really, I wasn't to blame. I never got with another guy, and even if I did, Justin and I weren't dating. I wasn't committed to him. He tricked me into thinking I was a selfish cheater when really, I was the one waiting for him in the arcade. He projected the blame on me to hide the fact that he was the one who disappeared all evening.

It didn't take long for Justin to see he made a mistake. Although he never apologized for falsely accusing me of being a player, he stopped dwelling on it. Just one day after our argument, he texted me, "hey." I found it difficult to forget his manipulation. Until, of course, he offered to come into the city to spend New Year's Eve together. Was he interested in me again? Was he planning on kissing me at midnight? My fantasies rendered me all in.

On New Year's Eve, I planned on having dinner with friends and meeting up with Justin after at a party. But a fun evening quickly turned into a night of empty promises. As the hours passed, Justin retracted from his plans to see me. Around seven, he insisted that he wanted to come but had no way of getting to NYC. I clutched my phone tightly at the dinner table, tapping my screen every few minutes to see if there were any new messages. "Stop checking your phone!" my friend scolded me, pushing a hot plate of prawns under my nose. "Enjoy your dinner. It's New Year's Eve." It was hard to enjoy the food display when my mind was elsewhere. When we paid the check at around eight, I finally received a follow-up from Justin. He said he preferred to hang out the following day and was an "idiot" for thinking he could come that late. Eager to see him again, I laid out a clear plan: he would meet me at my house at 2:30 p.m., and we would go ice skating. Justin promised, but it didn't take long for him to pull back. At 3 a.m., he warned me that there was a chance we would have to push our plans back a few hours.

Hours turned into days. I didn't hear from Justin until a week later. I was sitting at my desk, studying a pile of calculus assignments for an upcoming midterm, when he texted me. He was in the city and wanted me to meet him by his hotel in an hour. It was dark out, and I didn't feel comfortable taking a car alone to where he was staying at the opposite end of Manhattan. He never offered to come to me—I was the one who had to make the sacrifice on a school night. He wouldn't even meet me halfway. So I set my homework aside, grabbed black jeans and a sweater from my closet, and swiped on mascara. I blew my entire allowance on an Uber that took me to him.

Next thing I knew, we were hand in hand walking through Times Square. We considered climbing to the Top of the Rock, but Justin didn't seem too keen on spending his money (even though I had just spent mine). We stopped at a street stand, and as we waited for his hot dog, he began to bite my chin—again. The habit was starting to creep me out. As we strolled under the bright billboards, I wiped from my chin a smudge of mustard that he transferred from his lips. "Look at the New Year's Eve ball!" he exclaimed, pointing with a greasy finger. New York never seemed less glamorous.

The evening took a positive turn when we spotted a large seesaw in the middle of the street. We sat at opposite ends, and Justin pushed hard off the ground so that I went flying. I giggled. Biting fetish aside, he always managed to make me laugh. Witnessing the city from up above, I also saw Justin in a different light. He may have been a walking red flag, but he was a lot of fun. He was always unapologetically himself and encouraged me not to take life too seriously. After the weighted "I love you" of my previous relationship, he was exactly what I needed.

Entranced by his playfulness, I agreed to hang out with him the next day. This time, I was more prepared. I had already completed my homework, and I was dressed and ready to go for hours. The only message I had received from him that day was "hey." In fact, every time I asked him what time I should be at his hotel, "hey" was his only reply. It was as if he wasn't capable of having a conversation with me. I sat for hours on my bed with my phone in hand, waiting for some inkling of when or if I was going to meet Justin. I triple, sometimes quadruple-texted him (never a good sign). I passed the time by filming TikToks or neurotically touching up my makeup, so it would be perfect when he called. He never did.

## Double-Tap This:

**PRE-DATE HYPE PLAYLIST**

As I'm getting ready to go out with a guy, I have a special playlist of feel-good tracks I listen to. From Lizzo to Lil Nas X to Beyoncé, the songs below provide an instant confidence boost before leaving. Blast these tunes from your phone as you're swiping on lip gloss or dancing out the door.

1. "Pepas" by Farruko
2. "Around the World (La La La La La)" by A Touch of Class
3. "Panini" by Lil Nas X
4. "Party Up" by DMX
5. "Boss Bitch" by Doja Cat
6. "Bugatti" by Ace Hood (ft. Future and Rick Ross)
7. "Runaway (U & I)" by Galantis
8. "Bounce Back" by Big Sean
9. "SICKO MODE" by Travis Scott
10. "Hot Girl Summer" by Megan Thee Stallion
11. "Friday" by Riton and Nightcrawlers
12. "INDUSTRY BABY" by Lil Nas X and Jack Harlow
13. "MY POWER" by Nija, Beyoncé, Busiswa, Yemi Alade, Tierra Whack, Moonchild Sanelly, and DJ Lag
14. "Energia" by SOFI TUKKER
15. "Good as Hell" by Lizzo

It was getting late, so I texted him that I assumed we weren't hanging out anymore. His response was relatively unsurprising at this point: "hey." He asked me what I was doing, and I replied that I was waiting for him to tell me our plans. In the moment, I didn't care about how desperate I sounded. I allowed him to be in full control. I paced my room, infuriated by his lack of regard for my schedule. Finally, I texted him how I was feeling: "I can't keep sitting around my house like an idiot, Justin. I have homework. You can't keep flaking on me, it's not fair. This spontaneity thing is driving me crazy." The effort was always one-sided. I was sick of chasing someone who never made time for me. I wiped my makeup off and swept my perfectly straightened hair into a messy bun. It felt like I was punched in the gut. Justin apologized and even offered to pick me up at school the next day, but I knew that was never going to happen. Every time I tried to make plans with him, all he had to say was "hey." There was no "where," "when" or "what time." He always sent a delayed response, and although he expressed how much he wanted to see me, he never took the steps to do so.

There was no reason to keep holding my breath waiting for him to call. I learned that it's never worth pursuing someone who doesn't make time for you. If he doesn't treat you like a priority, then don't settle—he doesn't deserve you. I put so much energy into Justin, even when he wasn't physically there. Trying to decipher his bland texts and make solid plans with him was emotionally draining. He may have made me laugh when we were together, but the fun was fleeting. The positive memories we made together were overshadowed by the hours I spent agonizing over why he took so long to text me back. I needed to move on and focus on finding someone who made me feel seen and heard.

I later learned from a friend that Justin favors hookups over serious relationships, hence why he would only reach out to me when he felt like it. I was "something" he hooked up with—not "someone." In fact, I found out that he gets with strangers quite often. I had officially gotten the ick. With this knowledge, I felt lucky that I severed ties with Justin when I did. I never would have given him what he wanted and vice versa.

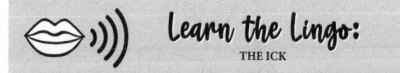

## Learn the Lingo:
### THE ICK

Your attraction to someone can be killed by something that suddenly flips your opinion—also known as an *ick*. Admiration turns into disgust, and you'll no longer be interested in the person. Icks are specific: perhaps your partner chews with his mouth open, or he has dirty fingernails. He may be obsessed with staring at himself in the mirror, or he never dresses well. One of my biggest icks is when a guy asks me, "Can I kiss you?" It makes the moment inorganic and completely ruins the chemistry if there was even any to begin with. Everyone has their own turn-offs—trust me, you'll know an ick when you see one.

While we were talking, Justin fell into a pattern of ghosting for several days. Now, it was my turn to cut him off. He made me feel like a desperate fling when all I wanted was to learn more about him. The right person will always put you first, not leave you in the dark. Someone who truly cares will stick around, not disappear into the night. It may also be best to avoid someone who bites (unless it's Damon Salvatore—then, you're excused). ♥

# Chapter 4

# The Aristotle Addict

FOR AS LONG AS I can remember, my dad has told me that life is like a roller coaster. Trust me, I know it's cliché. But he has a point—everything that goes down eventually rises. I used to believe relationships were like the track support of a coaster. They remain strong and stationary as life speeds by. But romantic connections are most similar to the coaster cars themselves. In fact, my relationship with Nathan, a fellow student at my university, was reminiscent of that roller coaster: turbulent, enthralling, and complex—all at the same time.

I've never been a fan of Greek philosophy, but for five months, I fell for a guy addicted to Aristotle—until I realized that he was *not* as intellectual as he led on. The boy seemed like a figure pulled straight from the Beat Generation, cooped up with a scholarly book and cigarette. His smoking obsession bothered me from the beginning, yet I ignored all doubts. He was smart, driven, and easy to talk to, so I was instantly drawn to him. We were to attend the same college in the fall, and besides discussing his daily Aristotle readings, we built a serious connection. He and I spoke of sex, death, serious past relationships, and even what it would be like when we meet each other's families. We never ran out of things to talk about. He FaceTimed me every night when he got out of the shower, wrapped in a single towel with water dripping from his spiky blonde hair onto his gold chain necklace. "Welcome to the show," he'd say, fully aware that I was attracted to him.

We first met when he visited New York. He was tall and very thin with slight scruff. I was floored by his 6'5" stature. When I went in for my first hug, a sense of power radiated from his presence. The fact that someone of such wisdom and strength—physically, emotionally, and intellectually—could challenge me was invigorating.

Subtle actions continually hinted that he was interested as we spoke: he'd play with the pom-pom on my beanie, reassuring that I looked "cute" despite the red poof situated atop my head. As the cold winter air washed over us, he wrapped me in his coat like a perfect gentleman (I drowned in the jacket). However, most of the time, he dominated the conversation and boasted about his own life, whether in person or on FaceTime. The tendency to talk was natural: some boys love to gab. Sentences upon sentences pass without the opportunity to utter a single word. The anxious foot-tapping and tongue-biting become all too familiar while waiting patiently for the opportunity to reply. The topic of conversation generally remains the same: it does not revolve around the weather or plans for the rest of the afternoon or evening. Typically, males dominate the conversation by discussing themselves. Conceited? Perhaps. But the ability to listen closely, ask questions, and stay engaged is the ultimate test. This standard has always frustrated me: why stay silent while boys fish for compliments so often? I was angry at having to hold my tongue while Nathan praised himself—his cars, his room, and even his appearance. I tried to talk about myself sometimes, but he didn't give much of a response. Constantly seeking his approval became exhausting. Why did I always have to be the one to boost his ego?

He never complimented me as I sat makeup-free, messy bun and all on my bed during our FaceTime calls. The strongest reaction I would get out of him would be a message with the heart eyes emoji when my cleavage was showing. It made me wonder if he wanted me or if he just wanted my body. Did he see me as a partner or prey? Most of the time, it seemed like he was more interested in my physical features than my personality.

Nathan's selfishness became especially clear to me when he stopped engaging in our budding relationship. Five months in, there was a two-week period where he suddenly ghosted me, cutting off all forms of communication without explanation. The sound of my phone vibrating always found its way to my ears as I anticipated his next text. Had I said or done something wrong? Was he talking to another girl he liked more? Perhaps I wasn't smart enough or pretty enough for him. During those fourteen days, I beat myself up over letting him get away. He hadn't provided any sense of clarity, so I blamed myself to secure some closure. Until I finally received a message from him: he was no longer interested in starting college with a girlfriend in tow. As he contemplated the next four years of his life, he began to realize that he couldn't see me in it. Any connection that he had established with me was shattered. All feelings were forgotten, and a relationship was no longer on the table. His flirtatious words echoed in my mind as I coped with the pain and shock, and I considered if our bond was simply a "show" all along.

The sudden change of plans left me winded, but rather than shed a tear, I found myself staring blankly at the ceiling, frozen in confusion. Why did he lead me on if he hadn't known what he really wanted? Why did I sacrifice my sleep schedule for weeks to speak to him (midnight and beyond) if nothing was to become of it? Most puzzling of all, I failed to understand how someone so intelligent could be so insensitive. The obvious irony of the situation left me wondering: where did his wisdom go?

Months later, he reached out via text: he was back in New York and wanted to hang out. Deep down, I knew I wasn't being rational in replying to his message. I kept my friends' words in mind ("You can do so much better"; "He doesn't deserve you"). But the next thing I knew, I was checking my calendar for my availability. The first time we tried to make plans, he canceled just an hour before because his couch arrived at his new apartment. The last-minute need to reschedule was a red flag that I blindly ignored, and I swore that I wouldn't be the one to initiate our next plan.

After a while, though, I was eager to see him. I texted him on his birthday and said I wanted to take him out to celebrate. We wound up meeting at a popular sushi spot, and I was under the impression that we were on a date. All the signs were there: he pulled out my chair, held the door open for me, and paid the check. We talked about his life, as usual, but one conceited comment particularly stood out. "How's school?" I asked. Nathan scoffed. "Too easy," he replied. Confidence is attractive, but not when it becomes borderline showy. I listened and nodded yet found it difficult to speak up.

After a bit of bragging about how his studies were "a breeze," Nathan suddenly asked if I was seeing someone. I smiled. Was he checking if I was single, so he could make a move? I told him I was on the market since I had been trapped inside my home for the majority of the pandemic, then asked him the same question. "Yeah, I'm seeing someone right now. We're kind of official," he replied. My smile faded, and I felt my chopsticks fall to my plate. I glanced down at my high-heel boots, which I had purposely worn to match his height. I felt defeated. How could I have been so clueless? Left with nothing to say but "Good for you," we parted ways.

After the date, I told myself I was done with him. There would be no more spontaneous Snapchats and flirty FaceTime calls. He wasn't available, and that was that. But, a month later, he randomly reached out, informing me that he was now single. He even swiped up on an Instagram story of me in full glam, replying with a wide-eyed emoji. His message clearly signified that I caught his attention—his eyes were finally on me. Nonetheless, I was still angered over the sushi night. I stood my ground, "liked" the story swipe-up and sent a mere "ok" in response to his declaration of singledom. I was proud of myself for not showing any signs of emotion; he hurt me, and I was not going to allow him to trigger my feelings again.

But when you're stuck in the middle of a pandemic, desperate for human connection, it's easy to think irrationally. And that's just what I did. In a moment of weakness (or perhaps it was just boredom), I messaged him and made myself available. The evening was an out-of-body experience. I was feeling vulnerable, and just a few hours after I reached out, I was in an Uber to his apartment. On the outside, I knew what it looked like: a 9 p.m. booty call and nothing more. Yet I imagined that maybe, just maybe, he still held onto the emotional connection we established a year prior. With faith in romance, I strutted out of the car and into the brightly-lit lobby. "Here for Nathan. I'm a friend," I announced to the doorman. As I walked toward the elevator, I clenched my iPhone and the chipper GIF of Carrie Bradshaw my friend had sent. I read and re-read her words: "Carrie Bradshaw. Carrie Bradshaw. Carrie Bradshaw." "It's Nathan," I told myself, feeling my hands shaking as I pressed floor twelve. "You know him. Everything is going to be okay."

At first, everything was okay. He greeted me warmly at the door. His scruff had transformed into a slight beard, and his head of hair was in the process of growing back from a semi-buzz cut. I was taken aback by the strong aroma of cigarette smoke in the living room. I asked him for a cup of water and sipped as we began our signature intellectual discussion. I cuddled up on the couch, and he sat a few feet away at his desk chair, nervously removing his glasses to adjust them every few minutes. We gave each other life updates: he showed me a video of another high-rise apartment he was moving into. I looked deeply into his eyes—they were slightly red. While I focused on him, he zoned out and often glanced out the window.

# Double-Tap This:

### IT'S YOUR FIRST TIME AT HIS HOUSE... HERE'S WHAT TO REMEMBER

Visiting your guy's house for the first time is a big deal, especially if you two are working towards an exclusive relationship. You're finally getting privacy together outside of dates or hangouts in public. If he invites you to his home, expect to explore your physical connection more than you have done before. No need to be scared—trust the connection you already have, and only do what you're comfortable with. Here are some tips to consider before pulling up to his place.

- Calculate how long it's been since you two started seeing each other. One week? It might be too soon to take things to his private quarters. In general, if you've been on five or more dates, you should be good to go.
- Don't come or leave too late. You don't want to seem like a booty call. Six or seven should suffice for the arrival. Head home before midnight, and do *not* sleep over at his place.
- Give his address and phone number to a friend or family member in case of an emergency. Tell them not to use it unless you're MIA for several hours.
- Wear comfortable clothes. Think sweatpants, a tank top, and a no-makeup makeup look.
- Consider that you might run into his parents or roommates. Make sure you're well-mannered and dress appropriately just in case.
- Treat his space with care. Take your shoes off, so you don't track in dirt, and ask before touching any of his things.
- Brainstorm a fun activity for you two to do—and no, Netflix and chill doesn't count (at least not until later). Perhaps he has a speaker you can play music off of or some snacks in the fridge you can share.
- Ask a friend to check in via text after an hour to make sure everything is going well. If you want to leave, have them call you with a white lie (i.e., a "family emergency") that gives you an excuse to go.
- Use the bathroom if you need to. This one may seem obvious, but some people are afraid to stink up their date's space. Holding it in will only make you uncomfortable for the rest of the night. Use an air freshener if there's one in the bathroom, and you have nothing to worry about.

Randomly, he started talking about how he loathes therapy: "We should walk through fire to get to the light. We have to deal with our own problems to get better, not rely on a therapist," he lectured. I clenched my teeth as he spoke. Therapy is a treatment I'm passionate about, and he carelessly dismissed the concept. I wanted to speak my mind, to assert that there's not one singular path to the light. I wanted to explain that the journey to recovery is more of a crossroads than a straight line: you can choose to go to therapy or go it alone, and both decisions have potential for success. I kept my mouth shut for fear of angering Nathan. My breath deepened in anger as we shifted topics.

He began to discuss the U.S. economy, fidgeting in his chair as he revealed what was weighing on him: "America is screwed." I know little about the economy, but I do know Nathan. "You like things complicated, though, don't you?" I asked once his rant was complete. He chuckled, then went silent for a few seconds. I couldn't tell if his stoned state had shut his mouth or the realization that I really understood him. "Damn, that was insightful," he said quietly. We were finally in sync.

After we exercised our brains, I suggested we watch a television show or movie. I moved to the side of the couch and suggested that he sit beside me. "I'm comfortable in the chair. That's why I got it," he bluntly asserted. Confused yet still confident, I directed my attention towards the screen. We agreed to watch *Bones* on Hulu. Throughout the pilot, we mocked the script and background music. "It's so cheesy! It sounds like music you'd find on the Haunted Mansion ride at Disney or something," I giggled. We both criticized the characters, and eventually, that connection drove him to sit next to me on the couch. All of a sudden, he began to stroke my hair. "Did you make it blonder?" he said. I glanced at him out of the corner of my eye. "Nope, it's the same," I replied. He removed his hand. "It looks good."

Soon after the compliment, Nathan finally took action. He leaned in, and we began making out—slowly, comfortably, and

with effortless sex appeal. As he kissed me, I could taste the cigarettes he smoked before I arrived. It bothered me, but I wasn't
going to let it disrupt the moment that I had been waiting to
occur for over a year. Not even five minutes into the hookup,
though, he directed me into a position on the couch where I
was straddling him. "Lower," he whispered quietly, pulling my
hips closer to his. I wasn't aware of what was going on, since we
both had our clothes on. Eventually, I realized he was teasing to
sex. "I don't want to have sex, Nathan," I declared. He maintained an almost eerie-looking smile across his face. "Why not?"
The answer was simple: I wasn't ready. He said he understood,
and we locked lips once again after I made my boundaries clear.
While I was in his arms, I took it upon myself to ask why he went
on a date with me as he was seeing someone else and why he
waited so many months to make a move. "I like to be a tease," he
said. "I like to build tension. I knew you were confused." It was
clear he craved a sense of control in his romantic engagements.
But how much control is too much?

When the couch became cramped, he suggested we move to
the bedroom. When we reached the bed, I stood stunned as he
unexpectedly unfastened his belt and dropped his jeans to the
floor. It was all moving so fast. "You're going to see what I look
like when I don't work out," he laughed while stripping down to
his underwear. "Stop, you look good!" I quickly reassured him,
although I knew he was just fishing for compliments.

With my consent, he walked behind me and gently lifted my
oversized sweatshirt over my head. I took a quick glance at my
reflection in the window with Nathan by my side. It didn't seem
real; it felt like someone else was staring back at me, like I was
watching a show or movie. Nathan and I were finally getting intimate, and it was hard to believe. "How comfortable are you?" he
asked. Honestly, I didn't know the answer. I advised him simply
to take things slow.

He picked me up and threw me onto the cold bed sheets. As I kissed him, I noticed he was out of character. "Yeah, get lower, baby," he advised. The word placed me inside my head for a moment—he had never called me "baby" before. Nathan situated himself on top of me and dug his fingers into my neck. Once again, he asked about my comfort level. I stared at the perfectly-white ceiling and suggested he "do his thing." At one point, I became uncomfortable, so I decided to be candid with him. "I'm scared," I revealed. He told me not to be afraid, and my heart rate began to calm.

But suddenly, I saw a shift in Nathan. He sighed and sat back on the bed, refusing to make eye contact. He stood up stoically and made a beeline for his clothes, which laid in a disheveled heap on the floor. I remained stretched out on the mattress, arms extended over my head, and watched him in confusion. "This was a mistake. Get dressed," he barked. There I was, lying there half-naked and more vulnerable than I had ever been, and it still wasn't satisfactory. To him, my presence on his bed was noth-ing. I felt like one of many when I had expected to feel like one in a million. I wanted a romantic connection that was special, not ritual in my partner's eyes. I put my leggings back on and walked towards Nathan. "It's not you, it's me," he said, leaning on the edge of the door. "I'm just messed up mentally. I've been in situations before when I wanted something casual, and the girl expected something more. I'm not going down that road again." My initial annoyance was quickly replaced with guilt. It felt like my fault: I was the one who wanted something more meaningful and didn't give him what he wanted. I wasn't enough for him. A sense of shame gnawed at my heart.

Once we were both dressed, we sat on the couch and contin-ued to analyze the situation. He told me I was inexperienced and that we were in different places romance-wise. His comment put me in defense mode. "Just because I don't give my body to every single guy I get with doesn't mean I'm inexperienced," I said, finally standing up to him. How could this be the same guy who opened up to me before? I asked Nathan if he had any feelings for me during those months of FaceTime calls. My heart stung as I witnessed his shocking response: "It was a long time ago. I honestly can't remember."

Instead of a meaningful experience, our hookup seemed like an everyday interaction to him. "Kissing is like shaking hands," he said. My blood boiled at his belittling behavior, but as the discussion continued, I realized that he was correct about one thing: we had completely different perceptions of love. "I'm one hundred percent never going to get married. I'm going to be like that crazy uncle!" he said.

At that moment, I closed the book. It wasn't the fact that he wouldn't want to marry *me* that was bothersome but that he rejected the principle of marriage in general. "You're going to remember when you're forty that conversation you had with me at eighteen," he said. "You're finally going to realize I'm right. Fairytales aren't possible." It took everything in me not to break down or consider that maybe he was right—perhaps everlasting love isn't reality. But then I pictured my first love and how safe, special, and loved my ex made me feel. Nathan may have been sexually mature, but I connected to a guy—a good one at that— on a more poignant level and developed emotional maturity as a result. That quality was something Nathan had yet to establish. I wasn't about to let a guy tell me what or how to feel—that was entirely up to me.

In a sudden detour from our discussion about love, Nathan said he was thinking about becoming a model. "I'm tall. I'm handsome. Why not? Do you think I could do it?" he asked. It was a desperate cry for reassurance. I searched my brain for the perfect reply until I finally found one that fit: "I think you could do anything you set your mind to. Even finding a fairytale romance."

Nathan's narcissism reached a head, and I decided to order my car home. He actually put it best: the hookup needed to happen for it not to happen. Romantic tension built up between us for months, and we needed to explore our physical chemistry to realize we weren't right for each other. He handed me my mini backpack, and we ended the evening with a hug. Just like that, it was over.

As I undressed for a shower that night, I felt dirty. It felt like I had lost my innocence. I kicked myself for getting undressed with someone who did not respect my vulnerability. Once clean, I rummaged through my drawer to find the most innocent-looking pajamas I have: a baby blue pair of Roller Rabbits with a pink pig print (they are now my signature post-hookup PJs). A part of me hoped that stepping into a childlike ensemble would reverse the events of that evening even though deep down, I knew I couldn't go back. I glanced in the mirror and traced my neck with my fingers, praying that a hickey was not present to mark the occasion.

After Nathan abandoned me while I was semi-naked, I felt insecure in my skin. In undressing for the shower, I avoided looking at my body, and I shoved my black lace bra I wore with him deep in my drawer after it was washed. I ditched crop tops for a while as well; anything that showed off my arms or legs took me back to that moment when I felt my bare limbs on Nathan's bed. I swore that I'd never let a guy make me feel uncomfortable with my body again—especially him.

I knew that a relationship with Nathan was finally out of the question. He wanted to stay friends, but I struggled with whether or not that was possible. What did it mean to remain friends with someone I once had an emotional connection with? How were we supposed to hang out without being reminded of our past? Cutting ties altogether seemed like the simplest option to avoid any more complications.

## Swipe Left:

← CAN YOU BE
FRIENDS WITH
SOMEONE YOU
HOOKED UP
WITH?

One time, I spontaneously hooked up with someone I had been friends with for years. We ultimately chose to avoid a relationship because we didn't want to ruin the strong friendship we had established. But when we hung out again late at night, it was awkward. What would happen when the sun went down? I held my breath, waiting to see what would occur when we relaxed in my apartment. He would flip through Netflix or play on his phone to avoid flirtation. Although we sat close together on the couch, neither of us ever made a move. We stuck to the narrative of being "just friends," but I struggled to forget what occurred between us before.

It's difficult to be friends with someone you were romantically connected to in the past. There's always going to be some under-lying feelings towards the person you kissed. You may never hook up with him again, but the sentiment is the same: every time you look him in the eye, you won't be able to forget what it felt like when he held you. It's up to you whether or not you're okay with that lingering over your friendship. In my case, I was friends with the guy before we became friends with benefits, so he was worth holding onto. I pushed my emotions aside because I valued him as a friend. It was a sacrifice I was willing to make because I didn't want to lose him.

Decide if you're comfortable hanging out with memories at the surface or if the emotions are too much to handle. Sometimes, suddenly seeing someone in a more platonic light can be confusing, anxiety-inducing, and painful. Are you able to maintain a friendship, or will your former feelings always get in the way? Just remember: once the physical boundary is crossed, you never really return to being "just friends." Even if you stay friendly, you won't ever see him the same. You two will always be friends with benefits, whether past or present. There's no turning back.

Little did I know Nathan would reach out. A month later, I was out to brunch when I received an impromptu text from him. "Hey. Are you back in the city? Let's hang," it read. All of my pent-up anger and disappointment over our last interaction suddenly vanished. He reached out to me. He was making the effort. Images of our late-night FaceTime calls and flirty texts flashed through my mind. Not only was I reminded of the intellectual conversations themselves but how they made me feel. The more we disagreed, the more I was turned on—hence why I kept coming back to him. Although the way we ended things made me feel undervalued, I tried not to think about what had occurred. You'd assume I was torn in deciding whether or not to respond, but I always saw the best in him. So I said yes…again. He invited me over to tour his new apartment in the evening, between 8:30 and 9:00 p.m., since he "had class." I wasn't about to repeat history. I told him I was nearby and could come in the afternoon if he was available. A pop of spicy cinnamon gum and a fifteen-minute Uber ride later, I was there.

"Here for Nathan," I said to the doorman. The déjà vu stung. Those were the exact words I uttered when I visited his previous building. The doorman rang his apartment, but there was no response. "You were here the other day, right?" the employee asked. I gulped. Perhaps I wasn't the first girl to visit the new space. I glanced out the door and considered ditching the situation. *Maybe this isn't the best idea*, I pondered. Nathan's intentions with me were unclear, especially because he asked to see me later in the evening. I stared at a text my friend had sent in the car: "Remember he was rude to you." I kept the memory tucked away in my mini backpack—the same one I carried the last time I saw Nathan—and proceeded upstairs.

When I exited the elevator, my ears were blocked from riding up over twenty-five floors. The hallways were long and winding. I saw one apartment and an entrance to a rooftop—all the other homes were hidden behind a wall. I wandered through the floor as if it were a maze in trying to find his apartment. Simultaneously, I attempted to navigate the maze in Nathan's mind to figure out what his motive was for the afternoon. Several knocks on the door gave me time to think, until finally, he came to greet me. I still got butterflies when I saw him—even after everything that happened between us.

The welcome was warm yet awkward as expected. Nathan extended his left arm for a hug while I reached out my right. We both aimed for the platonic side hug. I told myself to play it cool—things are only as uncomfortable as you make them. "Welcome to my new place!" he exclaimed, taking in the space with a wide smile as if he himself was viewing it for the first time. "Wow," I declared. "It's beautiful. Just like the videos you showed me." The apartment was surrounded by glass windows with sweeping views of the New York City skyline. The furniture was clean and minimal. It was as if he copied and pasted his old apartment. The desk chair from his previous home remained as well as the flat screen television. I kept getting flashbacks to our evening at his old place, but I tried to push them aside.

There was a small kitchen, a gray couch, two bathrooms, and window shades he was eager to fix. Upstairs, a string of clothing hung off the railing in front of a crisp white bed. A door also led out to Nathan's private roof that overlooked a busy street. "I like to sit on a chair in the middle of the roof and just look around or watch the people on the balcony downstairs," he said. I laughed at the plastic folding chair, still marked by its sticker from the store, that sat on top of pebble stones. "You know the doorman thought I was here before?" I laughed, eager to see how Nathan would respond. He scoffed. "Yeah, he probably thought you were some other girl. You're not the first person that's seen the new apartment." I wasn't surprised.

"How have you been?" he asked as I trailed behind him on the way back downstairs. His genuine interest in my life was refreshing. I plopped down comfortably on the couch, rested my head on the back pillow, and slumped in my seat. Likewise, the entire conversation was comfortable—I felt like I no longer needed to impress him because I wasn't expecting a relationship. Occasionally, I slipped through the cracks of the couch, and it reminded me of how the potential to date fell through the cracks of our lives.

We began to analyze how COVID-19 caused us to reassess our friendships. I was the one who initially raised the argument, and he'd occasionally point at me as I spoke to indicate he was in agreement over what I said. The validation made me feel good about myself. I knew I shouldn't have been seeking his approval, but it was satisfying when he thought my statements were wise. "The friendships we kept during the pandemic are the ones that will last," I said. Nathan nodded. "We only hold onto the people we value most in life." Did that mean he valued me? Even after everything we'd been through together? We said we were friends, but every time we locked eyes, I could sense something more was still there. Nonetheless, I kept my feelings hidden.

After a quick trip to the bathroom, I reentered the living room. Rap music now played out of a speaker. "Mood music?" I laughed. He was scrolling through TikTok when I returned. "Okay, I'm stalking your account now," I announced. His feed was filled with what he called "thirst-trap videos" that showed off his jawline, expensive suits, and overall handsomeness. "Okay, we're going to film a TikTok," I suddenly declared, scrolling through the dozens of sounds he had saved. Most were slow or ominous, unlike mine, which he declared were "all dance sounds" as he held my phone and looked through them. One of his sounds stood out from the rest: the way the man in the recording spoke was hilarious, although it was unclear what exactly he was saying (the only word I could make out was "sex"). "Okay, get up!" I said, placing his phone on the kitchen counter. A text popped up from a girl as I put the device down, but I didn't have enough time to read what it said. I considered that he may have been flirting with other girls, but I managed to shrug it off. After all, we had a TikTok to film.

Nathan and I laughed a lot. Not just while filming his video, but throughout the entire afternoon. It was the happiest I'd ever seen him. I searched for a sound about people with two different heights and placed my phone under the shades to catch the light emanating from his window. "This is your TikTok tutorial!" I teased as I explained when to squat and stand up. Nathan was grinning from ear to ear in the video, and so was I. "Go TikToker go!" he said as I watched the clip back.

We filmed our final TikTok together on my phone: a "group chat survey." The sound posed "who's more likely to" questions, and we pushed the person forward who the query applied to most. Neither of us listened to the sound before recording, so the questions came as a surprise. When the woman's voice asked who had the worst taste in guys, Nathan unhesitatingly pushed me in front. "You pursued me," he stated as I stood in front of the camera, indicating that I was not wise in going after him. When the sound asked who was the bigger simp, Nathan shoved me with even more force.

Endorphins still ran high as we decided to take another look at the roof. He brought a speaker and stood at the ledge admiring the sky, despite the fact that it was now dark and gray. The air was slightly cooler, the sun had disappeared, and Nathan pointed out a man who sat solo on the balcony beneath us smoking weed. "It's supposed to rain soon. I should probably get going," I said. "Yeah, I have some work to do," Nathan replied.

He adjusted a baseball cap that rested on the kitchen counter, so I assumed he was walking me downstairs. "Bye, Carrie," he said to my surprise. I slung my backpack over my shoulder. The exit felt more satisfactory yet far less eventful than the last time I left his apartment. "Oh, you're not walking me down?" I said. "Do you want me to?" he asked as he held the door open. I told him that he didn't have to, and we ended our three-hour hangout with a hug. This time, we embraced with both arms.

Long story short, Nathan and I never dated. We stayed friendly; he was kind enough to message me when I stress-fractured my legs to make sure I was okay. He called and asked if I wanted to rent his apartment when he was moving out (again). I even posted the TikTok we made on my Instagram story for his birthday, although he quickly made me take the post down. "I'm not big on birthdays," he DMed me. I suspected the real reason he wanted the video removed was so people didn't think we were dating. His behavior was predictable at this point.

Nathan and I never saw each other in person after that day at his new apartment. My heart stopped every time a tall guy passed me in the school hallway, and all the memories would come rushing back. I worried about what I'd say if it were him. We texted occasionally. Nearly a year after we hung out, I had just gone through a breakup and missed having a guy in my life. I wondered what Nathan was up to. I thought about having lunch with him and seeing if he had changed—maybe he was finally mature enough to engage in a relationship. I brought up the idea of lunch, but luckily, neither of us followed up about it.

One day, a friend dropped a bomb that left me shellshocked. She knew someone who had also been played by Nathan. Apparently, he had a habit of coaxing girls into his bed, and after they were intimate, he would get up, look in the mirror, and hype himself up. He was only interested in using girls for sex. I wasn't surprised—more so disappointed. All of my doubts about him were validated. In a twisted way, I was almost relieved. I wasn't crazy for seeing faults in the way he treated me because I wasn't the only one being mistreated.

I really did care for Nathan. We had a deep intellectual connection that's difficult to put into words. Perhaps I even held a bit of love for him, which is why I kept giving him chances. He entranced me; every time he spoke, it felt like he was staring into my soul. But it wasn't just me he sweet-talked. He had a talent for casting people under his spell. I felt foolish for having feelings for him, but I couldn't entirely blame myself. Nathan was a manipulator. With newfound knowledge, I considered if he didn't want to date me because he knew I lived at home. He wouldn't be able to exploit me if my parents were in the room next door. I'm grateful my friend shed light on Nathan's true colors because I likely would have fallen for his manipulation again. I'm someone who is open to love, but he was incapable of reciprocating feelings of love to me or anyone else. I always wondered why he was willing to sacrifice the deep connection we had when he left me on the bed that evening at his apartment. I finally had an answer: I was falling for a facade.

Despite occasional flirtatious messages (a "wow" or heart eyes emoji in response to an Instagram story), we never resumed our romance. A part of me will always harbor deep feelings for him, but a relationship would have never worked. This boy may have been able to recite Aristotle's *Nicomachean Ethics* by heart, but when it came to relationships, he was completely naïve to a girl's feelings and desires. I now recognize this as the inherent nature of many Gen Z males I have encountered: as boys begin a new phase of their lives, they don't lead with their brains. They often allow their sex drive to take the wheel. All traces of intelligence are overshadowed by a selfish yearning to play the field, leading them to stomp over emotions.

My former fling's hunger for a casual connection blinded him to what was right before his eyes: a girl willing to be vulnerable and open her heart, someone who found him interesting and hung on his every word. I gave him too much patience, time, and consideration only to be casually discarded and relegated to the "friend zone." I've found that Nathan didn't necessarily reject me because I wasn't good enough or even due to his arrogance. Perhaps he simply had low self-esteem, which explains why he struggled with sexual rejection.

Most girls seem to have significantly different desires as they enter their college years. Tired of high-school romance games, they want to ultimately love and be loved. Sex may or may not be a part of that picture, and both decisions are valid and acceptable. In retrospect, Nathan's selfishness made me understand my self-worth: I didn't need a guy to make me feel good about myself. I also learned not to set my expectations too high when it comes to pursuing college students. Age-wise, these boys are new adults, yet their emotional intelligence has not caught up.

In the twenty-four hours that followed my hookup with Nathan, the taste of his cigarettes lingered. But when the flavor finally dissipated, I came to an important realization: I deserve to find someone who is patient and holds out hope for a love that is special. If he makes me question my self-worth, the relationship will snuff out sooner than he can say, "goodbye." ♥

# Chapter 5

# The Pandemic Fling

ONE YEAR INTO ISOLATION, I was itching for rebellion. I lived with my parents and grandparents in the Hamptons for almost eleven months with no one to kiss but my dog, Maddie. I wasn't allowed to see anyone—not my friends, and definitely not potential boyfriends—unless from six feet apart. I was basically in hiding, lacking any sense of social interaction beyond hugs from the same four family members. I craved a sense of normalcy. All I had holding me together were my memories, which began to fade as the pandemic prolonged. Each day felt like Groundhog Day: I would wake up, work out, attend online college classes, film TikTok content, eat, write, and sleep. There was no variation to what I was doing. There was nothing to look forward to.

A few weeks after my eighteenth birthday, a belated gift arrived: new faces. I was outside my house, shooting a campaign for a fitness brand, when I noticed something different. Next door, several teenagers who looked about my age piled into a car with a university bumper sticker. I hadn't seen them around before. I continued to shoot photos but got distracted as they drove by. "Looking good!" one guy shouted out of the back seat. He and his friends then burst into laughter. I was humiliated—were they mocking me? I stuck my tongue out at them as they drove away.

That wasn't the last I saw of the college teens. I was walking my dog when I spotted some of the boys leaning on the same car.

"Where do you go to school?" someone asked from several feet away. I told him, and our conversation ended there. He didn't seem very interested in getting to know me, and honestly, my social skills were rusty after spending a year practically alone. I took my dog inside and pretended I hadn't seen the guys in the first place.

Around 11:30 p.m., I was doing an ab workout when the doorbell rang. Dripping in sweat, I panicked. I quickly wiped my forehead on my shirt, threw on a coat, and ran downstairs. When I opened the door, no one was there, but a napkin note was left on the ground. It read: "come to our place for a good time." I swiped on some mascara, put on a face mask, and ran out the door. Keep in mind, this was pre-vaccine, and much of the world was still quarantined, so my parents were paranoid. "Yo!" I shouted into the evening air. I heard EDM music playing faintly from a distance, but nobody was in sight. I walked over, and as I approached, four boys and a girl met me outside. "You got our note!" one of the guys said, slightly tipsy. I realized he was the one who told me I was "looking good" earlier. He was short, about two inches taller than me, with large ears that stuck out behind his hair. Several of his friends were more my type—tall with shaggy blonde hair—but this guy's energy was magnetic. The one girl pushed in front of her male friends. "Hi! I'm Julia!" she exclaimed, throwing herself at me for a hug. I introduced myself to the group, trying my best to play it cool. In reality, I was uncomfortable. It was clear I was the only sober one there. I twirled the strings of my hoodie anxiously to calm my nerves.

"What were those pictures you were taking earlier?" another guy asked. I didn't know how to respond. I could reveal the truth, but what if he thought it was weird? I figured I had nothing to lose. "It was for a brand campaign. I'm an influencer on TikTok," I explained. The rest of the group perked up. "Yeah, what's the clout?" someone asked. His wording threw me off—it was clear he was intrigued by online fame. "About one and a half mil," I replied. The guy ran out into the parking lot and took a lap. "No way!" he yelled, loud enough to wake the neighbors. Julia asked me for a picture. "You're famous!" she exclaimed. I was disappointed—all I wanted was a fun night with college peers, not a bunch of teenagers obsessing over my following. Despite the blinding camera flash, they didn't see me for who I was: a normal eighteen-year-old girl just trying to make friends.

## Swipe Left:

### THE CURSE OF THE BLUE CHECK

Most men don't know how to handle a successful young woman—some will fawn over her while others won't even make an effort to learn about her career. The downside about being an influencer dating a non-influencer is that some people get caught up with the blue check. Almost every guy mentions how I'm verified or that I'm "famous" (whatever that means) and have a lot of followers. I can't add a guy on Snapchat without him having to "subscribe" to me. If they snap me, they'll always see the verification star next to my name. Every date I go on in public, I worry that I'm going to get recognized (it's happened several times before, and it's very awkward, especially when the fan asks if the guy is my boyfriend). I don't want the internet notoriety to throw him off.

One time, I told my date a story about an event I went to in Los Angeles that Addison Rae attended. Hearing her name made the guy all googly-eyed. "Addison Rae? You know her? Do you have her number?" he exclaimed. He begged me to show him her phone number and send him a screenshot. It was crazy how quickly he forgot that he was on a date with *me*.

Now, I'm cautious whenever a guy hints that he's using me for clout. I've considered if it's better to date an influencer since I wouldn't have to worry about being used. Although I haven't sworn off doing so, most influencers' egos are too large to invest in a relationship. I search for someone—regardless of their social media following—who inquires about my life beyond how I got verified. My platform doesn't define me. I want someone to get to know me beyond my TikTok or Instagram.

"Looking good" guy pulled me aside. I learned his name was Tyler. He and his camp friends were renting a house for the weekend. They all lived in different states, and this was their winter reunion. While the rest of the group scrolled through and stalked my TikTok, Tyler wanted to get to know me. "How did you get started on social media?" he asked. I explained my background to him, and he listened intently. "Wait, why are you wearing a mask?" Julia interrupted, stepping between us. "My grandparents live next door, so I have to be extra careful," I explained.

I was talking to Tyler and Julia when all of a sudden, I heard a booming voice emanating from outside my house. "Carrie, where are you?" my dad yelled. It was incredibly embarrassing. "Sorry, one sec," I said, jogging to my door. "Wait, come inside and party with us!" another one of the guys shouted. I told them to hold on and proceeded to the door. "Dad, what are you doing? I'm wearing my mask!" I protested. "Why can't I have fun for once?" He shook his head. "No way. You don't want to get Bobbi and Papa sick. Come back inside," he maintained. My dad was usually pretty laid-back, but in this instance, it was clear he wasn't going to budge. I ran back to Tyler and asked for his Snapchat. "I'll snap you," I said. "Maybe we can meet up later." It felt like I was lying to myself, but I got his info in case of a miracle.

That miracle was my mom. She managed to make my dad compromise. I wasn't allowed to go inside their house, but I could hang out with them on my back patio if I was wearing a mask. I wasn't sure if Tyler would be down to stay outside in the thirty-degree weather, but I snapped him regardless. "Want to chill in my backyard around 12:30?" I typed. To my surprise, he agreed.

A few minutes after 12:30 p.m., my doorbell rang. I expected to see just Tyler—unfortunately, he brought his entire friend group along. The guys were holding giant bottles of Grey Goose, and the girls were tripping over themselves. "Let me show you around to the back," I said. Tyler and I walked ahead of the drunken group. "So what's your college major?" he asked me, yelling over his friends. I tried to tell him about my passion for journalism, but both of us were distracted.

Since it was wintertime, there were no chairs outside. "It's fine. Let's just chill in our house," Julia said, taking Rachel (the only other girl) by the hand. I panicked. There was no way I could go inside when my parents had a view of the back patio. They were probably spying on me to make sure I obided by their rules. I needed a backup plan. "My neighbors are gone for the season. We can just hang out in their backyard," I said, leading everyone to a setup of chairs around a long table. The guys set up the alcohol and started pouring into red cups. "Want some?" they offered me. I declined. I was the only teen without a cup in my hand and felt like a baby among the group. I was the only one staying smart, and my decisions made me an outlier. "Let's introduce ourselves!" Rachel said. They all knew each other. The game was only for my benefit. We went around, saying our names and what college we went to. There were so many personalities, it was hard to keep track.

After the introductions, Rachel and Julia pulled me aside. "So who are you feeling?" Rachel asked. Like me, these teens were seeking a good time. I looked around to make sure the guys couldn't hear. "I mean, I just met everyone, so I don't really know," I whispered. "Well, do you think anyone is cute?" Julia pressed me. I knew exactly who I was most attracted to, but I avoided those feelings because I knew I couldn't take action. "Well, I think Tyler is cute, but I can't do anything because of my grandparents. They live right there," I said, pointing to their house a few feet away. "Eww, you don't want Tyler," she said. I scanned the patio. Everyone else was coupled up or bouncing back and forth from their house. Rachel never told me why I should avoid Tyler—I was left to eventually find out for myself.

"Hey, Carrie, can we film a TikTok?" one of the guys asked. He wanted to do the "Corvette" dance that was trending on TikTok at the time. "We all know that dance!" Julia exclaimed. I sensed they wanted to film with me as a joke, so they could show me off when they got back to college. I did the video, but I still worried I was being treated like a trophy. To try to fit in with the group, I offered to film some TikToks on my page as well. I had been watching quarantine couples trends on TikTok for months. Now, I could finally try one for myself. "Wait, can we do this one?" I said, pulling up the sound, which I already had saved. Tyler and Julia hovered over my shoulder. It required two guys and two girls. Each girl would have to stand still while the guy runs into frame, sweeps the girl off her feet and continues out of the camera. Tyler and Julia volunteered, along with another guy that Julia dragged in with her. Obviously, I partnered with Tyler. It took several takes to get the video right, but it helped us bond. "You better not drop me," I said. He promised he wouldn't, and he didn't.

After we filmed the videos, the four of us returned to the table. The rest of the group went back to the house to warm up and never returned. Rachel gave me her number and said to text all the details on what happens with Tyler later. "When are you guys leaving the house?" I asked. They were to depart the following day. I only had one night to socialize, so I was determined to make the most of it. We talked about college life for hours. There was a temporary interruption so Tyler could pee—on my grandparents' lawn. The germaphobe in me was crying inside.

If that wasn't gross enough, I was in for a rude awakening. We were talking when Tyler's phone suddenly buzzed in his pocket. "Oh, shoot," Tyler said. "What's wrong?" I asked. He placed his phone down on the table. "My mom has COVID," he chuckled, as if it were a joke to him. My stomach dropped. "Um, okay," I said, pulling my mask up further over my nose. "When did you last see her?" He shrugged. "A few days ago." I started to inch away from him. "No, don't worry about it," he said, touching my thigh. "I had it a few months ago. I have the antibodies, so I'm good." It never fully registered to me in that moment that he could still be a carrier of the virus. I calmed my nerves and continued to let loose.

Our group conversations gradually narrowed until it was just Tyler and me talking. Sensing that we were connecting, Julia and the other guy went back to their house. It was now three in the morning. I felt my fingers turning numb. "I'm so cold," I said. "Feel my hands." I placed my hand on top of Tyler's, and our eyes met. He slowly started to pull back my mask, but I hid my head in my shoulder. "I can't," I said. He placed a hand on my arm and started stroking the goosebumps on my skin. I sensed he was seducing me. "Why not?" he asked. I recited my story like a broken record. I couldn't give in for the sake of my grandparents.

For over a half hour, he tried to kiss me, but I swerved every time. "I promise, you're not going to get sick," he said. I didn't trust him. After all, he was basically a stranger. I continued to pull my mask up while he was adamant on taking it off. "I'm not going to give in," I declared. He may have thought I was playing hard to get, but I was genuinely concerned for my family's safety.

At about 3:30 a.m., the lights on my patio flickered. I sensed my parents wanted me back inside. Tyler and I walked to my grandparents' backyard to say goodbye. It was a dark area, and I knew my family wouldn't be able to see how close I was to him. Tyler tried one last time to take my mask off, but I shook my head. "Alright," he said coldly, clearly defeated. "Nice meeting you." As I watched him walk away, I couldn't help but feel like I was missing out. "Wait," I called after him, yanking him back by his arm. I pulled my mask down and leaned in for a kiss. We only made out for twenty seconds or so, but it was exhilarating. After months of loneliness, I felt on top of the world. All I wanted was to be happy again if only for a night. Deprived of my in-person college experience, I was eager to explore. It wasn't about Tyler.

It was about what he symbolized: a sense of freedom and independence I craved as a new adult. What I failed to recognize is that being an adult comes with responsibility, which I completely neglected that evening.

I took the walk of shame back into my house. "How was it?" my mom asked as I headed upstairs. "It was good," I said vaguely, avoiding eye contact. In my mind, I ran through several ways to confess what I had done. Should I just lay it all on the line? Tell her tomorrow? Not tell her at all? I tiptoed into her bedroom. "Mom, I did a bad thing," I started. My dad was fast asleep, but he rolled over so he could listen. "I kissed someone." My mom sighed. "Alright. It's okay," she said. "No, that's not all. His mom has COVID right now," I continued. "Carrie!" my dad screamed, sitting up out of the bed. "Why would you do that?" I started to sob. "I needed it! It finally made me feel alive again!" I argued. My mom instructed me to get in the shower. "I'm glad you had fun, but now you have to live with the consequences," she said. At least she understood where I was coming from.

My dad, on the other hand, was in full-on panic mode. "I'm going to Uncle Charles's house for the next five days," he declared, stuffing his clothes into a bag. "I'll leave first thing in the morning." I didn't blame him—it was his parents I was putting in danger. He was ashamed of me. But I was so blinded by my euphoric evening, I dismissed any concerns. I figured I could just distance myself from my grandparents for a week. I was finally happy—that itself led me to think the risk was worth it.

Before bed, I texted Rachel as promised. In her drunken state, she made me feel like we were closer friends than we actually were. "We're basically besties," she said, although we had just met. "Call me tomorrow so I can tell you everything!" I messaged her. She promised she would. I pressed her to tell me what Tyler said when he came back to the house. "He didn't really say much. He just said he got with you," she replied. It had been a year since I kissed a guy, so I was insecure about what he thought.

"Did he say how it was?" I asked. Rachel claimed he didn't say anything after, or at least nothing she wanted to tell me.

The following morning, there was an energy shift between me and the other college kids. I messaged Tyler that I had a good time, and he said the same. But as soon as I told him I wanted to say goodbye, or asked when he was going to be in the Hamptons next, he ghosted me. Rachel never called either to find out how my time with him was. I texted her at 9 a.m. that I wanted to come over, and she didn't get back to me until six hours later. I gave a few of the people I met a hug goodbye, but our interaction was awkward. They were not nearly as friendly as they were the night before (I guess that's what alcohol does to you). Beyond a "nice meeting you," we didn't say much to each other. As for Tyler, he was nowhere to be found.

I never heard from him again. He went back to his college dorm while I returned to my life in isolation. We lived far apart, so the best thing to do was detach right away. I had to live with the repercussions of my actions: for nearly a week, my mom made me wear a mask around the house, and I couldn't come near my family. I kissed Tyler that night because I was lonely— the irony was that now, I was lonelier than ever. What made the situation even more frustrating was that Tyler's intentions were never pure. I realized he most likely kissed me so he could boast to his buddies that he locked lips with a "famous person." After all, Rachel was pretty adamant that I send her the TikToks I made with her friends. Kissing Tyler was one of the first difficult decisions I made as an adult—and it was a big mistake. I put my family at risk to make myself feel connected to the world again. He reminded me that there was a life beyond the depression of being stuck indoors.

Thankfully, I never got COVID-19 from him. But the guilt I carried from that experience made me sick to my stomach. It wasn't worth jeopardizing my parents' and grandparents' health for a few hours of socialization. Family always comes first. I was so busy trying to escape the pandemic that I forgot what was right in front of me: a loving, supportive family who always had my back. They were the ones who held me during my worst days in quarantine. They picked up the pieces on days when it felt like the world was crashing down. Tyler didn't even know me. I didn't need a boy to remind me what it means to show affection. My parents were setting the example all along. ♥

# Chapter 6

# The Surfer Soulmate (part 1)

WHEN IT COMES TO ROMANCE, I crave adventure. It doesn't have to be zip-lining in the jungle or backpacking in a foreign country. In my eyes, adventure is anything that makes you feel alive. It can be as simple as sitting in an hour-long traffic jam with the radio blasting or trying to fight the wind while strolling down a sidewalk. Adventure is a means of escape. It grounds you to the present moment and keeps you on your toes, no matter what else is happening in the world. Despite the adrenaline rush it gives you, adventure does not necessarily equal danger. In fact, when I first connected with Scott, our interaction was far from hazardous—the beginning of our adventure began with a mere mid-quarantine FaceTime call.

Scott was a California surfer boy—adventure was in his blood. The extent of my daily escapade was taking a new Peloton class while his was dunking under large waves. I found him on social media since we had mutual friends in his hometown. On a whim, I slid into his DMs, and within an hour, we started talking. Next thing I knew, we were Snapchatting each other photos and messages every day.

# Double-Tap This:

## HOW TO SLIDE INTO DMS

I've slid into guys' DMs more times than I can count. Seriously, I'm fearless. Influencers, actors… you name it. A little "hello" message never hurt anyone. If you want to indicate interest via social media, here are ways to slide in successfully, without looking like you're coming on too strong.

- Start off with a simple "heyy." I include an extra "y" for a touch of flirtation.
- Avoid emojis in your initial message. Red hearts and winking faces in particular can come off as too aggressive.
- Make sure you're following the person on Instagram. Nothing screams stalker more than if you aren't following, even if it's one-sided.

- If the person takes more than a week to answer, unsend the message for your ego's sake. Out of sight, out of mind.
- Don't reveal too much over DMs. It may feel easier to dish since you're not IRL, but you don't know this person well enough yet.
- Keep conversation simple. Ask where he's from, how his day is going, and so on.
- Wait at least fifteen to twenty minutes before answering your crush, so you don't seem desperate or obsessed.
- When the time feels right, carry the conversation over to Snapchat or iMessage. This shows that you're interested in getting to know the person more. He may not pick up on your flirtation right away, so don't be afraid to shoot your shot and ask for his number.
- Be authentic. In early stages of establishing a connection, it's imperative that the other person gets to know the real you, even from behind a screen.

After weeks of conversation, Scott and I finally decided to FaceTime. My heart raced as I shut the door to my bedroom, quickly concealed my pimples, and threw my hair up in an effortlessly messy bun. I held my phone in the air and walked around my bedroom to find the perfect lighting. It was the evening, so natural sunlight was out of the question, and using my ring light would make me seem like a try-hard. So I took a deep breath, switched on the light fixture above me, sat on my bed, and waited for him to ring. When he did, I was instantly taken aback. Although we lived nearly three-thousand miles apart, his dazzling blue eyes pierced through the screen as if he was situated directly in front of me. The long, dark brown hair I knew from his Instagram was reined in by a beanie, and he grinned from ear to ear as we got to know each other. He was the perfect conversation partner. I asked about his interests, and in return, he'd ask about mine. We each talked an equal amount, and I was at ease answering his questions ("What's New York like?" "How was it affected by the pandemic?"). A combination of sitting on my bed and Scott's down-to-earth personality made me completely comfortable.

I quickly learned about his passions. He loved his dog, who cuddled with him on FaceTime. He was also an ardent rock-and-roll fan and encouraged me to listen to Queen's "Don't Stop Me Now." A classic rock fan myself, I ran over to my Peloton, switched to the back camera, and showed him my favorite playlist. "Guns N' Roses are the best," I contended. He agreed with my choice of artist: "Yeah, they're rad!" I quickly picked up on Scott's surfer lingo. He worked in a surf shop, so phrases such as "rad," "gnarly," and "right on" were fixed in his daily vocabulary. It was like a culture shock: I was trapped inside my home in quarantine, but he transported me to California through his words and presence. As he recounted the details of a surfing photo shoot or afternoon in Los Angeles, I could feel the experience in my bones as well. I guess you can say that's when I first established a sense of trust in Scott. Although he wasn't physically present, I felt at home with him. When we spoke, it instantly put me in a good mood.

I'm often the one initiating text conversations, so it was refreshing to see Scott start iMessage chains. "Yo yo yo, what's up!" he'd say. His messages always came through at the perfect time. There were several days in quarantine when I was sad and alone, and when he texted, it reminded me that I still mattered. Somewhere, on the other side of the country, a person cared about how I was doing and was there to talk when I needed him.

We FaceTimed almost every night. One day, I wore a beanie to match his casual vibe. I found myself more playful on a video call than through text because I could be natural. I didn't have to think too much before talking. That day, I felt particularly comfortable—we had the beanies to thank for bringing us closer together. Feeling vulnerable, I opened up to him about something that was bothering me. "I feel like my writing isn't good enough anymore. I can't come up with any good ideas," I confided in him after an article I was proud of got turned down. I wasn't necessarily searching for an ego boost, more so a shoulder to lean on—and Scott provided me with both. He raised my spirits when I was in a funk and made my voice as a writer feel heard again. I texted him, "thank you," after the call, and he sent a message reinforcing what he expressed over FaceTime: "I speak the truth, Carrie Berk! The world seriously isn't ready for you and your talents. You're so accomplished already and are going to skyrocket to outer space and beyond, believe me. I'm excited to watch that process. You have awesome energy. Always a pleasure talkin' to ya."

Scott and I were there for each other when we both needed company most. The conversations were always easy and effortless. Even when we discussed hardships, there was never an awkward silence. At one point, I was struggling with anxiety while he was coping with his grandpa's death, and we gave each other virtual support. I knew I couldn't expect him to respond while mourning, but I checked in on him repeatedly, letting him know I was there in case he needed to talk. In return, when I received death threats on social media, he dropped everything to FaceTime me and make sure I was okay. I hid in my bathroom in tears, but he could care less that the bed was replaced by a toilet seat. "I'm sorry," he told me with an intense, empathetic look in his eyes. "You don't deserve any of the hate."

# Double-Tap This:

## TIPS FOR A FLIRTY FACETIME CALL

- It's not the Oscars. Getting too glam can be a turnoff. Guys want to see your natural glow—a little concealer and lip gloss are all you need.
- Look effortlessly undone. A messy bun makes you appear easygoing and confident.
- Don't get distracted by your phone. It's very clear if you're texting someone else or scrolling through social media while you're talking.
- Maintain eye contact even though you're speaking through a screen. This will make it clear you're paying attention to what they're saying.
- Laugh at their jokes. Laying on the couch while chatting can be tedious, but your personality can enliven the call.
- Ask for a room tour. Seeing his personalized space is a good way to get to know him.
- Play twenty-one questions. It may sound stupid, but it's ac-tually a fun way to warm up to each other. Ask questions back and forth—you choose how casual (or sexy) you want the game to be.
- Take smart risks. Talking from behind a screen may give you an extra boost of confidence, so don't be afraid to flirt. Just make sure you're subtle and not too forward. Allowed: "I really like talking to you." Not allowed: "Do you have a crush on anyone right now?" Opening up to someone over time will indicate that you trust them and are interested in deepening the connection.
- You're most likely going to be FaceTiming at night if both of you are busy during the day. Chatting when it's dark out is a vibe, but ensure you have his undivided attention. If he only calls you when kicking it with friends on a Friday, stop answering.
- Don't stay up all night on the phone. Leave him wanting to know more about you so he calls again soon. Plus, there's such a thing as getting too comfortable. If you're chatting for several hours, you may wind up revealing information about yourself you wouldn't have otherwise shared.

The next morning, he texted to ask how I was doing and if there was anything he could do to help. He was busy at the surf shop, yet he kept me at the forefront of his mind. I could tell that he really cared, and the prospect of having a boy that thoughtful and attentive in my life drew me in. Nobody had ever been that pro-active in protecting me and my feelings. It was almost too good to be true. Why is finding the qualities we deserve so hard to believe?

Scott left me old-school voicemails if I didn't answer my phone, whether on my birthday or simply to catch up. In one message, he struggled to catch his breath as he ran out of the surf shop yet made it a point to ask about my day. He was always unfiltered, and he encouraged me to be confident in doing the same. After I conquered my fear of swimming in the ocean, I sent him a selfie as proof and apologized for the mascara run-ning down my face. But Scott did not pay heed to my imper-fections. "I don't care about the makeup. I'm so proud of you! Does this mean I get to take you to the beach in Los Angeles?" he texted me. His tendency to be transparent carried into family matters as well. Scott introduced me to his mom and brother on FaceTime. I had never done a virtual "meet-the-parents" before, but I was excited that he was comfortable enough to let me into his home—even if it was only through a screen. I later intro-duced him to my mom on FaceTime as well. Unsurprisingly, Scott couldn't have been more polite.

He was always charming and authentic. On New Year's Eve, although three hours behind, he was the first person to call me after the ball dropped. "Here's to hailing cabs in New York and surfing adventures in Los Angeles!" I exclaimed. Not only did I say what I hoped was in the cards for us in the new year, but I saw it as well. I envisioned us dodging waves hand in hand, the sun beating on our faces as we splashed around. The more I dreamed, the deeper I fell.

As months passed, Scott and I continued to develop a deeper connection—yet I could never tell if he was flirting or just being friendly. I tried my best to pick up on subtle hints, although there were very few. When a friend slept over at my house, I handed her my phone while on FaceTime with him and pretended to "go to the bathroom." I listened closely from a few feet away as my wingwoman tried to get Scott to indicate any romantic interest. "You guys are so cute!" she declared, eager to see how he would react. "I like talking to her a lot! Hopefully I can take her out when she gets to L.A.," he replied. I nearly tripped over my own feet while walking back to the couch. He said he wanted to take me out—that had to mean on a date, right?

I continued to keep track of flirtatious moves. One day, I replied to a Snapchat selfie of him with the text "qt" across my own photo. His response: "that's YOU." Additionally, when I was on vacation in Palm Beach, Scott responded to a Snapchat story of me in a bikini several days later—the delay didn't matter when I saw his message. He always sent me neutral emojis via text: a smiley face on holidays, an eye-roll after an embarrassingly late reply. But this time was different: the text "looking good ;)" accompanied three fire emojis. It felt like a breakthrough. I didn't know where to start in deciphering the message. The fire emojis? The compliment? The winky face? I finally had some clarity: he was interested in me. I still wasn't sure if he wanted a relationship or casual fling, and to be honest, I didn't know what I wanted either. All I knew was that I liked him, and he liked me, even though neither of us explicitly admitted our emotions. We would take it from there.

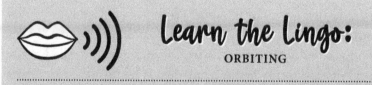

## Learn the Lingo:
### ORBITING

The person *seems* like they're into you. They follow you on social media, comment on your posts, and swipe up on your Instagram stories with flirtatious messages. But they never indicate their interest outside of the online sphere—it's as if they're *orbiting* you. In Scott's case, he was active on my Instagram and Snapchat, but he didn't flirt when we were on FaceTime.

In the spring, I planned a trip to Los Angeles at last. Scott lived a few hours away, but he said he would make the drive to see me. The effort was incredibly romantic—I knew he wouldn't have traveled all that way if he didn't care about me. In one of our first conversations, we agreed that adventure is key in a relationship. His ex never wanted to leave the couch. Scott and I believed that exploring the world with someone is essential. "We'll go on an adventure. I'll let you surprise me with where we go," I expressed flirtatiously over FaceTime. I couldn't wait to find out what his plans were, so he disclosed the details ahead of time: we would go to the beach, walk around Hollywood, and grab dinner at one of his favorite L.A. spots. On a FaceTime call, I asked him where he would sleep. "Do you have your own room?" he said. Was he implying that he wanted to stay the night, so he could make a move? "I want to sleep over," he confirmed. The nature of what was to happen in the hotel room always remained unspoken. When I first discussed it with him, I wasn't thinking about sex. After all, it was going to be our first time meeting face to face. I soon realized that an evening alone in a hotel room naturally has that association. I knew it, and so did he.

I always wanted to wait to have sex until I was a few months into a relationship, head over heels in love. But the second I recognized sex was potentially on the table with Scott, I began to seriously consider it. We weren't in love, nor were we exclusively dating, but I trusted Scott more than any other guy I had previously been associated with. We had been talking for eight months. I knew that I would feel comfortable in his arms. I preferred to have my "first time" with a friend with benefits I trusted over an inconsiderate asshole any day. It felt like the hotel room with Scott was the right moment to lose my virginity—call it a gut feeling. The events to follow were still unwritten, but I promised myself to keep an open mind and listen to my heart. Little did I know, not even my heart could have prepared me for the emotional pain I was about to experience. ♥

# Chapter 7

# The Surfer Soulmate (part 2)

MY TRIP TO LOS ANGELES quickly approached and my time with Scott along with it. Twenty-four hours before our adventure, he texted me that he would be arriving an hour late. "I have to get a few things done at my house before I drive down in the morning," he texted. Initially, I worried he would flake and tempered my expectations. But this was Scott—he was someone I could trust, so I had faith that he would make the trip.

I woke up in the morning with a pounding heart, shaky hands, and sweaty palms. I had never been so anxious over a date—nearly a year of texting and FaceTiming led to this moment. Each call felt like a date. It felt like we had been seeing each other for almost a year and that we were further along than we actually were. I put pressure on myself for the day to be everything I ever dreamed of. I knew he was special from the start, yet I worried about potential sources of disappointment. What if he canceled at the last minute? What if he wasn't as easy to talk to in person? What if he only saw me as a friend? I took all my stress out on the hotel treadmill, then showered afterwards to bring myself back to reality. Effortless beach waves, light makeup, and a bikini left me feeling confident. As I swiped on lip gloss, my phone dinged from the other room: he texted that he was almost there. I popped a piece of gum in my mouth and quickly threw on a graphic tee with a rock band on it, paired with a white mini skirt. Luckily, my trust in him was never broken, and he arrived ten minutes ahead of schedule.

Other hotel guests rode the elevator downstairs with me, but it felt like I was elsewhere. I was trapped inside of my mind, a prisoner to endless questions about how the day would unfold yet no answers. I picked at my knuckles, a nervous habit I couldn't shake, and chewed my gum extra fast to ensure the mint flavor was properly dispersed. As the elevator doors opened, I chose to lean into the unknown and believe that he was as kind, caring, and trustworthy as I perceived him to be on FaceTime.

Scott was parked outside the hotel in a black Jeep. He walked towards me and greeted me with a tight hug. He was dressed in a fedora with a red and beige embroidered rim, neck scarf, tee, and black jeans. The look was also accessorized with several rings, a long necklace, and aviator sunglasses. Despite the load of jewelry, I assumed this was his casual attire for a beach day. Seeing him in the flesh was surreal. Although I couldn't connect to his bright blue eyes behind the sunglasses, the fact that he was finally standing in front of me was exciting.

Once I buckled into the passenger seat, he programmed the directions on his phone to the Santa Monica Pier. I was his navigational assistant; his car didn't have a GPS on screen, so I held up his phone with Google Maps directions as he drove. The conversation instantly flowed: he asked what I was up to in L.A., and I asked about his recent surfing competition. I listened and nodded enthusiastically as he recounted the details. Oftentimes, I struggled with what to talk about because we already knew each other so well from our phone calls, but the California highways were a continual savior. The roads were filled with billboards and movie posters, and each one gave us a new topic to discuss.

Even though my conversations with him were interesting, they lacked flirtation. "I wore a rock tee for you," I said, attempting to get a rise out of him for caring about his love of rock music. "Aye, that's awesome," he said indifferently. We laughed beside each other as friends. It wasn't clear to me yet if he saw us as anything more.

Once we parked in Santa Monica, he took a large black backpack out of the back seat and swung it over his shoulder. "It's as if we're going backpacking," I joked, although we only had to hike up one flight of stairs to get to street level. The streets were loud, and people walked shoulder to shoulder. One ear listened to what he was saying while the other was distracted by the sounds of children's laughter and screams from the rollercoaster in front of us. The wind swirled around me, forming a halo of disheveled hair strands. We tried to resist the harsh breeze as we made our way past several restaurants, shops, and entertainers. By the time we reached the end of the pier, my perfect hair was destroyed. I was shivering, and I hoped he would put his arm around me. Clearly, he wasn't ready to make such a flirtatious move. I crossed my arms to cover my goosebumps while he commented on the ocean ahead: "The waves look crazy today!" Scott laid a blue and white towel he brought out onto the warm sand. We kept up a conversation for a long time, sitting side by side, our legs extended in front of us. I wasn't sure how many minutes passed, nor did I care to glance at the clock.

He said he was writing a book of personal essays, and he read to me some of the pieces written in his notes. He poured his emotions onto the pier—his words were authentic and believable. I was captivated. I punched his shoulder playfully when he finished—his writing was brilliant, and I complimented the metaphors he came up with. I also gave him feedback from writer to writer: "You should stick to metaphors related to one topic only. If you draw metaphors from too many different areas of life, the essay will lose focus." I was worried I'd hurt his ego, but he appreciated the constructive criticism. He held onto every word, nodding and validating my recommendations. "What's your favorite thing you've ever written?" he asked. I gulped. He didn't know that I loved writing about relationships, and I wasn't keen on telling him. But he was always truthful with me, so I admitted that my favorite piece of writing had come out of pain in a relationship. "I was really proud of this piece I wrote about a bad experience with a guy from the past," I vaguely explained. I didn't want to reveal details, and he was completely understanding. "It's awkward telling you this because we're…talking," I said. I didn't know how to label my relationship with Scott. Were we friends? Friends with benefits? Future boyfriend and girlfriend? The term "talking" was broad enough to encompass all three options.

I read him an essay about my connection to fitness instead. I felt shy in reading the piece aloud after his heartfelt, poignant monologue, so I handed him my phone and let him scan the words himself. Mine read like a testimonial while his was a personal diary, and I was insecure about his being better quality. I leaned over his shoulder as he scrolled through the document. Our faces were mere inches away. While I wondered what he thought of my writing, I also considered if he was feeling any romantic attraction. "I love it. I can tell how much fitness means to you," he said, turning his head so close to mine that I instinctively turned away. The deep eye contact was uncomfortable, desirable and enthralling all at the same time. I quickly switched the conversation back to his personal essay. "Mine definitely wasn't as good as yours," I said, continuing to flatter his work as I placed a hand on his arm. Scott, on the other hand, avoided physical contact throughout the day. Every time he'd accidentally bump into or elbow me while walking, he'd apologize and instantly scoot over. He seemed nervous to come in close contact.

As we strolled to the other side of the beach, I noticed Scott's rings. "Wait, let me see your jewelry," I said, gently lifting the hand that rested at his side. "I'm sure each of these pieces means something to you." He passionately walked me through the symbolism behind his jewelry: the necklace was purchased at the beach, and one ring was a gift from his ex-girlfriend (he claimed to still wear it for aesthetic purposes only). The attachment to his ex was concerning, but I was too focused on the temperature shock of the ocean to care.

Our day was lackluster so far—but I knew exactly how to increase excitement. "This is our adventure. Let's dunk in the water!" I suggested. It was cold and windy, yet we would be taking it on side by side. My fearlessness made Scott perk up. He wrapped a towel around his waist while dropping his jeans down to the sand and pulled up a colorful, printed pair of swim trunks. I scanned his body from head to toe: at 5'8", he wasn't exactly a tall drink of water. Nonetheless, his strong arms caught my eye. I admired his bulging biceps as he picked his heavy backpack up off the ground to put his clothes inside.

Scott sped ahead of me into the waves. I stood static, my hands clasped as I tiptoed into the water. Once he was in the ocean, he'd shout encouraging words back at me: "Come on! You can do it!" I kept reinforcing that I was scared, so he quickly took my hand to pull me deeper into the water. I wanted him to stay and splash around with me where it was shallower, but he returned to his spot further in the ocean. Frustratingly, I was forced to go underwater on my own, and he threw his arms in the air to celebrate—from several feet away.

After we were both soaked, we ran back to the sand, and he politely offered me the towel. I knew he must've been cold as well, so I saw an opportunity to be flirtatious. "Want to share the towel with me?" I asked. He wrapped himself around the second half of the towel as my arm draped over his chest. But once again, he broke free of our physical connection after a few seconds.

As the salt water dripped off our bodies and onto the sand, we glanced up at the sky. "Look how blue it is," he pointed out, noting how the clouds were all perfectly aligned. "Do you ever read clouds?" I asked. He didn't, and I said I could teach him. "What does that one look like to you?" I pointed at a relatively flat, circular cloud that rested higher above the rest. "A penis," he blurted. Scott was looking at a different cloud than the one I pointed to, but what he saw was telling considering the sexual context of our day. "I'm not talking about that one," I laughed. I shifted his attention toward the cloud I meant for him to see. "I think this one looks like a flying saucer," I claimed. "I can see that!" he replied. There was something sincere about the fact that we were seeing through the same pair of eyes at that moment. He knew exactly where I was coming from, and even though we were only discussing clouds, I read deeper into his desire to understand. I believe everything is a sign, and we're surrounded by billions of signs each day. The sexual symbol Scott found in the sky, coupled with the flying saucer, seemed like a sign, suggesting that our sex lives were ready to take off. "Good! I taught you how to read clouds!" I exclaimed, while I myself learned a thing or two about Scott.

We hiked up the boardwalk, which was bustling with salt-water-soaked bodies. The path was covered with shards of glass and snack wrappers that we dodged. My legs ached as we climbed. Suddenly, we suddenly came across a sports field. In contrast to the pier, the area was secluded—the nearest group of people was at least ten feet away. Bits of sand from the beach transferred to the ground, which was lined by several gates and benches. "Let's jump the fence!" I declared. Scott didn't have to think before he jumped while I got stuck and couldn't swing my legs over to the other side. "Ouch, that hurts!" Scott said, witnessing the top of the fence digging into my upper thighs. He didn't bother helping me over. We took a seat on a bench, yet a large green block in the center separated us. "Come sit next to me!" I encouraged him, scooting to the side to make room.

We never got too comfortable. After ten minutes or so, we decided to grab an early dinner. We walked over to the parking lot, got comfortable in the Jeep once again, and hit the road. The GPS calculated one hour of travel time. What would we talk about for another sixty minutes en route? Scott passed me an aux cord so that I could plug in my phone and play my classic rock mix. I knew he probably liked most of the artists on the playlist, but part of me feared that as a rock aficionado, he judged my song choices. Gwen Stefani's pop-infused "Sunday Morning" played repeatedly on shuffle, and I worried that my song choice was too far a stretch from the hard rock he loved. I was relieved when Scott turned the volume up. "Gwen Stefani is awesome!" he said and started to sing along.

Suddenly feeling overheated, I wanted Scott to open the windows, but I feared coming off as too demanding. When I casually mentioned I was hot, he said I should have told him before. "Sorry!" I laughed. "I'm not much of a straight shooter." It turned out we were pretty similar. We're both straightforward when asked a question upfront, but we circumvent certain topics until they're brought up by others. Being straightforward is essential when communicating in a relationship though, so we agreed to no longer hold anything back.

The evening was approaching, and Scott still showed no signs of flirtation. I took it upon myself to finally make a move. Several Sexwax air fresheners dangled from his rear-view mirror, providing me with the perfect opportunity to transition into a conversation about intercourse. "Sexwax..." I pondered as we sat in bumper-to-bumper, rush-hour traffic. "What is that?" Scott claimed that it smelled good—he rubbed some on his hands and encouraged me to take a whiff. The aroma was undeniable: it smelled like a mix of pineapple and coconut, reminiscent of a tropical cocktail. As I leaned down to smell his hand once again, my nose gently tapped his fingertips, and he pulled away upon realizing we touched. I assumed physical chemistry would come naturally to us after so many months, but he was in his head throughout the entire day.

I rubbed the scent onto my hand and took a third inhale. "Why is it called Sexwax? Is it made during sex or something?" I joked. Scott laughed, finally giving me the chance to ask the question lingering on my mind: "Wait, are you a virgin?" Scott replied quickly and abruptly. "Yeah, are you?" I confirmed that I was a virgin as well and that I felt like I needed to ask. "I wanted to ask you too," he said. He explained that we were at the beach, and it wasn't the right time to bring up the topic. I blushed and pointed at the Sexwax. "Yeah, I thought I'd slide it in now." Something clicked in Scott's mind, and he realized I only mentioned the air fresheners to bring up our own sex lives. "Oh, that was sly!" he admitted.

Scott's virginity came as a surprise to me. "I'm insecure about my inexperience with girls," he confessed. The golden-hour sunlight wasn't needed to illuminate his discomfort—it was clear from his faint tone of voice that he was vulnerable. I told him he had nothing to be insecure about and that I understood where he was coming from. We were on the same wavelength about our "first times" in particular. Both of us were not necessarily waiting for a relationship to lose our V-card—trust, safety, and some "feeling" or attraction was most important. I believe that if the right person comes along, you will know. Your partner can either be more or less experienced than you. There's no rule book when it comes to love—you write your own rules because only you have access to your heart.

Scott and I continued to discuss sex in a broad sense, but he gradually narrowed in on our relationship. "Maybe you can help me with my inexperience," he said, glancing at the highway outside his window. I looked down at my feet. "If you want..." he continued, sensing my silence. "...Maybe later." His candidness left me speechless. I was processing the fact that he was finally starting to open up. Scott had dropped a clue as to what he was anticipating that evening in the hotel room—and I wasn't exactly opposed to it. "Okay, straight shooter," I joked.

Now that we were "straight shooters," I searched for more clarity as to what Scott's intentions were. "Do you speak 'Gibberish?'" I suddenly asked, although I assumed his answer would be no. Gibberish was a language I spoke with my best friend when we wanted to gossip about boys in public. We spoke it fast and understood each other perfectly while nobody around us had a clue what we were saying. "I'm going to say something in Gibberish, and you have two guesses as to what it is. If you guess it, then I'll tell you it's correct," I explained. I knew the second I told him I was saying something secretly, his mind would go to the one topic neither of us asked about in English until recently: sex. The words I actually uttered had no significance: I said we went to the beach, were on our way to dinner, and were going back to the hotel room to do "something." "You'd love to know what I said," I teased, implying that I said something else. Scott was forced to think about the words left unsaid during the day, and he finally shared what was on his mind: "You asked me if we were going to hook up tonight in the hotel room." We previously discussed how the definition of "hooking up" is different based on where one grows up. In his town, the term signifies sex.

Despite the previous lack of flirtation, I now figured Scott saw me as more than a friend. Like me, he was most likely nervous. While my anxiety is channeled through adrenaline, his caused him to withdraw. In fact, throughout the day, he was so in his head, he would struggle to finish sentences. We called each other Dory (like the fish from *Finding Nemo*) every time either of us had a "brain fart." But Scott seemed to have drowned Dory and swam to the surface: he was focused at last with nothing to hide.

I laughed at the fact that I tricked him into admitting what he was thinking. "So do you want to?" he asked sincerely amid my laughter. I didn't want to give him a straight-up answer about whether or not I wanted to hook up with him—even though I knew exactly how I felt. After all, he left his feelings ambiguous with me during our adventure. A smirk and shrug were perfect responses—it wasn't a no, but it wasn't a yes either. "I guess we'll see how the night goes," Scott said, offering a vague reply of his own.

When we got to the restaurant, we waited in line, only to find out when we got to the front that eighteen people were ahead on the list. I had to rethink our plan: I knew the manager at another popular L.A. eatery and quickly called her. I spoke confidently when she picked up, eager to impress Scott with my connections. "I need a table now please for me and my…date," I explained. I glanced over at Scott to see if he was uncomfortable with the label. To my surprise, he didn't flinch. "That's how it's done," I said, holding out a hand for Scott to high-five. "You my date?" Scott looked at his car ahead as he slapped my hand. "Hell yeah!" He didn't maintain eye contact and seemed disconnected. I couldn't pinpoint exactly what was wrong—was he nervous about the hookup to occur? Was he stressed about us going out on a formal date? It wasn't the first time his eyes wandered during the day. I slammed the car door and simultaneously shut all worries. We coasted along West Sunset Boulevard. The ambience was the perfect picture frame for our evening. I needed to trust.

The restaurant had an upbeat-yet-chill aura that matched Scott's energy. The majority of seating was underneath a large white tent, reminiscent of a camping excursion with a West Hollywood upgrade. Lights were strung across the ceiling, and several fire pits lined the space for a s'mores dessert special. Sports games played from several televisions, and the restaurant's song selection was controlled by guests via an app. As we waited for a table, the tent shaded us from the sun, but I still asked Scott to let me borrow his hat. "It fits with the vibe here," I said playfully.

While securing the fedora on my head, I noticed the music that was playing—classic rock. The songs perfectly aligned with the playlist that I had just played in the car. "It's like they knew we were coming!" I exclaimed. Little did he know I queued some of the songs.

When we finished our meal, Scott swept the check off the table and put a one-hundred-dollar bill inside. "I got it," he confidently stated. Since he paid for dinner, I figured he definitely saw it as a date. My gut was telling me to keep hanging on, to continue trusting the universe and move forward in my evening with Scott. As I climbed back into the passenger seat of his car, I alluded to the future. "It's so cold, I'm going to change into sweatpants right when I get to the hotel room," I declared. "Do you have anything comfy to change into?" Scott admitted that he only had a spare change of clothes for the following day. Apparently, pajamas weren't his thing: "I sleep naked," he said.

When we got to the hotel, I popped in one last piece of mint gum before exiting the vehicle. "Should I bring my backpack with me?" he asked, circling around to the trunk. Initially, I wasn't sure how to respond. He wasn't changing into other clothes, but what if certain objects inside could come in handy if we were to have sex (i.e., the condom)? I told him to bring the bag "just in case."

The hotel lobby was relatively empty; only a few people sat on couches or waited outside for a car. We rode the elevator upstairs quietly and entered my room together on the third floor. Scott appeared disengaged as he slipped his shoes off. I changed into a sweat set, dusted off the mascara flakes under my eyes, and smoothed hair flyaways. I had left a pineapple body spray on the sink so that I smelled fresh. A quick spritz on the inside of my wrists, behind the ears, and in the air to walk through, and I was ready to go.

"My hair literally looks like a lion," I laughed. The wind did not bode well for my mane, but that didn't matter to either of us as we relaxed indoors. As I placed my clothes from the day into a laundry bag, he removed his jewelry and fedora. Seeing him in a simple t-shirt and jeans made him appear more casual, relatable, and even vulnerable. But the accessories were import-ant to him—they were a part of his identity. "I admire that about you. You do your thing," I said while scanning the jewelry on the table.

Once we were both comfortable, I suggested watching TV, assuming it would help us ease into conversation (and poten-tially more). He grabbed the remote, and we sat backwards on the bed, lying on our stomachs. Our heads faced the bottom end of the mattress, and our feet floated up in the air towards the pillows. Scott flipped through channels, but nothing was of interest to either of us. *Wheel of Fortune* would have to do. "My grandma watches this," I rolled my eyes. "Mine watches it too!" Scott replied. No matter how tedious the show was, somehow, we found a way to relate. We always did.

"So what did we do today?" Scott suddenly asked, encour-aging us to recap our adventures. "We went to the pier, did the ocean…" I contributed my own standout memories as well: "… jumped a fence, ate dinner, and now, we're here." I could feel the bed elevate with Scott's breaths. "It was a fun day," he repeatedly said. The declaration seemed pretty conclusive—every time he said it, I expected him to lean in and kiss me. Our bodies were not in sync. We laid just inches away from each other, but it felt like we were miles apart.

Feeling anxious, I headed to the bathroom once again. I glanced in the mirror, combed through my hair and faked a laugh so I could see what Scott saw. I gasped. My pearly whites had a green surprise inside: a sole piece of kale right in the center of my two front teeth. As soon as I finished washing my hands, I stormed into the other room. "Scott!" I exclaimed. "Why didn't you tell me I had food stuck in my teeth?" It was probably there for at least an hour—I was mortified. "You did? I didn't notice!"

he said as I plopped down on the bed next to him. There was no way he didn't notice. He was just being his usual, polite self in overlooking the green stain.

Scott glanced out onto the balcony, and my eyes followed. A full moon shone brightly over the hotel pool, which was illuminated by an array of alternating colors. "It's so pretty," he maintained. I suggested we go out and look. We stood side by side in the chilly air. "There's a moon! We have to make a wish on the moon!" I said. Scott didn't seem too familiar with making a wish upon a moon (perhaps stars were more his forte), but I proceeded. I shut my eyes and dreamed of the future both near and far. The images that flashed through my mind lasted at least sixty seconds, although I kept my eyes closed slightly longer to see how Scott would react. I hoped that he would come up behind me and wrap his arms around my shoulders or that he would pull me in while my lids were still shut and kiss me for the first time. Eventually, I gave up and opened my eyes. Everything was exactly how I left it: the pool was still illuminated in pink, palm trees swayed with the wind, and the sun had almost left the sky. One thing, however, was different. Scott was no longer next to me. He stood a few feet behind, waiting patiently to go back inside.

Scott took a seat on a sofa chair as I shut the door to the balcony. "What did you wish for?" he asked. There was no way I was going to reveal my wish—then, it wouldn't come true. I leaned against his chair. "You still don't know what I said in Gibberish earlier," I teased. It was time to tell the truth. "I literally said nothing. I was just trying to see what you thought I'd say." Scott sighed as I returned to my spot on the bed. "But it worked!" I exclaimed. "You were being so vague about everything all day." He bit his lip. "Yeah, I know," he said. I tapped the left side of the bed and encouraged Scott to sit beside me. I could finally see his eyes, which were concealed by his sunglasses all day. He no longer had adventures to hide behind. Finally, he began to reveal how he felt about us.

"Obviously, I had a great time today, and we've been flirting for a while now. I feel like there was a lot of anticipation leading up to today," he started. My heart skipped a beat. "Yeah, it has been eight months," I said. "This is kind of crazy." There was a long pause. We glanced off in different directions. *Wheel of Fortune* still played faintly, and I could hear palm trees rustling outside. I looked at Scott out of the corner of my eye, and when I caught his gaze, I shyly turned away. Neither of us knew what to say or do. All we knew was that we liked each other, but we were too afraid to admit that. There was a lot of pressure on us to achieve an epic conclusion to our adventure, an event that was almost a year in the making. We worried that one wrong move would ruin the connection we established, which is why neither of us wanted to instigate what came next. "Let's turn this off," I said, breaking the silence by pressing power off on the television.

"So what do you want to do?" Scott suddenly inquired, although I could tell through his passionate stare that he could foresee what was coming. "What do *you* want to do?" I asked. He shifted in his seat. "I guess we can have some fun," he replied. It concerned me that we lived on two different coasts and would hardly ever see each other, yet we were on the brink of losing our virginity. As soon as I raised my doubts, I could tell that Scott retreated inside his head. "Well, I'm not looking for a relationship because I'm so busy," he clarified. I wasn't either necessarily, but I couldn't help how I felt about him. "Well, I like you," I said. The sentiment was mutual. "I wouldn't have kept up the conversation this long or driven four hours to see you if there wasn't any chemistry," Scott professed. Yet he still appeared reserved. He squinted and scratched his head while contemplating where we would go from here. We sat quietly and gave each other space to think. After a few moments of silence, his energy shifted. It was as if a voice inside suddenly gave him a push forward, and all doubts were dismissed. I decided to place my fears aside as well. "Okay. So do you want to have a little fun?" he asked. He leaned in to begin our sexual adventure. Surprisingly, no sex was ever involved.

Scott kissed my lips more passionately than any guy I had been with before. He bit my bottom lip hard, to the point where it felt bruised, but I countered the pain by tensely pressing into his back. Our long hair kept covering our eyes and getting in our mouths. I stroked his brunette strands and pushed them aside. He genuinely cared about making me feel good, and I indicated my appreciation by pulling his shirtless body in close. There's no feeling as exhilarating as skin on skin. But suddenly, Scott stopped and rested his chin on my shoulder. "I can't get hard," he declared abruptly.

My innocent, inexperienced self didn't fully comprehend what was happening. "Are you nervous, maybe?" I asked. "There's no need to be! I was so nervous about today." He revealed that he was tense about the evening at first, but he was comfortable now. I immediately assumed his inability to perform was my fault. "Is there anything I can do?" I asked. He said he didn't know. I figured that maybe Scott wasn't aroused because he didn't feel sexually attracted to me, regardless of how passionate our make out was.

I told him to take a step back for a second so we could cuddle. Maybe moving too fast was stressing him out, and he needed a moment to breathe. The fact that he spooned me was sweet. Not all guys are patient enough to cuddle. I gave him a quick peck on the tip of his nose or cheek, and he did the same to my lips or chin. The kisses were cute and playful, and they raised what we referred to as "chemistry bubbles." "You're so cute," I said at one point while our faces were just centimeters away. Scott rolled his eyes. "No, I'm not," he responded. I insisted that he was, attempting to boost his spirits. "You too," he said with not nearly as much passion as my previous declaration. I gently tapped his cheeks and pointed out his "big blue eyes." "Your eyes are like caramel pools," he complimented me. I laughed. "Well, your eyes are like oceans," I one-upped him.

Despite the compliments, Scott had no luck. He proceeded to speak to himself out of frustration and desperation: "Come on!" It was almost like a game to him. I felt like the prize at the end of the line when I should have been an equal companion. At one point, Scott even went into the bathroom to help himself, and I followed for support. "I wish I had Viagra," he sighed. "I'm sorry. Wait, I'm not sorry!" His mental dilemma was ever-present. Scott claimed he lived with no regrets because everything is a learning experience, but I could tell he was disappointed and ashamed. He hopped off the bed to pace the room. Once he stopped, I wrapped my arms around him, and he placed his hands on my waist. "Is there *anything* I can do?" I asked again. Scott shook his head. "No, you killed it," he claimed. "It's not you, it's me." The sentence struck a nerve. Every time I heard a guy say those words, it seemed like a false excuse. I found it difficult to separate myself from the phrase's negative connotations and believe Scott was being genuine.

All in all, he appeared too discouraged and "bummed out" to continue. He sat on the edge of the bed, and I placed my hands on his shoulders as I stood above him. We glanced at ourselves in the mirror directly beside us on the wall. "Look at us," Scott said. "Look at us," I repeated. "Eight months in the making. It's been a long time, eh?" Scott added. In the mirror, we looked like a couple. It was as if we were glancing into a future that could be, yet one I knew was impossible. As I felt his cheek against mine, our bodies pressed together as one, I didn't want to let go. But he did. "Do you want to watch TV?" he inquired, abruptly jumping off the bed. Sensing his disappointment over what had just happened, I told him that was fine. He reached for his t-shirt, and I put my sweatshirt back on as well. I had some hope that things would be okay between us. "Tango?" he proposed, leading me into a quick dance around the hotel room. He spun me by the tips of my fingers, and I did the same for him. But only for a moment.

Scott started to get fully dressed, jewelry and all. Watching him go through the motions was quite poignant: as he slid rings onto his fingers, he was slipping outside of his vulnerable self and back into a more public front. The Scott that finally confessed his feelings was gone. All that remained was my distant crush who sat tensely at the edge of the bed with a glazed expression. His feet were crossed, and he remained silent. We were in the same room, but I knew that I already lost him. "Is it okay if I lean on you?" I asked, tilting my head in towards his shoulder. I couldn't tell if Scott was still feeling romantic, but he allowed me to lay gently on him. I then rubbed his shoulders, encouraging him to recline. At first, as I rested my head on his chest and draped my leg around him, his arms were crossed. I nudged him to uncross them and he got the hint, as he wrapped his arm around me instead. I placed my hand delicately on his stomach, and he put his on my forearm.

Scott's mind started to move beyond the bedroom and back into the real world. "I have to tell my friend what happened. He'll think it's hilarious," he said. I didn't want to admit it, but the fact that he immediately wanted to spill threw me off. We were vulnerable both physically and emotionally. It was as if dishing the details was his way of being in denial. If he laughed it off, then he wouldn't be as embarrassed. The trouble was that in the process, my feelings were trampled over. I reinforced to Scott that there was more to our day's adventure than just the attempt at sex. "We still had a moment," I stated, although it felt like I was trying to convince rather than remind him. "Yeah, we had some fun," he said. The word "some" stung my soul. I could tell his heart was no longer with me.

After flipping through television channels, we landed on *The Blind Side*. Simultaneously, Scott seemed blinded by his humiliation. He was so distracted by his own embarrassment that he didn't stop to ask how I felt. I didn't need an apology—I needed empathy and understanding that the evening was just as disappointing to me. I closed my eyes as I laid on his chest, playing with his bracelets and occasionally opening my eyes to see if he was glancing down at me. But he remained fixated on the scenes from the movie—I was of second importance. In fact, after he got dressed, he never kissed me again. Scott seemed to have altered time. The entire day sped by throughout our adventures, but it suddenly slowed down as he wallowed in humiliation. The mood shifted for the worse as we both realized that all the anticipation was for nothing. Scott anxiously checked the time on his phone. I tried to soak up every second while he wanted to be alone with his thoughts.

Around 10:00 p.m., he abruptly hopped off the bed and slipped his shoes and jacket on to leave. "I'm heading to my friend's house," he said. So he wasn't sleeping over. The change of plans came as a shock. As I laid on the mattress, watching him flip his hair over to put on his fedora, I experienced déjà vu from my experience with Nathan. Scott may not have ditched me mid-make out or said the evening was a mistake, but the sensation was the same. He stood a few feet away in the room, and I felt vulnerable and abandoned.

Scott leaned down and gave me a one-armed hug goodbye. I was puzzled. A semi-embrace was not an appropriate way to conclude our several adventures. "Let me get up and walk you out," I offered. He insisted I didn't need to leave my spot and appeared in a rush to exit the room. He didn't just walk—he *bolted* out the door and down the hallway. "Come back!" I playfully shouted after him. In chasing after Scott, the door shut behind me. Not only was I locked out of the room, but I stood in the hallway desperate and barefoot with a messy mane. I rode downstairs in the elevator with him because I needed a new room key, yet he was silent. "This is not a good look on me," I joked, pulling down my shorts and smoothing the top of my hair. After another quick embrace to say goodbye, I was alone—although I felt isolated for at least thirty minutes prior. Scott and I never spoke again.

Once I got back to the room, I sat on the bed so that I could process my emotions. I scanned the space: the sheets weren't that disheveled, yet I could still see the indentations of where Scott was. I pictured the shadows of his shirtless self moving through the space in my memory. In the mirror, I glanced at my cherry-red bottom lip, tinted from where he kissed passionately. To my surprise, I burst into laughter. Why had I placed so much pressure on our first interaction? It was silly.

I lied to myself in pretending I was okay. The next morning, when I woke up, I was struck with a sudden tsunami of emotions. I don't know what triggered the tears, but they wouldn't stop coming. I sat on the balcony of the hotel room and stared with blurry eyes out at the pool. The water was no longer illuminated. The moon had disappeared. It didn't feel the same. I believed my heart should have been enough to carry me through a successful evening. Scott's inability to perform wasn't my fault, but I blamed myself. I self-criticized over what went wrong—was I not sexy enough for him? Was he just not into me? I wondered what ran through his head. Was he uncomfortable because it was our first time meeting? Was he nervous because I was older than him? Did he lack the experience in age? Did he feel overall pressure to impress? The fact that I couldn't pinpoint a single answer was distressing.

It turns out that none of the above was to blame. Another reason arose later on: during all those months of flirty FaceTime calls, I most likely wasn't the only girl he was dialing. Just one month after our connection collapsed, I saw an Instagram story of Scott kissing his new girlfriend on the cheek. She couldn't have been any more different than me, with a nose ring, thick eyeliner, and a red streak in her hair. She referred to him as "the love of [her] life." It always stings to see the guy you like falling for someone else.

It's rare to meet someone and fall in love in just one month (although Jack and I seemed to have accomplished this). I assumed that Scott and his girlfriend had to at least have been talking beforehand. Did that mean he was thinking about another girl while we were hooking up? Was that why he seemed so in his head all day? I envisioned his internal monologue: *I want to get with Carrie, but I'm talking to this other girl too, so I feel bad. I don't know if I should go through with this.* I was never the one for him. He was never mine. I was most likely a distraction while he figured out his feelings for another girl. That realization hurt.

Besides the fact that I could have been a mere option to him, I knew the prospect of sex lingering the entire day must have psyched him out. Sex sat like a cloud over us throughout our adventures, just like the ones in the sky that we admired at the beach. While those clouds disappeared with nightfall, our reflections on sex lasted until the very last one-armed hug, and even in the days that followed. The hotel room was always at the end of the line—all of the events that occurred earlier were just a means to that end, leading up to a physical and metaphorical climax. On one hand, I liked that we trusted each other so much, we were comfortable losing our virginity to one another. But it bothered me that sex was the lingering end goal for us. Did he genuinely like me and trust me enough to be his first time? Or was that all I was to him—a "first time"? Did he only drive in that day to be intimate in the bedroom? Considering these questions was upsetting to me because Scott meant more to me than just sex. As he pulled me in tight and kissed me slowly, I secretly hoped that one day, we would become more than just each other's "first time."

The fact that he rushed out proves that sex was at the forefront of his mind—not me. I wished that he had stayed in the moment instead of bolting. Scott was not the type of guy to pull away and be "done for the night" if he didn't get what he wanted sexually. I just think he was embarrassed—the evening most likely made him nervous, anxious, and insecure. Our hookup was the farthest he's ever gone with a girl, and vice versa. We explored together more than we ever had with our exes.

As I sat on the sofa of the hotel balcony (eating my feelings through a large cup of Greek yogurt with dates and blackberries), I spoke to friends and close family members to analyze the evening. One friend kept telling me everything happens for a reason. I generally agree with that sentiment, but now, the thought just made me angry. I didn't believe her. Nobody understood just how special the moment was to me. It felt like my feelings were invalid. "Good job. You took her on a sex trip," I overheard my dad protest over the phone to my mom. His words hurt, especially considering the fact I cried to him over the phone just hours earlier about being hurt by a boy. Yes, it was my first time meeting Scott. Yes, we lived on opposite coasts. Yes, we weren't dating. Yes, it was *really* soon. But somehow, the moment felt right. There was something precious about the fact that we were both inexperienced and going through "adventures" together for the first time. It was a mutual exploration, which made me feel more comfortable if I "messed up" anything. My heart told me it was the right time to lose my virginity, and I wasn't going to fight it, nor did I need to defend myself to anyone.

We discussed how much I believed in signs, so naturally, I paid attention when the universe sent me one. I'm not a very religious person, but I felt like God was watching out for me. He forced me to doubt the gut feeling that told me it was the right time for a "first time." He made sure I didn't make a mistake by rushing the moment. He gave me a do-over when a lot of people don't have the opportunity for one. I wanted sex to be easy and simple, but in reality, it isn't.

# Double-Tap This:

## HOW TO KNOW IF YOU'RE READY FOR SEX

Sex is something sacred. Growing up on *Sex and the City*, the characters suggested otherwise. They made it seem like sex was an integral part of one's everyday routine, like brushing your teeth or making your bed. One character in particular (Samantha) became so accustomed to intercourse that it lost its meaning and significance. When thinking about losing your virginity, don't let *Sex and the City* set the example. Sex is symbolic; it represents a progression into adulthood that isn't achieved by age—only experience.

When you are about to have sex for the first time, the decision has more to do with you and less to do with your partner. It's a choice you must make yourself—don't let the other person pressure you before you're ready. Try not to let peer pressure affect you either. Just because your friends are losing their V-cards doesn't mean you need to rush. You have nothing to prove—it's not a competition as to who gets laid first. Sex should feel safe. Only you know when you feel comfortable enough to move forward.

Don't jump into sex just because you're lonely or because you crave the endorphins. You have to be careful whom you give your heart to—save it for someone you really care about. It takes a lot of time and trust to be vulnerable with someone. Wait for something real, not something fleeting. Waking up next to someone who doesn't care about you will hurt. Recognize your self-worth and make sure the person who takes your virginity values you.

# Learn the Lingo:
## ZOMBIEING

Consider a person who ghosts you, only to return months later—as if he came back from the dead. *Zombieing* is when someone you dated resurfaces months (or sometimes years) later in a subtle manner, like through a sudden text or Instagram follow. In my case, Scott returned in the form of a happy birthday text six months after he ghosted. Oftentimes, the "zombie" will bring up old emotions and ignite painful memories.

Nothing happened that I regret. In fact, it was Scott who encouraged me to live regret-free. But if I could go back to that night, I would probably caution my innocent mind that life doesn't always go according to plan. People are unpredictable, especially when it comes to sex and relationships. The narrative of the day leading to a potential first time fell apart and out of my control. While weeks of anticipation built positive tension, there was also a ton of pressure for the moment to be perfect. Perhaps if we were more spontaneous and less in our heads in forcing sex to occur, then we would have transitioned into it organically and successfully. My heart may have led me to that hotel room, but the heart can't predict the future. One must lead with both the heart and head in pursuing romantic connections. I was so blinded by our chemistry, I forgot to consider what could go wrong. If I used my brain more, with greater reason and rationality, my expectations would not have been set so high.

When confronting waves in the ocean, a person has two options: to float to the top or dunk under. My relationship with Scott functioned similarly. As we approached sex, the wavelength was too immense; pressure prevented us from making love, and the universe forced us to dunk under and avoid the situation. But in analyzing our time together, I found a third option in facing the tide of teenage relationships: to surf. What does it mean to surf? To let go, ride the wave, and trust the universe wholeheartedly. If Scott was the right person to be my "first," the universe would have brought us back together. Trust is everything—trust in a partner, trust in the universe, and (most importantly) trust in yourself. There was no need to fret: waves ebb and flow, and the tide always rolls in. ♥

# Chapter 8

# The Best Friend's Ex-Boyfriend

"WHAT ARE THE BOUNDARIES?" I asked my best friend Stella several times leading up to a date with her ex. Her response was always the same: "No boundaries," she'd say passively. "Do whatever you want." Stella is known to hide her emotions, but deep down, I know she's human—she hurts and goes through emotions like the rest of us. I assumed her tough skin left her bulletproof when it came to ex-boyfriends—but I was in for a rude awakening.

I was virtually introduced to Adam during my weekly walk down 5th Avenue with Stella. He FaceTimed her, and I stuck my face in the camera to see who was on the other line. The spring air was surprisingly cold, but I instantly felt the heat between the boy and me. His personality was refreshing: he was friendly, attractive, funny, sarcastic, and charming. I encouraged Stella to give him my Snapchat, and she willingly obliged. He lived a couple hours away, but a little flirtation was harmless, right?

After he added me on Snapchat, my first impression was that he was very good at flirting. He always knew exactly what to say, whether it was that I looked "cute" or that "we'll have a fun time in New York" when he comes to visit. I became familiar with his texting habits: he'd use a combination of punctuation marks such as ";)" over emojis to indicate his emotions. Maybe

I was reading too much into it, but his choices showed me that he was putting more effort into our conversation by avoiding basic smileys and symbols. I also warmed up to his signature Snapchat face: he'd purse his lips and squint his eyes slightly to appear picture-perfect. "Boys don't know how to pose," Stella rolled her eyes. As I told her about my frequent communication with Adam, she told me to be careful: "He's flirty with everyone, even me. We used to date in ninth grade."

Their relationship history came as a shock to me—I thought they were just close friends. Stella was six months into a relationship with her boyfriend at the time. My best friend was seventeen going on thirty: she'd already picked out her wedding dress and venue, home designer, and the names of her children. With this in mind, I immediately assumed the Adam connection wouldn't be a problem. Stella had clearly moved past him. My understanding was that she and Adam were in an informal relationship during their first year of high school. I figured fourteen-year-old romance tends to be casual. I had nothing to worry about in pursuing her ex. "It's fine. You have my blessing," Stella said repeatedly.

One weekend, Adam came to New York to visit his grandpa and attend Stella's birthday dinner as a friend. He asked me to hang out alone when he arrived. While my heart was eager to accept his offer, my head told me Stella would be uncomfortable. Nonetheless, I asked her permission. "Do what you want," she declared like a broken record. Stella's other best friend was in town, and with another person to keep her company, I thought it was the perfect time to see Adam. His flight landed at around 6 p.m. on a Friday, and he raced back to his hotel to shower and get ready. He planned to meet me on the cross-street near my apartment at eight but texted that he was running late. He sent several updates and screenshots of his Uber ETA, so I knew when he'd arrive. Used to boys canceling or showing up whenever they felt like it, I was pleasantly surprised by Adam's accountability.

At 9 p.m., he asked me to come downstairs to meet him. I spotted him from across the street and gestured for him to cross to my side. He looked tiny in a sea of yellow taxis, but as he inched closer, I noticed he was tall—5'11" to be exact. His face, however, was young and innocent. Like me, he could easily pass for either twelve or twenty-one. He greeted me with a brief hug and led me in the wrong direction towards the restaurant we planned to go to. We laughed over our shared poor sense of navigation, even though I've lived in New York City all my life. "You'd think I'd know where I'm going at this point," I said. Little did we know, we would soon discover the restaurant was closed for the evening.

We needed a new plan. Adam explained how much his grandma loved a lounge in the city, so we spontaneously decided to walk over. The spot was not close, but one mile had nothing on us, even if we only had thirty minutes to get there before it closed. As we speed-walked down the sidewalk, I joked that he was in the presence of a "professional runner." "I ran eight and a half miles the other day," I boasted as I walked a few feet ahead of him. He gloated about how he ran on the track team the year before. Our skills clearly came in handy. We made it to the lounge before its 10 p.m. closure, but they weren't taking any new customers.

So Plan C—the final and most successful plan of the evening—was devised. We rushed to a movie theater to purchase tickets for their last screening of the night. The movie itself (a rated-R action film) didn't matter—we only wanted to be alone together, and spending time in a theater was the perfect opportunity to cuddle close. Before we left for the movies, Adam told me his credit card wasn't linked to Uber, and he needed to call his mom to order the car. I raised an eyebrow as he walked towards the curb to talk to her, leaving me standing alone in the middle of the dark street. This wasn't the only time he phoned his mother during our date—he called about ten times, whether for a check-in or car services, throughout the evening. Adam didn't shy away from their connection: he was a self-proclaimed "mama's boy." It was cute, but I'd be lying if I said the frequent calls didn't throw me off.

Once the car let us out in front of the movies, we ran inside to make the final showing. The theater was isolated: two employees swept popcorn and candy scraps, and one staff member returned to his counter when he spotted us. Adam took charge, from the movie title to the seats to the payment. Paper tickets in hand, we rode up the escalator, illuminated by a multicolored film strip that hung from the ceiling. He selected seats in the back of the movie theater, a more secluded area that allowed us to chat and grow closer without others' eyes on us. We sank in the theater seats. My heart began to pound in anticipation of whether or not he would make a move.

We were thirty minutes into the movie, and Adam's eyes remained glued to the screen, with occasional sarcastic commentary. He even stepped out to dial his mom at one point, never explaining the reason for the call. When he returned, I reacted to every jump scare in the film, even if the scene wasn't scary, in hopes that he would put his arm around my shoulder. It wasn't until the first action scene in the film, a sudden burst of fire, that he decided to take initiative. He leaned in abruptly, catching me off guard. The kiss was unusually fast-paced. I opened my eyes for a split second to see if he was slowing down any time soon. His lips were relentless. I moved my hands from his hair to his neck, but his remained static on my waist. It didn't help that my arm was tangled in the mini backpack on my lap. I moved my head away for a breather, and so I could untangle the bag, but it was difficult to pull away.

Midnight quickly approached, and my eyes began to shut slowly. As I drifted off to sleep, I laid on Adam's lap, and he gently rubbed my back. The moment was no longer awkward. It was only our first time meeting, but strangely, being with him felt easy. Several yawns later, we decided to leave halfway through the movie. The weather was significantly colder, and a chilly breeze blew strands of hair in front of my eyes as we exited the theater. "Come here," Adam said, opening his arms to me. I wrapped my arms around his waist, and the wind no longer held as much power. While we waited for the Uber he ordered to take me home, we slow-danced on the street. My head rested delicately on his chest, and we swayed slowly from side to side under the lights of the theater awning. Once we stopped, we held each other in a tight hug. The disappointing kiss from inside the theater quickly became less significant. The present moment was magical.

The connection continued onto the car ride. We held hands the entire trip back to my apartment to drop me off. When leaving the vehicle, we were once again smacked by the wind. As I leaned against the white wall in front of my building, I realized that very spot was the site of my first hookup. There I was, standing there on a date five years later. It was as if my brain transported me back in time, and the familiarity left me with a strange sensation that washed over my body. But Adam's warm caress grounded me to the present, and my revelation led us to recount the details of our first hookups—first names, last names, and all. As we told our stories, it wasn't the slightest bit awkward, and we laughed over the fact that we lost our "kiss-card" at the same time. A quick glance down at my iPhone transformed my mood—it was getting late. We wrapped up our conversation and solidified our plans for Stella's party the next day. He suggested I pick him up at his hotel, and we would walk to the restaurant together. A quick peck ended the evening on a positive note, and I skipped upstairs, eager for our next interaction.

I texted Stella to divulge the details of my date as soon as I showered, but to no reply. Was she angry? Upset? Had she simply fallen asleep already? I drifted to sleep with questions still in mind and waited until the morning to call her. She answered casually, with no mention of my time with Adam. All she uttered was a "hi" and "how are you?" I called attention to the elephant in the room: "So are you going to ask about last night?" She finally asked about how the date went, and I recounted the evening as vaguely as possible: "We walked around, and a bunch of places were closed. Then, we went to the movies, kissed, and he dropped me off at home." My quick summary shook Stella. She glanced uncomfortably off to the side of the screen and pursed her lips. "I wouldn't have done that if I were you. It just looks bad on the outside that you're going out with my ex," she explained. Both Adam and I received her blessing repeatedly, so why the sudden change of heart? I brought my confusion to her attention, and she clarified her opinions. "Do whatever you want," she said passively. "Just don't be showy at my birthday party. It's supposed to be all about me." She backpedaled on her disapproval of the date. Still, I was unsure whether or not to continue pursuing Adam. The mixed messages were overwhelming. I was floating the evening before, only to be shocked by reality in the hours that followed.

Instead of letting Stella's doubts throw me off, I decided to go with my gut and resume my budding connection with Adam. I promised to limit flirtation at her party, which Adam and I agreed to over the phone that afternoon. We kept our original plan of meeting at his hotel. As I watched him step out of the elevator in a mismatched grey button-down and brown loafers, I worried if we would be able to pick up where we left off. I also wondered if Stella's words affected him at all. Clearly, they didn't. "You look incredible," he declared, spinning me around in my baby blue mini dress. As we walked to the party, we decided it wouldn't be the best idea to leave the restaurant together. We didn't want to further hurt Stella's feelings and ruin her evening. When we were a block away, I stopped and placed a hand on Adam's shoulder. "Let me give you a kiss goodbye now since I'm not going to be able to later," I asserted, shocked by my own confidence.

We arrived ten minutes late to an already-full table. Stella rolled her eyes as we greeted her. To redeem ourselves, we made an effort to talk to other attendees. We were seated next to each other, so Stella's request to rein in the romance was difficult. I wanted to get to know him, and it pained me to be mere inches away without engaging in conservation. At times, though, we couldn't help ourselves. We'd whisper to each other and gossip about the people around the table, giggling about how certain interactions with the guests were awkward and uncomfortable. I talked about my love of football, and we searched on our phones under the table for a quarterback I liked. When the cake was brought out, Adam knew I didn't eat dessert. He dug his fork into my plate, so it looked like I ate it—and also inhaled a chocolate slice himself.

The dinner finished sooner than I expected. It was only 9:20, and with forty minutes before I needed to head home, I asked Adam if I could walk him back to his hotel. However, we couldn't let Stella see us leaving together. Adam came up with the first part of the plan: he would say goodbye first, and I would leave a few minutes after. He intended to wait for me on the corner of the nearby avenue, but I sensed that Stella was onto us since we would be walking in the same direction. I pretended to order a car and faked a phone call with the driver where he told me to walk to the opposite avenue. Adam and I circled around to meet each other in the middle. I felt guilty for lying to my best friend, but still, my sights were set on Adam.

We strolled side by side down the busy city streets. I still wondered if he saw me the same way as he did the night prior. I subtly slid my hand through his arm, and his response provided me with clarity. "Here," he said, offering a hand to hold. Our fingers were interlaced for the entire fifteen-minute walk as we recapped the highlights of the evening. On the street of the hotel, a woman shouted at us out the window of a car—it was Adam's mom, and she was on her way to a comedy club with his father. "Nice to meet you!" I exclaimed, smoothing the top of my hair and charming her with a grin. She called Adam shortly after—I wasn't positive if it was to elaborate on her plans for the evening or to recap our spontaneous encounter. Adam relayed his mother's words: she asked if I was the girl he was with last night and if I was a model. The label was extremely humbling, and it gave me an extra boost of confidence.

Since we never took photos together at the party, we asked a woman in front of the hotel to grab a few shots. As the camera snapped away, I felt Adam lean his head in close. I knew that I could never post the pictures nor show them to Stella, but the memory was all that mattered. "Why do you have to leave?" he whined. His urging me to stay was sweet, and I told him we would see each other soon. We kissed goodbye and parted ways, leaving me with nothing but an adrenaline rush. Sure, we were sneaking around Stella, but I loved the feeling of living on the edge—it only made my connection with Adam deeper and more adventurous.

Once Adam boarded the plane back home, I planned on seeing him again on vacation a month later. We weren't officially dating, but I loved bouncing flirtatious messages back and forth with him. Perhaps there was relationship potential? I soon realized that wasn't what he was looking for. I sent him kissy-face selfies via Snapchat, but he replied with photos of half of his face. I texted him potential dates to meet up, and when the message sent in green, I grew concerned. Did he block me? Stella told me that he bought a new phone: he notified her, not me, about his new number. After I asked her for his digits, I forwarded him the dates I was visiting. "I'm not sure. I thought this was a one-time thing," he typed. I froze. What happened to slow dancing under the stars at the movie theater? Where did the magic go? It vanished as quickly as his airplane took off into the sky.

Part of me knew that dating a guy in a different state would never work—I wanted someone I couldn't have. But still, his words stung. Girls can usually tell whether or not a guy is in it for the long run. Adam, however, was always unclear about his intentions. His message made me feel like I was used and discarded. He tricked me into believing I was special so that he could get what he wanted out of me during the twenty-four hours we spent together: a casual hookup and nothing more. It took everything in me to muster the courage to respond calmly: "Lol, we live in different cities. I wasn't expecting to date." He then proceeded to tell me he liked someone else, and he didn't want to give off the wrong message. Not only was I angry that he played with my feelings during the time we spent together, but I was also frustrated for the girl he was pursuing. Little did she know he was a player. Adam had little care or consideration when it came to others' emotions, and that reality made it easy for me to detach from the situation. "No worries, totally get it!" I replied. I placed my phone down on my dresser and felt proud for owning my power in the face of his selfishness.

## Learn the Lingo:
### SITUATIONSHIP

Ever felt like you were in a relationship with someone, but you never put a label on it? Those engaged in a *situationship* are in a confusing in-between status of not friends but not boyfriend and girlfriend either. They have fun and fool around as if they're dating, but the connection is casual and commitment-free. There's no pressure, since the situationship is not necessarily going to turn into something serious. Adam and I epitomized a situationship. We clearly had chemistry, but we never identified ourselves as an exclusive couple. We kept the relationship light and informal. Situationships are destined for failure, because no matter how much you tell yourself you don't care, you do. You will, especially when he's gone.

I told myself I would never get with Adam in the future. But a year later, I was in a place where I was desperate for a rebound. I was just getting over a breakup, and I wanted to feel desired again. I happened to be in his hometown, and seeking validation, I reached out to him. We started talking and quickly redeveloped a friendship. I acted out of pain and insecurity and used him to fill a void. I contradicted my previous distaste for a casual fling. But I was in a vulnerable place, so I gave in. Sometimes, it takes something reckless to learn and grow.

Both single, we reunited. Our time together can be summed up with this: two days, one concert, and one porta potty make out (it was the only place we could find privacy). When we weren't kissing in the bathroom stall (gross…I know), I enjoyed swaying to the music with his arm around my waist from floor seats. He was always charming, often romantic—holding my hand, opening doors, keeping me close when someone squeezed by us at the concert. I felt comfortable being myself around him because the stakes weren't high. It was just a fun, spontaneous fling between two friends with benefits—although it felt more like he was my fake-out boyfriend for the weekend. I prevented myself from catching feelings this time around because I knew a relationship would be impossible. Distance (and his track record as a player) would not allow it.

Adam and I met up one last time a few months later when he visited New York. We people-watched (okay, maybe mocked) the ice skaters wiping out at Bryant Park, and then went back to his hotel room to "hang out." Not even one minute into our make out, Adam stopped me and suggested I get in the shower before we continue. Apparently, I looked hotter to him when mascara was running down my face (ew).

Later that evening, he told me he wanted to have a "deep conversation." I wasn't sure what he meant, and frankly, neither did he. He said it seemed like I was eager to say something, even

Carrie Berk

though I was simply laying in his hoodie on the couch of his room. I wasn't planning on telling Adam, but I wound up confessing that I had feelings for him once upon a time when we first started seeing each other. I asked him if he ever had feelings for me, and he quietly shook his head no. "That's fine, but then why do you get with me? If it's not feelings, then what is it?" I asked. There was a long pause. "Nothing," he whispered. His response took me aback. He could've said he liked me as a friend and had fun with me. He could've said he was physically attracted. Anything but "nothing." When he said "nothing," it felt like *I* was nothing.

Adam was hooking up with me mindlessly. I knew that in my heart, but hearing him say how he felt aloud made it more real. It made it hurt more. I started to change back into my own clothes. "What's wrong?" he said, sensing that something was off. "Well, I feel kind of objectified," I asserted. "It feels like you're just using me for my body." He told me he didn't know what "objectified" meant, so I explained it to him like he was a child. "I'm not using you for your body," he eventually said. I looked him dead in the eye. "If it's not feelings, and if it's not my body, then what is it? Why do we keep hooking up?" It took him a while to muster a response. "I don't know. It's you." It was clear we weren't getting anywhere, so I stopped trying. He was taking advantage of me and trying to avoid admitting it. Perhaps he saw me as an easy target. I was sick of being accommodating so that he could feel superior.

On my end, he was a friend I was physically attracted to; his flirtatious words and actions made me become attached. But the romance was just a ploy to get me in his bed. It felt good in the moment when he was affectionate, but his intentions weren't pure. He didn't care about me like I cared about him, even as a friend. Our "deep convo" was eye-opening—after that, I never saw him the same.

140

## Swipe Left:

### SIGNS THAT HE'S A PLAYER

- He's too nice. He'll do whatever it takes to make you feel special so that you'll give him what he wants (usually sex).
- He avoids getting to know you better. Adam kept wanting to do a group FaceTime call with our friends. Normally, being introduced to your guy's friends is a good sign. It means he feels confident enough in your relationship to incorporate you into his social life. But my FaceTime calls with Adam were *only* in groups. If he was interested in you and only you, he would call you alone.
- He sweet-talks his way out of things. Adam would always find excuses, whether it was the hickey he already had on his neck when we met in his hometown ("that's in the past") or why he didn't want to tap into his feelings ("I'm not a dating type of guy").
- He's eager for a hookup. If you sense he only wants to get laid, chances are you're not his only victim.
- He's keeping secrets. If you don't know anything about his life or hobbies, maybe he doesn't want you to.
- He doesn't send personalized Snapchats. Pictures of the ceiling that say "streaks" are definitely being sent to several people. If you're only snapping someone to keep up a streak, that person is not worth your time.
- He only hits you up after you post in a revealing outfit or swimsuit. You deserve someone who loves all of you—not just your body.

After our weekend together, Adam stopped texting and snapping me (he lost our streak). The guy who had messaged me every ten to twenty minutes while we were planning hangouts now left me on open. Sure, our time together was fruitless, but I was still human. Since we hooked up sans feelings, he didn't respect me. I planned on continuing to talk to him as a friend, but we rarely spoke. It was as if we were strangers.

Hooking up with a guy gives me the ultimate endorphin rush. It makes me feel more present. But I feel far worse afterwards if he stops talking to me because a hookup is all he was in for. I'll feel hurt. I'll feel dirty. I never know how far to go with someone I'm "vibing" with. What if I just met him, but I'm feeling a connection? Sometimes, you have to take a step back and be rational. Do you like the person, or do you just like how he makes you feel? I didn't *really* like Adam. I indulged because I liked how he made me feel when I was with him: fun, flirtatious, outgoing, and sexy. When a guy makes me feel good about myself, I lose my head. There's a difference between hooking up with someone because you want to explore a deeper connection and hooking up with someone because he flatters your ego. You also don't have to jump in a guy's bed early on to show you want to be more than friends. Use other physical cues to indicate your interest. One of the biggest indications of interest is time. Obviously, spending more time with the person is only possible if he lives within a convenient distance (sorry, vacation flings!).

I'm not saying to avoid hookups at all costs. I can't just sit back and not kiss guys because I'm afraid they're going to leave or that I'll get my feelings hurt. Because one day, someone is going to stay. Among the emotionally or geographically unavailable guys, you may find the diamond in the rough: someone who makes you feel comfortable when you're around him, so you your personality can shine without fear of judgment. Adam always made me feel comfortable, but we weren't poised to last. What I've learned is that your person is most likely not going to live in another state. They're also not going to be someone you kiss too soon—then, they won't respect you.

So is the temporary endorphin rush from a spontaneous hookup really worth it? Sometimes yes, sometimes no. Having fun with someone you're attracted to isn't wrong. Hookups are healthy because they help you learn about what you want. But if you're only hooking up because you're bored, insecure, and want to boost your confidence, quit it. Your joy should not depend on anyone else. There are other ways to make you happy besides a make out.

When Adam stopped communicating with me, I was surprised by how much I cared. After all, we agreed to keep no strings attached. I considered if perhaps he worried about getting too serious. The man next to us at the concert asked if we were dating. He said he could tell I liked Adam from the way I looked at him with passionate eyes. Adam generally avoided kissing me in public to avoid relationship assumptions. Then again, he posted a photo of us on Snapchat after the concert. At first, I didn't think much of it, but I soon wondered if he only shared the image to show me off to his friends like a trophy.

## *Swipe Left:*

### MIXED SIGNALS

Men change faster than the seasons. Just look at Adam: he kissed me goodbye, begged me not to leave, then abruptly stopped texting. The mixed signals he sent me were contradictory, confusing, and seriously anxiety-inducing. I would agonize over how he felt about me, and I let the rumination interrupt my everyday life.

If this sounds familiar, try to clear your head. A guy who's giving mixed signals is the one with the mental conundrum, so don't let his feelings carry on to you. He could be trying to figure out his emotions, which is why you're getting conflicting messages.

So does he like you or not? There's no way of knowing. One guy told me he missed me and then never reached out when he was in town. What you can learn from the ambiguity is that the person has poor communication skills. They're not being direct with you about how they feel. Perhaps they're avoiding commitment and don't know how to let you down easy. Or they're just indecisive and stringing you along while making up their mind. Either way, that person is not someone you'd want to date.

Thankfully, Stella didn't hold my superficial fling against me. "It has nothing to do with me or my emotions," she explained. "It just seems like you're at a time in your life when you're exploring your options and enjoying being single. I don't know why you wanted a relationship out of this." I liked spending time with Adam, and in the beginning, I genuinely wanted to see if our connection would go anywhere. But the time and distance were never right.

I may have disagreed with some of Stella's words, but deep down, I knew I hurt her in pursuing her ex—and that was never my intention. Sometimes, people say things they don't mean, and perhaps she gave me the go-ahead as a test of friendship. She was in a relationship, so technically, she couldn't have said no. Forbidding my date with Adam would have indicated that she still had emotional ties to him and that her boyfriend should have been worried.

In the moment, I was selfish and insensitive to her feelings. She was out and about with her boyfriend for the six months prior while I was single and lonely. I didn't wholly consider how me seeing Adam made her feel before moving forward. We were no longer just sisters in friendship but spit sisters as well—that reality was most likely strange and difficult for her to swallow. I was always good to Stella. But I tend to lose my head around boys, even when my best friend is involved. She opened the door between Adam and me and saw how I'd handle that situation. I made a poor choice. I shouldn't have gone out with him and allowed myself to catch feelings in the first place, but since I did, it was difficult to abandon those feelings in the moment.

The experience made me wonder: is there ever an exception to "sisters before misters"? In love, do invisible boundaries exist, ones that are not explicitly drawn but assumed through logic and instinct? Looking back, I recall the emptiness in Stella's eyes as I recounted my date with Adam. The way I hurt her, whether or not she explicitly admitted it, was not okay. You should never ignore your best friend's emotions. She didn't have to say anything for me to recognize that what I did was wrong. A person will always hold mental ties to their ex, whether positive or negative.

When my other friends asked about Adam, I always referred to him as "my best friend's ex-boyfriend" to remind them who he was. In pursuing a relationship with him, it would have been difficult to get a fresh start and detach from his dating history with Stella. Besides, sisters always come before misters, and nothing—not even a magical moment under a movie marquee—can change that. ♥

# Chapter 9

# The Big Shot

HE WAS TWENTY-SEVEN. I WAS eighteen. Age is nothing but a number—or is it?

As I stood outside the doors of a party, scouting for a new guy was the last thing on my mind. Instead, I focused on Liam, the seventeen-year-old my friend Ava brought along to set me up with. At dinner that night, Ava had handed me her phone, so I could scroll through their text messages about me. I couldn't believe what I was reading. He already planned out our entire future: we would lock eyes, mutually agree to make out in a bathroom, and be exclusive for a few months until he left for college. The fact that someone I'd never even met wanted me so badly was hard to believe. My skepticism held me back from the start, but I agreed to give it a shot. Little did I know that an older, more exciting option was waiting just behind the glass doors.

Initially, the party looked empty. It was mid-pandemic, so guests roamed with masks draped beneath their chins. A large abstract sculpture decked out in silver glitter stood in the center of the room, with a winding white staircase hidden behind it. I grabbed Ava by the hand and dragged her to the steps, with Liam following not too far behind. We made our way through a large crowd of guests who waved their hands wildly in the air. I was blinded by the lights, deafened by DJ sounds but instantly drawn to the dance floor. The room was lit by geometric projections and lined with an array of plants. Professional dancers in crop tops and skirts stood on the surrounding platforms, shaking their hips to the beat of the music. The far left of the space featured a roped-off area for event VIPs, and I glared enviously as guests enjoyed a private celebration. A man brushed past me in a light-up rainbow fur scarf and took center stage in front of the DJ. A woman from Brazil spontaneously embraced me, and we began singing along to booming EDM tunes together. The party had a surplus of spirited people, and I wanted to become one of them.

After an hour of jumping and screaming over the music to talk to Liam, I realized that we were incompatible. "Teach me how to dance!" I exclaimed, placing his hands on my waist. He didn't seem to pick up on the flirtation, and his eyes darted nervously around the room. At that moment, I noticed two men standing directly behind us. One of them had piercing green eyes, and I shot him a subtle smile as I continued to let Liam guide my hips. The music crescendoed while my connection with Liam diminished.

Bored, frustrated, and fed up, I fibbed that I lost my lip gloss and walked towards the back of the room. I was making a bee-line for the bar when I felt a sudden tap on my shoulder. "Your boyfriend seems pretty soft," the guy with the green eyes said. I laughed. "Definitely not my boyfriend. He won't even make a move." The new man's name was Brandon, and he was a twenty-seven-year-old college graduate and entrepreneur. He was also bicoastal; his other residence was in California. He asked about my career, and I told him that I was invited to the event as a social media influencer. "What do you have, like two million followers or something?" It almost seemed like too much of a coincidence. At 1.8 million followers and counting, the proximity was pretty scary. But I didn't have enough evidence to prove his guess was not by chance. Instead, I showed him my TikTok and assumed it was the first time he'd looked, quickly scrolling past the age "18" written in my bio. "Okay, big shot!" he joked. I shook my head. "You're the one who's a CEO of a company," I clapped back.

He offered me his phone to type in my phone number, insisting that I include my middle name as well. I raised an eyebrow at the odd request. "My best friend doesn't even know my middle name," I informed him. I chose to leave out that detail from his contact list yet playfully insisted he include it in mine. I was eager to continue our conversation, but our exchange was halted by a small hand on my back: Liam's. The two of them shook hands, and Liam grabbed my arm to drag me back to the DJ booth. I considered strutting away from the older guy without looking back. But something inside of me felt like I was giving up a good thing. So my insecurity spoke: "Come find me later."

As we continued to dance, I became even less interested in Liam. My eyes shot past the strobe lights in search of Brandon. Next thing I knew, I was asking the Brazilian woman, a complete stranger to me, for advice: "What do I do? I'm supposed to be going out with my friend's friend, but I really like this older guy I met here." The situation seemed complex, yet she made it simple: "Which guy do you like more?" Her words took me out of my head and into my heart, where I remained for the rest of the evening. I knew Brandon was the answer.

Once again, I snuck out of the crowd. I pretended that I was "too hot" and needed to cool down when in reality, I hoped Brandon would find his way back to me. And he did. "Where's your boyfriend?" he teased. I told him I wanted to talk to him instead. "Yeah, me too. I think you're cute," he said. Brandon (or perhaps the alcohol in this case) proceeded to ask me a few of the same questions as before—where I grew up, which university I attended, and my career path. The party was packed, but our conversation transported us out of the crowded space. We were solely focused on each other, as if we were in a vessel of our own. Eventually came the question I feared most of all: "How old are you?" I anxiously scanned the room. The attendees were tall, intimidating, and seemed to be over the age of twenty-one. A couple directly beside us was smoking pot, and the smell of mixed alcohol permeated the space. I didn't belong, but I sure could fake it. "Twenty-one," I replied, cautiously optimistic.

Brandon placed his hand on my back and led me to the bar. "What do you want to drink?" he asked. He didn't know I hated alcohol. My sober self was bubbling with stress, but I knew I had to say something. "Surprise me." His green eyes glanced to the side as he tried to find his words. I was proud of myself, an eighteen-year-old stumping a full-on adult with a flirtatious remark. "Whiskey sour or ice water?" he finally said. To me, the answer was clear, but I thought very carefully about how to respond. I didn't want him to think I was a baby. "I already had a lot to drink tonight," I lied.

"Thanks for treating me. The other guy made me buy him a Sprite earlier," I said in between sips of boxed water. Brandon's mouth dropped to the floor. "Can I go punch this guy?" he said. I laughed, but part of me actually felt like he was being serious. I felt guilty that he was hating on a younger guy, but then I realized—Liam's not much younger than me. I had to tell Brandon my age before he set unrealistic expectations for the evening. Images of bar-hopping and hotel room hookups flashed through my mind. I didn't want things to take a turn for the worse. "You're going to kill me…I lied to you," I said.

Just as I was about to reveal my age, Brandon's friend approached us. "I'm leaving to go to another party. You're welcome to bring your new friend if you want," he encouraged Brandon. I knew going alone to a crowded space among strangers was poor judgment, so I placed the blame on Ava and Liam. "You go ahead! My friends wouldn't want me to abandon them,"

I claimed. Brandon shook his head. "They can come too. You know, I can be pretty convincing in making them leave," he said. I shot down the suggestion. "It's okay. Call me another time." But Brandon refused—it seemed like he genuinely wanted to continue getting to know me. He rejected his friend and stayed by my side, waters still in hand.

"About what I wanted to tell you," I started. "I'm eighteen." To my surprise, Brandon didn't flinch. He stood with his feet planted firmly on the ground—it was clear that he was unfazed and not going anywhere. "Really? I actually believed you were twenty-one," he said casually. I told him I was telling the truth and that one quick Google search would serve as proof. But no internet search was needed. He trusted me, and strangely, I trusted him too.

We didn't want to bump into Liam on the dance floor, so instead, I led Brandon into an emptier room with projections. I watched in awe as the colorful lights zig-zagged across his face in different patterns. There was something profound about being in an artistic, semi-private space with a complete stranger. Across the room, I spotted a couple whom I had observed earlier on the dance floor—they went to a less crowded room to continue their make out session. It felt like I shouldn't have been watching, but I couldn't help myself. I watched as the man's hands traced the woman's entire body, and he pulled her full head of curls closer. They seemed so into each other that nothing—not the music, projections or surrounding people—could ruin their moment. My fascination was interrupted by Brandon's frankness: "Honestly, I'm surprised they just want to make out and not have sex." So sex was on his mind. Was that all he wanted?

The teenage brain ignores what's risky when you're enamored with someone. With Brandon, I got swept up in the heat of the moment. He literally swept me off my feet: he placed his arms on my waist, lifted me up in the air and spun me around in circles. As I watched the projections speed by, I spiraled deeper and deeper into infatuation. It felt like I was on top of the world, and I didn't want to come down from the endorphin high. When he lowered me, my spirit was still soaring. My fingertips dangled from his gentle grip as I twirled, dancing to the DJ beats that played in the room next door. Overcome with joy and laughter, I fell into Brandon's arms, and he finally leaned in for a kiss. The music boomed around us, yet our make out was anything but "techno." It was slow, careful, and full of chemistry. His scruff gently brushed my chin as our lips touched in a steady rhythm that challenged the EDM. My mind never wandered elsewhere—I was completely present in the moment.

I was focused on Brandon when I suddenly realized Ava and Liam were walking up to us. Liam stared at his feet and refused to look me in the eyes. He appeared embarrassed by my rejection—I felt bad for him. "We're about to head home. Ready to order the Uber?" Ava asked. I didn't want my evening with Brandon to end. So I hugged her goodbye, and I let Liam go without any explanation as to why I was no longer interested in him. "I'll make sure she gets home safely," Brandon assured them.

We breathed a sigh of relief as we watched them walk away, and after a few minutes, Brandon guided me to the dance floor. Now that Liam was gone, we didn't have to worry about exploring our connection in the crowded room. As I felt sweaty bodies brush past me, I put on my face mask, suddenly feeling uncomfortable. Like a perfect gentleman, Brandon took out his mask to mirror me and drew me closer. "What are we supposed to do with these?" he shouted over the music while pointing to his mask. My spontaneous heart held the answer. I pulled my mask down, removed his and leaned in to lock lips. I was always careful during the pandemic, but I was tired of restraining myself. It felt good to be bad. When Brandon receded, I released my neck towards the ceiling and closed my eyes. My hair grazed my bare back, exposed by my strapless dress. As he held my waist, he began to kiss up my neck and towards my ear. "You're stunning," he whispered. "All I want to do is keep kissing you."

# Double-Tap This:

## PARTY ETIQUETTE

After my evening with Brandon, I learned a thing or two about the dos and don'ts of going to parties. I found a friend group to party-hop with whenever I need a fun night out. They encourage me to get outside of my comfort zone, let loose, and be flirtatious. I'm not afraid to inch closer to someone in hopes of striking up a conversation. That said, parties often make me feel insecure, especially when I don't get picked up by a guy. Males don't always approach females anymore (perhaps they're scared of rejection), but that doesn't mean you can't take charge. Waiting too long to talk to someone you're crushing on will not serve you well in 2023 and beyond. We were in lockdown for several months, so don't take your time for granted. Here are some helpful tips I learned for a night out on the town.

- Go to parties with people who watch out for you. Showing up solo is almost always a bad idea. Have someone by your side in case you're confronted by an unfriendly stranger.
- Never go to the bathroom alone. The last thing you want is to be followed by some creep. Employ the buddy system.
- Share your location with your friends during the night in case you get lost. Taking a car home late can be dangerous. Let your parents and/or friends know your whereabouts; you can stop sharing when you're home.
- Don't succumb to peer pressure. In high school, I held an empty red solo cup and pretended to sip so it looked like I fit in. Safety always comes first.
- Wingwomen are overrated. Guys are much more interested in a confident girl who makes the first move herself.
- Put your phone in your pocket. Looking up from your screen forces you to live in the moment. Just make sure your device is accessible in case of an emergency.
- Never put down your glass. Be cautious of others slipping unwanted substances into your drink.
- Don't be too aggressive in pursuing a potential suitor. My favorite way to catch a guy's attention is by lightly tapping his shoulder and saying "excuse me" when passing by.
- Don't take yourself too seriously. I've had lots of slip-ups. I spilled a drink on a guy's shirt as he was talking to a girl. A guy even knocked into me and spilled my drink down my shirt by accident. Laugh it off and keep dancing.
- Never go home with a stranger—period.

Soon after dancing, he offered to take me home. "I'll pay for your ride. Here, put your address in," he offered, handing me his phone. I typed in a location across the street from my house to get dropped off at. It didn't feel right to give a stranger my exact address. We climbed up the winding staircase, our fingers intertwined, and he held the door open for me as we left the venue. Speeding through midtown in an Uber, my eyes were on Brandon and Brandon only.

He handed me his phone to show an advertisement for his company. "Okay, big shot, this is insane!" I said, using the same words he previously used to describe me. Our conversation constantly shifted as we got to know each other. At one point, Brandon expressed his distaste for dating apps. "Yeah, I'm a no-bullshit kind of guy. I'd rather meet a girl organically," he said. "And when she texts me, I respond right away." He was saying all the right things. Not focused on his age, I asked what his expectations were when it came to the two of us. "I don't have any expectations," he maintained. "Things happen naturally. Whatever happens, happens." His mindset was promising. "Yeah, I agree. I'm not the type to pursue someone only for sex, though," I said, afraid he was looking for something more that evening. Brandon nodded and affirmed my opinions. Perhaps I was just paranoid. It seemed like sex was never even in the picture.

The conversation shifted as Brandon brought up one of his favorite movies about a Met Gala heist, *Ocean's 8*. "I've never been to the steps of the Met," he admitted. "No way—you have to!" I exclaimed, encouraging him to change the destination on his phone. Within minutes, our car glided down an isolated 5th Avenue to the Metropolitan Museum of Art. Brandon and I climbed to the top of the steps and took a seat. No one was in sight. Strangely, our Uber decided to stick around for a few minutes. It was as if the driver were waiting for us to kiss. The second Brandon leaned in, I listened to the car quietly whoosh by.

I took in the panoramic view of the city. Manhattan had never looked so stunning and wide-spanning. "What a treat! Let's take a selfie so we can remember this moment," Brandon said, snapping two images from a low, unflattering angle. He then started playing Kendrick Lamar's "Money Trees" from his phone for mood music. "Catching feelings…" he mumbled. I leaned in to capture Brandon's gaze. "Catching feelings for the music, or me? Or both?" I sought to clarify. He shrugged playfully and leaned in for another kiss. Occasionally, we'd both come up for air. My cheek rested beside his, and I listened closely to us breathing in harmony.

I promised my mom I'd be home by 12:30, and it was already 12:10. My Cinderella moment was quickly coming to an end, but Brandon ensured I felt like a princess until the last second we spent together. "Can I give you a piggyback ride home?" he offered. He once again swept me off my feet. I was draped friskily over his shoulder as he carried me down the steps. "Big shot," I mumbled in response to his strength.

# Learn the Lingo:
## LOVE BOMBING

Think twice next time the person you just started dating is being extra romantic. *Love bombing* is characterized by overt displays of affection in hopes of getting something from you. Oftentimes, it's sex or the ability to control you. The person assumes that if they do something for you, you'll provide something in return. Early on in a relationship, it's easy to get caught up in flattery, extravagant gifts, and loving words ("we're soulmates"; "I'm falling for you"). But beneath the surface, the person may be manipulating you to win your trust. You'll know a person is love bombing versus being genuine if their actions are extreme. One time, a guy treated me to a $300 Omakase dinner on the second date. Little did I know, we were a block away from his apartment, a convenient distance if he wanted to lure me there after dinner. Don't lose your head if your date is over-the-top or overly affectionate—even if it feels exciting. Sometimes, his actions aren't pure.

When we reached the street, I jumped on his back, my feet flailing in front of him. He wound up carrying me for over a mile—it was as if I had my very own horse-drawn carriage in the middle of Manhattan. I had never felt so special in my home city. When Brandon's back got tired, he lowered me onto a car and began to kiss me. What if the owner of the car was watching? What if I dented the trunk? Nothing mattered as I soaked in my fairytale.

When I pointed out that my apartment was across the street, Brandon scooped me up and carried me all the way to the glass doors. "Want to take me upstairs?" I asked, staring longingly into his eyes. We entered the elevator, and he pulled me in for one last make out before we parted. "Let's do dinner tomorrow," he whispered as we stood in the hallway, just a few feet away from my door. I tried to play it cool by asking him to text me the time. To my surprise, he wanted a firm plan in place. "So six..." he said hesitatingly, waiting for me to indicate what time worked best. The arrangement was perfect, and we sealed it with a kiss goodbye.

I ran inside my apartment, kicked off my shoes and could hardly contain my excitement. "Mom!" I exclaimed, trying to keep my voice down while Brandon waited for the elevator. "I'm literally in love." She was on the couch, looking down at her phone, but I continued. "I met a boy at the party, and he was so sweet. He took me home!" My mom pursed her lips skeptically. "Yeah, how old is he?" she asked. I gulped. I knew hiding his age from her would eventually backfire. "He's twenty-seven," I confessed. She glanced up from her phone with fear in her eyes. "No way," she quickly stated. "No, no, no." The sudden negativity felt like a slap in the face, and I felt my heart sink to the wooden floor. I had just been on top of the world, floating under strobe lights and soaring down the streets of New York City. Yet as I recounted the story to my mom, she made my emotions feel invalid and knocked me back down to reality. "I hate you!" I screamed. "This only has to do with you not wanting me to grow up." She told me I couldn't go to dinner with him and that my actions were dangerous. "You don't even know this guy. He could've kidnapped or groomed you!" she maintained.

Grooming was something to be taken seriously—that never even crossed my mind when I was with Brandon. I was familiar with the concept from a series I watched, *Cruel Summer*. In the show, a high-school student forms a close relationship with her principal only to be kidnapped by him later on. Similarly, everything seemed perfectly safe with Brandon when we met. There may have been a large age gap, but I was eighteen, a legal adult. He was a nice guy, and all we did was talk and kiss. I didn't see where anything could've gone wrong.

My inability to initially recognize that I was at fault made my mom panic. Her screams quickly turned into a flood of tears, and I watched her breathe heavily. "You betrayed my trust!" she sobbed. Not to mention, it was Mother's Day, which made the situation more tense. She didn't speak to me for the entire night, and any words uttered the day after reflected her anxiety and disappointment. I still didn't see my shortcomings. I hadn't lied to her. All I did was hide what I was up to with Brandon in the moment, keeping things under wraps until I was back in the apartment. I love my mom, but no matter how much she cried, shrieked, and hyperventilated, I disagreed with her. I couldn't empathize with her while she was hurting, and that made me feel selfish.

Our mothers have a natural inclination to protect us at all costs. They want to preserve our innocence. However, I needed to focus on myself and my own emotions that night. Her pain reflected onto me. She was struggling with her own fear about my having been in a potentially dangerous situation with a stranger. At the same time, I struggled with the fact that my happiness was fleeting. Not even my own mother could see through to my soul to understand what I had just experienced and the difficulty of what I was about to do. I knew I had led Brandon on, and a single tear streamed down my cheek as I rejected him over text against my own will. "I have a lot of finals. I also did some thinking and I think the age gap might be too large. Keep in touch!" I typed. His response: a mere thumbs-up and cool-face emoji, along with the affirmation that it was "great hanging at the Met." His text choices seemed soulless compared to the stirring events of the evening. Still, I was hung up on our in-person interactions.

You always want what you can't have, and Brandon was no longer within reach. It felt like I was an adrenaline junkie, and I wanted to be taken back to my perfect night. Brandon and I had a chemistry that was hard to explain. It was a sensation unlike any I'd ever experienced before. But beneath the allure of the party lights and 12 a.m. piggyback rides, deep down, I knew my decisions could have been dangerous. I had simply been lucky, and it took eight hours of sleep, a morning cycling class, and a whole lot of screaming matches to recognize that.

I try to live with no regrets, but in this case, there are a few things I would have done differently. First off, if I could go back in time, I would have pulled Liam aside to explain the situation before he left. I would have mustered the courage to admit I didn't think we were compatible. It was difficult to tell whether or not he was actually pursuing me. That's why I directed my attention towards Brandon instead. He made his interest clear. Secondly, I shouldn't have climbed into a car with a stranger. Although I felt like I could trust Brandon, my ability to reason was clouded by my infatuation with him. He could have very well been a pedophile or sex trafficker who changed the address on his phone to a different location. Thankfully, that wasn't the case, but I learned it's always smart to consider the worst-case scenario. I also recognized that drawing him close to Central Park in the wee hours of the morning was not the best idea. The area was quiet and isolated. I couldn't see it at the time, but I barely knew Brandon. What if he led me behind a tree in the dark and took advantage of me? I even let him know where I live, which was a poor choice. What if he had written down my address and stalked me outside my building in the days to follow?

# *Swipe Left:*

### HOW TO LET A GUY GO GENTLY

Calling things off is never easy, but sometimes, it's necessary. Despite how you feel about the other person (disgust, indifference, or in love), you should let him go with grace. Even if he treated you wrong, don't stoop to his level in dumping him disrespectfully. If you're no longer interested in pursuing a relationship, here's how to split seamlessly.

- No ghosting. The guy deserves an explanation. You wouldn't want to be left in the dark, so why would he?
- Have the conversation IRL if possible. Especially if you've been dating for a while, there's nothing worse than breaking up with someone via text message. It shows that you lack empathy. No matter how scary it might be, it's best to chat in person. He'll respect your maturity. (The exception: if you've only been on one or two dates with the person, a phone call or polite text will suffice.)
- Be straightforward from the start. Don't dance around how you feel, so he doesn't assume you'll come around.
- Keep a calm tone. You may be pissed about that "other girl" he's been talking to, but try your best to stay level-headed and respectful. You can be firm with him, but don't come unhinged.
- Avoid rehearsing your lines. You can think generally about what you want to say, but stay away from stereotypical breakup excuses ("it's not you, it's me"; "I just have to focus on me right now"). Speak from the heart and tell him how you really feel.
- Don't apologize. This may seem like the natural thing to do, but saying sorry may make the other person feel like you're taking pity on them.
- Give him an opportunity to respond. Be prepared for any kind of reaction: anger, upset, or confusion. Acknowledge his feelings, but don't let his emotion (particularly if he's disappointed) coax you into changing your mind.

That evening in Manhattan, I wasn't thinking. I lost my head and became addicted to Brandon's charm and praise. His compliments placed me under a spell. As a young woman, I often struggle with self-esteem. He washed away my insecurities with flattery and the warmth of his physical touch. But that's just what groomers do. They tell you everything you want to hear and try to make you feel special—only to manipulate and exploit you later on. Any twenty-seven-year-old who preys on an eighteen-year-old has questionable morals. Brandon was approaching his thirties, and a relationship with a teenager was inappropriate. Someone that age doesn't just go out and kiss girls for the fun of it. He was either looking for sex or for a wife.

The fact that we kept our romance private from my friends and parents for the evening also could have set me up for a potential grooming scenario. He distanced me from my mom and best friend: they remained stashed away in my mini backpack on "vibrate" as he wooed me. I hid his age from my mom for the whole night because I knew she would have a strong reaction. My initial inclination to keep our connection a secret was an issue in itself.

In the words of Carrie Bradshaw, I couldn't help but wonder: did I really need Brandon to validate my self-worth? In his absence, how else would I make myself believe I'm special or beautiful? As I walked through the party, I couldn't see my own value. I could have danced solo under those blinding lights, but instead, I surrendered to my desire for a significant other. I could see through the minds and hearts of the couples surrounding the space and assumed that several were only in it for a one-night stand. Straight out of quarantine and seeking some fun, I pushed aside my dreams of a lasting relationship to embrace a casual hookup.

My rash decision raised another important question: in searching for love, should we savor the temporary or wait patiently for a lasting relationship? Sometimes, living in the spur of the moment is worth the excitement, adrenaline rush, and spontaneity. I'm not saying that safety should be sacrificed, but part of life is living on the edge and taking risks on occasion. The world is ours, but only if we let it. Staying chained to a fear of the unknown holds you back from unlocking new adventures in a quest for love.

That evening, reveling in the present was all I cared about. Any sense of rationality was abandoned. Sometimes, you need to lose yourself (even just for a few hours) to find what really matters—honesty and integrity. I didn't consider the potential consequences of my actions until Brandon was gone. He may have temporarily numbed my mid-pandemic anxiety, but continuing to pursue him could have hurt me in the future. He began to "love bomb" me from the moment we met by expressing his affection. This strategy was obvious in his over-the-top attempts to make me feel special: spinning me in the air, giving me a piggyback ride, and declaring he was "catching feelings" after just a few hours. The speed at which he shared his emotions was overwhelming—but that may have been his intention. Thankfully, I stopped myself before getting caught up in a potentially dangerous situation. Reality hurts, and so does heartbreak—luckily, I spared myself of the latter before it was too late.

Brandon may have been older and more experienced, but I was the one who made the mature decision to sever ties (even though I was hesitant). When the heart takes over, it's difficult to lead with your head, but doing so is crucial for your emotional, mental, and sometimes physical survival. Sure, Brandon may have been twenty-seven, but I was the one who had the strength to walk away. Guess I'm the big shot after all. ♥

# Chapter 10

# The Shy Guy

EVERY GUY HAS A TOOL kit. In wooing someone, they take on certain strategies and channel their most flattering traits to make the first move. One boy may utilize his sense of humor while another styles his hair or clothing a certain way. Logan was a mess at making moves. His tool kit featured kindness and physical touch but was notably lacking in courage and gusto. Not that the deficit stopped me from pursuing him, of course.

He looked like a stereotypical TikTok boy, with long, shaggy black hair that stood up in several different directions. He sported a single cross earring in his left ear, a style top content creators often employ that irks me. He also had five fading tattoos, most of which were on his arms. They didn't look like the intense ink I was typically opposed to. Logan's markings were small and sweet, and they appeared as if they were drawn in pen.

With another summer social media tour on the horizon, I looked at Instagram to see who would be attending. When I saw Logan's photo, I slid into his DMs and sparked a conversation. It started with a "heyyy" and quickly transformed into a Snapchat exchange. I began to learn more about his life and hobbies. He sent me close-up selfies, either smiling, winking, or playfully sticking out his tongue. I would detail my daily happenings in New York City, and he described his job in his small town. I'm not one to keep up with Snapchat "streaks," but the string of days we talked added up effortlessly.

The day before the start of the tour in L.A., I tried to stay level-headed. If friends inquired about whether there was a particular boy I had my eyes on, I shook my head. "Nah, I'm not going to be in a relationship," I said. "I'll only be on tour in L.A. for two days and another week on the East Coast in August. That's not enough time." Unlike me, Logan was touring the Midwest, and he wasn't going to be on the East Coast leg. L.A. was our only crossover.

Jordan and I were rooming together in Los Angeles leading up to the tour. Before we ordered our car to the tour hotel, we had a separate event to attend. As I styled my hair and completed makeup in the bathroom mirror, I heard my phone repeatedly buzz on the nightstand in the other room. I placed my lipstick on the sink and ran to my bed to read Logan's snaps. "Good morning! What time are you getting to the hotel? I'm waiting for you." He clearly intended on connecting with me—making friends with the other guys seemed like an afterthought. But I knew better. I made that mistake when engaging in a relationship with Jack and abandoning all friendships in the process. Two years, a heartbreak, and one pandemic later, I was older, wiser, and more mature. No matter how handsome Logan was, I knew I needed to keep the relationship at surface level.

A little flirtation, however, couldn't hurt. To keep us occupied, I proposed that we film TikToks together in the hotel. "As friends or as a fake couple?" he asked. Anything was fine by me. "I think fake couple content would be fun and do really well," he typed. Our videos would spark online conversation, but in reality, there would be no official commitment. We sent several sounds to each other on TikTok. At first, I messaged him romantic songs we could lip-sync, but we eventually began to propose other sounds with piggyback rides or almost-kisses.

Pent-up tension transcended the screen and into my hotel room as I prepared for the tour. I tried to focus on styling my outfit, but at the same time, scenes of what could potentially take place with Logan lingered. I didn't want a romance like my prince of two years past, but I couldn't help but fantasize. *Don't give in*, I told myself. Old Carrie would have tried to pursue a relationship. But I knew that I only had two days with him, and he lived far away.

My friend and I skipped the tour orientation to spend extra time at the event in the Hollywood Hills. Rushing to get to Logan didn't sit right—it made it seem like I was chasing romance, so I stayed in the Hills to prove myself wrong. Nonetheless, Logan sent me short clips and selfies from the orientation, which took me out of the present moment. "Be there soon!" I typed, digging my nails into the palm of my hand to prevent myself from booking a car.

Eventually, I gave in and ordered an Uber to the hotel. The lobby was quiet and quaint, and a long white tour bus was parked in front. I left my luggage at the front desk and scanned the space to see where Logan was. There was a sea of boys seated on couches, and I was embarrassed for not having been able to tell which one he was. I took Jordan by the hand and dragged her down the hallway. "Maybe he's in the gym?" she suggested, pointing to a group of boys lifting weights behind a glass door. We entered the room and shook hands with each of the guys as they introduced themselves—still no Logan. Finally, we made our way to the orientation room, which was packed with staff now that the influencer meeting had concluded. One teen remained at the check-in desk, alone and looking down at his shoes. He was dressed in unique pizza-printed sneakers, a playful touch I didn't expect from a "TikTok boy." "Logan!" I shouted from across the room. His blue eyes were intimidatingly gorgeous, and I found it difficult to maintain eye contact. "Hey! How are you?" he said, pulling me into a casual one-arm hug. I noticed Jordan drifting off to say hello to the tour director, but I yanked her back to me for moral support. "I'm good! Just got back from this party at a content house," I explained. He smiled, and I watched his earring gently swing back and forth as he nodded. "Hell yeah. That's awesome!" he said in a soft voice with a tinge of swag. I nervously fiddled with the frayed hem on my denim shorts as we spoke.

"What are you up to?" I asked. He pointed to the stage manager hovering above a computer a few feet away. "We're trying to figure out a game I can play with the audience on stage since I'm not singing. Got any ideas?" he said. Jordan punched my arm. "What if you guys played Truth or Dare on stage together?" The manager overheard our conversation and started typing away on his keyboard to seal the deal. I envisioned what the game would look like: Logan and I would walk onto the stage side by side, and the audience would most certainly dare the two of us to kiss. The crowd would erupt into thunderous applause, and our lip lock would not only break the internet, but it also would draw me closer to Logan emotionally. I was afraid of catching feelings, but I ignored my concerns. "Let's do it," Logan said, and I immediately agreed. I asked if any other influencers wanted to join us on stage, but no one was interested. "It's going to look like you guys are a couple," Jordan whispered when Logan wasn't looking. I wasn't going to let that happen. "I'm smarter than that, I promise," I said, shutting down her suspicion. But was I?

Once our on-stage plans were solidified, we started roaming through the space we would be staying in for the next two nights. The entire evening, it was always us three: Logan, Jordan, and me. He trailed behind my friend and me and never strayed. At one point, we headed to my hotel room to unpack, and he tagged along. Jordan laid out her outfits as I took a seat beside Logan on the bed. "Wait, how old are you again?" I asked, embarrassed that my poor memory did not serve me well. "Nineteen. What about you?" he replied, running a hand through his hair. "Guess," I smirked. He gazed off, seemingly unsure. "You're sixteen," he said, "and she's fifteen." Baffled by his guess, Jordan made her presence known from across the room. "I'm sixteen," she rolled her eyes. "I'm eighteen," I continued. Jordan looked up from her suitcase. "Yeah, she's legal," she said. Logan laughed, yet I was busy ruminating over his age approximation. Did I seem young to him? Was I coming off as immature?

"Show me some of your TikToks!" I suggested. He opened his phone and scrolled through his page. "Which ones do you want to see?" he asked quietly. He seemed nervous to show me, although I would never judge. I selected a video that had over one million likes. His content was not overly sexualized like other male influencers' accounts on the tour. In fact, there were hardly any "thirst traps" to be found. I showed him my videos as well. "Hell yeah. That's awesome," he said as I selected clips. The two phrases were at the forefront of his daily vocabulary— he repeated them at least twice per conversation. Sometimes, I mocked him for his repetition. "Hell yeah," I echoed, which made him chuckle.

"Okay, let's go back downstairs! Come on, Mr. Logan," Jordan perked up in a false British accent. She was a pro at flirting, with an endless supply of playful actions and dialogue to keep guys on their toes. I couldn't help but adapt her strategies. "Yeah, Mr. Logan, let's go! Why are you walking so slowly?" I said in the best British accent I could muster. The three of us continued our exploration in the lobby, where we came across two male influencers at the water station. As I poured myself a cup, I wasn't paying attention to what the group was saying. Instead, I stared at Logan out of the corner of my eye, wondering what he was thinking. Was he vibing with me? "Let's exchange phone numbers!" one of the guys said, snapping me out of my trance. We passed our phones around in a circle, but when Logan's was planted in my hand, I suddenly had an idea. "Here you go!" I chirped. He was puzzled—I only gave him three digits. "What do I need to do to earn the other seven?" he asked. I came in close to answer his question: "I guess you'll have to wait and see."

I glanced outside the sliding doors of the hotel and noticed that the sun had finally set. I was waiting for it to be dark before we filmed our TikToks. A shadowy space would set the mood for filming. "Alright, guys. We're going to head up and film some TikToks now," I said, attempting to wrap up the conversation. I inched my way towards the elevator, and Logan followed close behind. We rode upstairs, and he suggested we go to his room to shoot. "It's much bigger. We'll have more space," he said. But the room was anything but spacious. It was packed with his roommate Cooper and four friends, who sat on the bed, table, and desk. I swept Cooper's dirty t-shirt off the sofa to make room to sit down. Logan stood in the corner on his phone, leaning casually against the sink. "My back hurts," I complained, causing him to look up. "Can you give me a massage, Logan? I'll give you another three digits." He walked over to the couch and began rubbing my shoulders. It was the first time the two of us came in physical contact. We didn't face each other, but I could feel sexual tension bubbling beneath the surface.

I realized that Cooper and his friends weren't intending to leave the room anytime soon, so we needed a new plan. I snapped both Logan and Jordan what I was up to before executing the strategy. "I forgot my phone charger. I'm going to go get it in my room," I said so that it wouldn't seem like a grand exit. "I'll come with you," Logan followed, making his way to the door. "Me too," Jordan said, grabbing her phone from the edge of the bed. I set the temperature of my room to seventy-three degrees before we left, so it was cozy upon our return. I'm always cold, so I reached for my favorite hot pink Victoria's Secret hoodie to keep me warm. Likewise, Logan and I sat on the bed to warm up to each other. We laid on our stomachs with our toes tangled, and he rubbed my back as we watched YouTube videos.

After I made a quick trip to the bathroom, Logan did the same. He and Jordan talked while I was away, and she hopped on the bed to offer her observations. "He said he doesn't usually like to make moves on the first day, but he's being flirty!" she dished, showing me a video she snuck of us cuddling on the bed. The clip was adorable, and I found myself wanting to spend more quality time with Logan. "If I want to be left alone with him, I'll just give you a signal," I declared, crossing my fingers in the air. "Got it," she said while mimicking the hand motion. As soon as I heard the water in the sink running, I shouted over the noise. I found it far easier to be bold when we weren't face to face. "Alright, Logan," I declared. "Let's film."

Shooting videos was a great way to become more comfortable with one another. "What sound do you want to use first?" I said, taking a seat beside him on the couch. "I don't know. You choose," he shrugged. No matter how many times I urged him to pick a trend or song to lip-sync, he reversed the question. His indecisiveness was a bit of a turn-off. Perhaps he was just shy, but I'm drawn to men who know what they want and speak up. I could only be so much of a leader.

Thankfully, Jordan interceded. Sensing the awkward interaction between Logan and me, she took charge of the situation and proposed a sound. "You guys are going to stand next to each other and say the lines," she explained. "When the music part starts, Logan walks away and Carrie pulls him back into an almost-kiss." The first take was uncomfortable: I didn't pull Logan in on time, and we giggled for the rest of the video. "Can I give her my other arm to pull me back with?" he asked Jordan. "Why are you asking me? It's your arm," she scoffed. He was bashful, and it was apparently up to me to make him feel at ease breaking out of his shell.

In between drafts, Logan vaped. He'd raise the pen to his mouth, only to immediately stow it inside his pocket when he caught me glaring. In fact, he always did what my friend and I ordered him to do, whether it came to TikToks, hotel adventures, or his vaping habit. But I was uncomfortable assuming so much control. Why was everything always left to Jordan and me?

After filming, Logan retreated to the bathroom again. As soon as the door shut, Jordan perked up. "You have to go in there with him!" she encouraged me. It seemed like the only way we would be able to get privacy that evening. But I was too scared to make the first move. I wanted him to want me. I wasn't about to force anything. I considered the best way to deal with a shy guy. Was I supposed to take the leap or wait patiently for him to initiate? I dropped hints: every time Logan and I laid next to each other on the bed, I inched closer. He'd smile whenever he caught my gaze. It was my friend who gave him the extra push. As I took my turn in the bathroom, I eavesdropped on Jordan's loud whispers. She instructed Logan to do the same as she advised me to do.

## Swipe Left:

### IS HAVING A WINGWOMAN EVER A GOOD IDEA?

In pursuing a guy, I've always loved having a wingwoman by my side. There's a lot of fear surrounding making first moves, and a third party can help expedite the process. However, there is something to be said about being your own wingwoman. The person you're pursuing will appreciate someone who is unafraid to make a move. Handling your own romance is simply the mature thing to do.

If you insist on keeping a friend in the picture to help you, train her to be just the right amount involved. There are two types of wingwoman: one who organizes (introduces you two, facilitates an Instagram exchange) and one who incites the connection. The latter is the wingwoman you don't want to endorse. Jordan told Logan exactly what to do, when really, he and I should have moved forward naturally and on our own terms. It's best not to force a connection so that it forms organically. (Although in my case, without Jordan, nothing probably would have ever happened between Logan and me.)

You're your own best cheerleader in pursuing a romantic connection. Find courage and confidence from within instead of relying on a friend to intercede on your path to love. Only then will you show the most authentic version of yourself—not the version your friend paints for you.

My heart pounded in anticipation of what would happen next. I considered if he was too "chicken" or afraid of coming on too strong like me. It felt like I got sucked into a time warp, sent back in time to my tour with Jack. Our epic love began the same way—a simple make out after mere hours of meeting, followed by intense feelings and a full-on relationship. The last thing I wanted was for similar events to follow now. Although falling in love is magical, it takes you out of the moment when there's a predetermined conclusion. Logan lived several hours from me via airplane. Although not impossible, long-distance relationships are extremely difficult. If I were to kiss this guy, we would have to keep it casual, and I didn't know if I was capable of doing that. I know myself well, and I was aware that I would fall hard and fast. But at the same time, my knowledge from my first tour experience would hopefully keep me grounded. Would I be able to tame myself and remember that our connection was only temporary? Was it possible for me to choose summer fling over fantasy? I considered if a summer fling was even worth my time.

I held off turning on the bathroom faucet because I knew it was the sign Logan was listening for. I also waited until after I brushed my teeth, scrubbing quietly yet ferociously to spread the mint flavor. Eventually, I turned the faucet on, allowing the water to flow and my thoughts and fears to simultaneously run wild. Like clockwork, Logan knocked on the door. *It's just a kiss*, I told myself.

But our chemistry was ever-present. He shut off the light and locked the bathroom door behind us—just as Jordan suggested. All I could see was Logan's silhouette, so I used my hands to find him in the dark. When he held me, all I focused on were his soft lips and the way his hands swept across my body. The intensity escalated as he picked me up and placed me on the edge of the sink. His hands remained pressed against my back as I ran my hands through his hair and kissed his neck.

I remembered Jordan's comment about how Logan did not typically make moves on the first day. "Why did you decide to make a move after all?" I asked. I couldn't see Logan's facial expression, but I felt him pondering amid a brief silence. "You're cute, so I thought, 'Why not?'" he said. I pulled him in close, and he proceeded to explain his choice. "I don't usually get with girls, you know. I don't really do casual hookups." The statement was shocking—I guess I didn't expect someone so handsome to avoid playing the field. "Really? When was the last time you got with a girl?" I asked. Another silence passed. "Four months ago. I had a girlfriend for two and a half years," he replied. So he was a relationship guy. I always wanted a boy who isn't afraid of commitment. Yet now, I was the one holding back because I worried about getting hurt again.

Kissing in the dark helped us become more relaxed—especially when it came to Logan and his reserved personality. At one point, his stomach rumbled as his body was pressed up against mine, and we started cracking up. "Let's turn on the light. If we don't, it'll just be awkward when we leave the bathroom," I said. Once I flipped the switch, we squinted for at least a full minute. The lights were blinding. "What do you want to do? I'm bad at deciding," he said. Once again, he placed our fate in my hands. "What do *you* want to do?" I asked. The exchange of questions started to become like a game. "Do you want to go back out?" I said. Logan fiddled with his earring. "I'm okay here." The feeling was mutual, and I leaned in to further savor the moment—after giving him the last four digits of my phone number.

Finally, Logan and I unlocked the door to the bathroom. The awkward duo who needed help filming together never returned. Two friends with benefits now walked in their place. "Don't mind me! I'm proud," Jordan announced. So was I, but not for the same reason. Logan and I were exploding with physical chemistry, and I was still guarding my heart. I didn't want to lead him on, though, so we needed to have a talk—when the time was right. That evening, the timing was inconvenient. After walking him back to his room, we found ourselves helping him clean up an unexpected mess his roommate left. The sink was filled to the top with empty beer cans and White Claws. Gathering the trash distracted me from delving deeper into my connection with Logan. We ended the evening with a brief kiss and hug goodbye.

"It's not fair. You get every guy. Every guy you want wants you back," Jordan mumbled as we fell asleep later that night. Her statement should have inspired self-confidence, but something didn't feel right. Sure, I've gotten lucky when it comes to smooches, but more often than not, the kiss doesn't amount to anything, no matter how much I want it to. A make out without meaning can only be chalked up to physical, not emotional experience. I feared that my fling with Logan, especially since it was inherently short-lived, would be no different.

The next day, I tried to keep my distance. My mistake with Jack was making him the center of my universe. I hardly socialized with others because I was so fixated on him. To make up for my past errors, I tried to hang out with everybody on the tour. On the bus, I sat next to Jordan and talked to several other guys on the way to the venue. I didn't ignore Logan completely, but I also didn't cuddle him in public or spend all my time with him.

At the venue, Logan often sat alone on the bleachers. I could've had him all to myself during the day if I wanted. I chose to restrain. The booming music and bright lights of the tour stage distracted me. I danced with friends in the crowd, so I wasn't tempted to hang out backstage with Logan. The adrenaline forced me to focus on putting on a good show. However, my on-stage Truth or Dare game with Logan turned out to be more awkward and uncomfortable than exciting and affectionate. The crowd could hardly hear us, so they resorted to their phones while we spoke. Eventually, someone dared us to kiss, just as I suspected. I swerved Logan, even though fans applauded as if we were going for it. One audience member then asked if he had a "sneaky link." "Maybe," Logan replied. I realized the phrase was relevant to our connection.

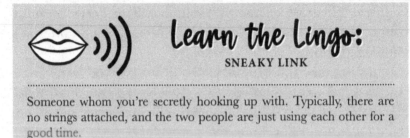

## Learn the Lingo:
### SNEAKY LINK

Someone whom you're secretly hooking up with. Typically, there are no strings attached, and the two people are just using each other for a good time.

After the show, I made my way to the meet-and-greet line solo. A male friend greeted me with a long hug, and I watched Logan stare in envy as he took a spot next to me. Once I broke free of my friend's embrace, I sympathized with Logan and realized that I may have been a little cruel in ignoring him all day. There's a difference between being selfish and being smart. I didn't have to take up an official relationship with him, but I also didn't need to tease or discard him like a piece of dirt. As fans made their way down the line to take photos with us, I made an effort to make him feel special. I held out my arms and pulled him into a tight embrace. "About time," Logan said. It seemed like he had been waiting hours to hold me. The sentiment was extremely sweet, and I regretted not having spent more time with him.

It was difficult to not get too invested, especially when we kept up the flirtation. I playfully poked his shoulder when he wasn't looking, and he did the same to me. At one point, I crouched down to grab my phone from my mini backpack on the ground behind him. On my way to stand, I ran my cold fingers under his shirt and up his back, careful that no influencers, staff, or fans saw. He jumped, and in return, he tickled my waist in between fan photos.

When the event wrapped up at 8 p.m., we boarded the tour bus back to the hotel. I sat with someone else to once again indicate that I didn't want to pin myself down, even though it stung to see Logan sitting alone scrolling through his phone. I didn't want another elaborate bathroom hookup, so I Snapchatted him to lay down the law of the evening: "When we get back, I'm going to stop by your room to say goodbye." Our connection would end there—no future commitment in sight. He sent back a selfie with a thumbs-up. Little did I know that our quick farewell would transform into an all-night journey.

After the bus pulled up, Logan, Jordan, Cooper, and I headed straight to the boys' room. The two guys inhaled pizzas they ordered on the way back to the hotel while Jordan and I prioritized relaxation. I crawled onto Logan's bed and laid on his pillow. I didn't expect him to cradle me from behind. "Cooper, we need to go outside," Jordan suddenly declared. "I think the hallway is calling our name." The alone time was not ideal, since I knew my attraction to Logan would take over if we were in private. "Only ten minutes! Don't go far!" I yelled as Jordan shut the door. We took much longer than ten.

As soon as they left the room, Logan leaned in for a kiss. I looked deeply into his eyes, and gently placed my hand on the tattoo on his leg. "Why me? Why me over the other girls on tour?" I asked. He placed his hand on top of mine. "Because I got to know you. And you're beautiful. And I like your little smile," he said. His words were genuine. He didn't call me "hot" or "smokin'." In his eyes, I was more than that. I was "beautiful." Logan didn't seem sexually driven. He was actually tentative. Our evening was a series of kissing and stopping. During one pause, as I sat on top of him on the bed, I almost fell asleep, my head facing the sheets while he stared up at the ceiling. But each kiss left me wondering, *what's going to happen tomorrow?*

Logan stopped mid-make out to vape while we were switching positions. I sighed. It was upsetting that his cotton-candy-flavored pen took priority. Each time he pulled out the device, I grew more frustrated. "Okay, I guess I'll leave then," I said. "No!" he complained, gently pulling me back as I made my way to the door. I proceeded to put my sneakers on. "Yup. I'm bored. I think I'm going to go," I continued. He placed his hand on the wall to encourage me to stay. I rested my arm on his shoulder and pretended I was reaching for the knob. "Make me want to stay," I teased. I imagined he would push me up against the wall or throw me on the bed, but my fantasies did not come to fruition. He did neither—he just stood there and whined. My shy guy had very little game. I started to grow tired, and I didn't see the need to continue exploring a connection if this was our last day together. Jordan messaged me that she was in our room with Cooper and needed more time, but I ignored the text. I wanted to shower and head to sleep, and I wasn't going to let my two-day fling interrupt my intentions.

"What's up? What were you guys doing in here?" I asked as we pressed open the door to my room. A wry smile spread across Cooper's face. "Oh, we were making out everywhere. The bed, the couch, on top of the lamp. Everywhere," he laughed. Sarcasm aside, Jordan was determined to stay with the boys, so I sat on the couch and let time pass. Logan and I laid on the sofa with our arms wrapped around each other as we pondered what the four of us would do next. I suggested a game of Cards Against Humanity that Jordan brought along. Nobody wanted to play, so we sat relatively silent, scrolling through our phones instead.

At around 11 p.m., Cooper left to attend a party with other boys. "Text us when you're back!" Jordan said. Logan stayed behind with us. It was getting late, and I didn't want him to be in our room much longer. "I'm giving you the boot!" I declared at 11:30. I walked him to the door, and he pulled me in for one final kiss. "See you on the East Coast in August," he said, alluding to the fact that he might add more cities to his tour agenda. I knew that more time with Logan would deepen my emotions. Nonetheless, I secretly hoped he would attend in August.

I reunited with him much sooner than I imagined. That evening, I was showered and in bed when I received a Snapchat from Logan: "Cooper is back. He wants to know if you guys still want to hang out." I sighed. It was 1 a.m., and all I wanted was to sleep. But I knew that Jordan was a good friend in setting up my hookup with Logan the day before. It was only fair to come along if she wanted to explore a connection with his roommate. She had not yet showered, and her hair and makeup from her on-stage performance still remained intact. "Come on! Please, Carrie!" she begged. I rolled out of bed and yawned. In a tour merch hoodie, Roller Rabbit striped pajama shorts, wet hair and not a swipe of makeup, I schlepped back to the boys' room.

Jordan pounded on the door aggressively so that the boys would be quick to open it. Two hours had passed, but the wee hours certainly had not gotten to them. Both guys were glowing as if they didn't need any sleep. I headed straight to Logan's bed and laid under the covers. He crawled in and spooned me once again. An awkward silence passed, and Jordan made a point to break it. "Why is everyone so quiet?!" she shouted to no reply. She impatiently sang the Jeopardy theme song, and Logan tapped my arm to the rhythm. I felt his hair brush my cheek as we cuddled. "Get a room!" Cooper shouted, jolting me awake as I dozed off. I felt myself going under, and I didn't feel like waking up. At one point, I squinted to see what was going on in the room. Cooper was mouthing something to Logan and gesturing towards the door. I couldn't quite tell what he was trying to say, but I had a hunch based on Logan's actions that followed. "Come on, let's go to your room," he said, taking my arm and pulling me towards the door. Jordan later notified me that Cooper wanted some alone time with her, and that would only be possible if Logan and I went elsewhere. "Please don't take too long. Be back by 2:30," I told Jordan in Gibberish so that the boys were not aware I was rushing their evening. An hour was more than enough time for her to explore a connection of her own. I didn't want to stay solo with a guy so late, and 2:30 was a fair compromise.

When Logan and I got back to my room, we cozied up under the covers. "Sorry I look like such a mess," I pouted as I rested my head on his shoulder. "I was about to go to sleep. I don't have makeup or hair done or anything." He shifted his head to look me in the eye. "You still look beautiful," he said. That was the second time he called me "beautiful," and the authenticity in his eyes made me actually believe him. The more sincerely he spoke, the more I became enamored with him. Nonetheless, the reality of the situation still lingered. I wasn't ready to fall asleep next to a guy I just met.

To force myself to stay awake, I sparked a conversation. Eager to get to know something other than his lips, I asked about his favorite TV show. "*Riverdale*," he confidently announced. I scoffed. A cheesy teen drama was not the answer I expected from a nineteen-year-old boy. "No way. I love *Riverdale*. Why is it your favorite show?" I asked, pressing for a deeper discussion. "It's very old-fashioned. Why do you like it?" he said. My answer was easy: the brooding boys. Cole Sprouse and KJ Apa's shirtless scenes kept me coming back every Wednesday, but I wasn't about to admit the source of my guilty pleasure. So I came up with another reason: "the mysteries."

We transitioned into talking about love and relationships. He made his intentions clear. "For the past few months, I've focused on myself and social media," he explained. "I told you, I'm not that into casual hookups. I guess I like relationships more." I raised an eyebrow. Did he see us as something more than just a one-time make out? "How about now? Where are you at now?" I asked. He shifted slightly in the bed. "I don't know."

I looked at my phone and read a text that Jordan sent: "a little more time." I sighed and told her to hurry up. I was exhausted, and it became difficult to keep my eyes open. I took a deep breath and tried to continue our conversation. Since he opened up about his feelings, I felt like I needed to disclose mine. "I'm nervous because the last time I was in a relationship on tour, it ended badly," I confessed. "That's why I'm holding back. That's why I'm so skeptical." He nodded understandingly. I wasn't necessarily saying "no" to spending time with him, but I did clarify that I wasn't looking for a serious relationship—no matter how much I liked him.

Jordan said she would be back soon, so I decided to close my eyes. "I'm going to sleep for a few minutes until she gets back," I said. He cradled me close, and I fell into his embrace. The rumbling air conditioner served as white noise, and soon enough, I was out cold. The moment was simple yet special—hence why I eased into his arms and fell asleep.

When I opened my eyes, Cooper, Jordan, and Logan were hovering over me. I now had morning breath, and the pimple I had been hiding under my hood was revealed. "Did I fall asleep?" I asked, darting my gaze anxiously around the room. "Yeah. You kicked me in your sleep," Logan laughed as he slipped his sneakers on. My mom always told me the same when we shared a bed on vacations, and her words reverberated in my mind: "like a soccer ball." "Well, it's 4:30. Logan and I should try and get some sleep before we get on the tour bus tomorrow," Cooper said. His declaration knocked the wind out of me. I swore to myself that I would not fall asleep, let alone for hours. Logan kissed my hand goodbye, leaving behind the faint smell of his musky cologne on my pillow. I sat on the bed, paralyzed in confusion, yet my brain buzzed with fear over what the worse-case scenario could have been. I hardly knew this guy—what if he took advantage of me while I was knocked out? I felt my hands start to shake under the covers, and tears formed at the corner of my eyes. I'd never fallen asleep next to a guy or let him sleep in my bed. I believe the decision is intimate and vulnerable—letting a guy hold you while you're unconscious is a form of surrendering yourself. A lot of trust is required to do so, and I wasn't ready to trust Logan just yet.

Jordan, however, had previously won my trust as my best friend—and that evening, she broke it. The situation could have been extremely dangerous if it had gone a different direction. I was attracted to Logan and felt like I could trust him, but in reality, I really didn't know much about him: what city he lived in, who he lived with, what a typical day in his life looked like beyond his job. We had spent very little time together, and I didn't know all there was to know about him. I relied on my friend to come back and wake me before I fell asleep, and she didn't.

In the hours that followed, I locked myself in the bathroom and cried. It was the middle of the night, and no one whom I wanted to talk to answered their phone, not even my best friend from the city or my mom. I blamed myself for having made a poor choice. *You shouldn't have been in bed with him so late in the first place*, I criticized myself. I also considered another side to the situation: was I being too sensitive? Was I overreacting because I had been so "gung-ho" with Jack, and I wanted this time around to be different? The scenario was complex and confusing, and frankly, I was too exhausted to continue contemplating. I climbed back into bed and fell back asleep with my arms cuddled into my chest, just as I did when Logan held me.

After twenty-four hours of rumination, I decided to forgive Jordan. We all make mistakes. We all live and learn. Just because someone breaks girl code once doesn't mean they're a bad friend. Besides, Jordan was the one who initiated the entire first evening with Logan. She had my back when the two of us were afraid to move forward. It would be unfair to ignore her and hold a grudge any longer. "I understand what I did was wrong. I know for next time," Jordan acknowledged, and I accepted her apology with a hug.

After the L.A. show, I had two weeks to spare in California and New York—and the days flew by faster than I anticipated. Logan and I FaceTimed and kept up our Snapchat streak as he considered whether or not to spend more time on tour. "I'm scared to ask about it," he said. "I really want to see you again, but I don't know if I can do all the extra cities. I have to ask my manager." Every time I followed up for an update, the answer was the same: "I'm waiting for the right time to ask." Eventually, I acknowledged that Logan was too timid to make the effort. If you didn't tell him exactly what to do, he wouldn't do it. If he wanted to see me like he said, he needed to have his options laid out for him. "Add a few more cities to the tour, or you could come to New York at the end of the month and visit me," I typed. As I texted Logan, it felt aggressive being the one in charge. I worried if my message made me seem too eager or insistent. Thankfully, he eased my doubts. "Would you pick me up at the airport if I came to New York?" he asked one day over FaceTime. I smiled. It felt nice not being the only one romanticizing for once.

I expected Logan to add more time on tour, but his choice caught me off guard: his manager informed him that he could do the whole tour, all twenty-four cities. Suddenly, I regretted my efforts to help him make the decision. What if he bonded with the boys and ditched me upon my return? What if the fans and fame got to his head? I was now faced with a difficult decision of my own: I could add as many cities as possible to be with him or stick with our week together on the East Coast. On one hand, I knew that if I joined more cities solely to be with him, I would be chasing something that wouldn't last. I was chasing a feeling more than I was chasing him. I was pursuing a sensation—not a person—that made me feel special, beautiful, and wanted. We all just want to feel loved. Nothing makes you feel more special than a guy who holds you in his arms and calls you "beautiful."

I craved that feeling, and being with Logan for an entire month would grant me easy access.

I could have dove in heart first, making memories while being emotionally invested. Or I could have held back, staying true to my original plan of a casual one-week fling without complicating things. I found a compromise: only join the tour for a week yet dabble in a bit of romance along the way. I liked him, and I owed it to myself to explore that—but it was also my responsibility to buffer heartbreak. I decided to own my emotions yet remain rational.

## Double-Tap This:

### SECOND-GUESSING

Right person, wrong time? Sometimes, the one we want most isn't what's best for us. Acknowledging that reality can be painful, but it also shows how mature you are.

One summer, I was seeing a guy who had to leave for college at the end of August. He asked me to be his girlfriend the day before he left. Although I was elated, the moment was bittersweet. All I ever wanted was a boyfriend, and now that he was in front of me, I needed to turn him down. There he was, gazing lovingly into my eyes, and I had to push him away. Long distance is difficult, and by cutting things off early, I was preventing myself from future pain. I had strong feelings for this guy, but time and distance made me second-guess our compatibility. Turns out, my concerns were valid. We planned to keep in touch after he left, but after a month of Snapchatting, he ghosted me.

Second-guessing is smart, so address any doubts you may have. My guy moved too far away, but maybe yours is too close for comfort. Perhaps he doesn't make time to see you enough, or you're questioning whether you're ready to give up singledom. You know yourself better than anyone—so trust your gut. Sometimes, you have to just wait. Wait for the right person, the right moment for you to embrace love wholeheartedly. Don't rush. Your time will come.

In an unexpected turn of events, I didn't spend a second more with him. Once the tour manager was hospitalized with COVID-19, and several influencers also became infected, I knew it would be too risky to attend. "I don't know if I should come. Do you still want me to come?" I said on a group FaceTime call with Logan and Jordan. He didn't flinch. "I don't know, that's your decision. You guys are taking it too seriously," he said. "If you want to come, come. If you don't, don't." He seemed irritable and uninterested. "If you get COVID, so what? It's just ten days of being sick in bed," he continued, rolling his eyes. The lack of care and consideration for my wellbeing made me furious. Logan changed, just as I had feared—and I wasn't going to let him get away with it. "Why are you being so rude?" I said. He yawned. "I don't know. Do what you want," he stated.

The boy who cuddled me until the wee hours of the morning was gone. Now that he was behind a screen, he had the courage to be brutally honest (not to mention obnoxious). At first, I blamed myself and considered if I gave him the wrong impression. Perhaps my attempts to avoid heartbreak made me come off as someone I was not: a girl who fools around for the fun of it and does not care for meaningful connections. In reality, I'm the exact opposite, which is why I took the time to get to know him aside from the hookup. I wanted to communicate my intentions with him from the start. In fact, that final evening together, I pressured myself into opening up because I feared leading him on. I explained how my history with Jack played into why I didn't want us to be official (summer flings rarely amount to anything). However, it didn't feel right sharing in depth why I was holding back. I wasn't ready to reopen the wound, especially to someone I just met. Your past is your past—it's your decision if or when you want to share it with others. I wasn't hiding my history, but he didn't need to know *everything*.

Over ten cities into the tour, Logan's ego seemed to have taken over. I find that often, if a guy is hot, he knows it, and he most likely feels like he's too good for anyone else. It's very rare to find a humble hot guy. Logan was no exception. But how could he have been so short with me after our romantic rendezvous? Had he already forgotten about our two evenings together? I wanted to figure out what changed. When I hung up the FaceTime call, Jordan dug for details, which she relayed to me later on. "I'm just not feeling it anymore," he told her. "I don't want a girlfriend, and I don't want to do things just to do them." I knew all along that he didn't like casual hookups. But the fact that he wasn't into me "anymore" indicated that what was once there between us had transformed. I felt like a failure. Where had I gone wrong?

## Swipe Left:

### HOW TO DEAL WITH BEING FRIEND-ZONED

It hurts to hook up with someone only to have him tell you he just wants to be friends—especially if you caught feelings. It feels like you're jumping from one extreme to the other: locking lips to barely even touching (or sometimes even speaking). The switch-up can feel sudden and shocking. When a guy doesn't want you anymore, it gnaws at your self-worth. A loud voice in the back of your head will likely tell you it's your fault. You may ruminate over all the potential reasons why he didn't want you: maybe he found someone prettier, or perhaps he wasn't physically attracted to you.

Whatever his reason was, it doesn't change anything about who you are. Believe it or not, his decision has more to do with him and less to do with you. If you started off as friends first, perhaps he doesn't want to ruin the strong friendship you already established. If you went straight to the hookup, he could be afraid of commitment. Either way, you shouldn't take the withdrawal too personally. Remain respectful of the other person's decision and move forward.

Don't hold your breath waiting for your relationship to turn into something more. Someone who's having second thoughts is not the type of person you want to date anyway. Most importantly, don't let fear of rejection hold you back in the future. Just because one person renders your relationship platonic doesn't mean you're incapable of forming a deeper connection. Romance awaits outside of the friend zone—all you have to do is put yourself out there.

Jordan asked Logan if he wanted to break the news to me. "If I tell her, I'm going to say that you told me to," he admitted. Ultimately, he allowed the responsibility to fall on her shoulders. Was his ego so fragile that he couldn't muster the courage to look me in the eyes and tell me how he felt? The situation frustrated me, and I spent several days trying to analyze his sudden change of heart. Jordan told me not to overthink things, to keep an open mind and let the universe handle the rest. That's exactly what occurred. I no longer needed to agonize over my decision to attend the COVID-19-infested performances—the rest of the tour was cancelled altogether. Now that I no longer needed to pull myself together and confront him face to face, I had time to consider why he no longer wanted me.

It turns out my shy guy was not so shy after all. In the end, I stood tall and proud that I didn't allow myself to get in too deep with him on a temporary tour. Furthermore, I knew he would have changed after several weeks of meeting his supporters. He didn't want a girlfriend. He didn't want a casual hookup. Instead, he wanted to stroke his own ego and have fans fawn over him. The reality is that we're living in the age of social media. Lots of guys are obsessed with themselves, whether they have two hundred or two hundred thousand followers.

After the tour, I started to trust my instincts more. Although I didn't acknowledge it in the moment, Logan's personality didn't sync well with mine. I pursued him because he was hot and convenient—and because there was a physical attraction. He may not have been my soulmate, but he helped me know myself and the guy I deserved better than ever: someone who was all in, not someone who bailed the second he was "not feeling it."

Don't settle for someone just because you like the feeling of his skin pressed against yours. Seek someone who truly sees you. Someone who refills your glass every time it's empty. Someone who makes you laugh until your stomach hurts. Someone who wipes away your tears when you don't have the strength to.

Someone who loves you unconditionally, without question or hesitation. Someone who feels like home. It may take time, but when you find that person, it will have been worth the wait.

Ironically, my shy guy taught me how to be confident. He brought out a self-reliant, more assertive side to me, summoning a girl who knows what she wants rather than waits for a guy to validate her feelings. A shy guy can encourage you to take on a leadership position in the relationship and provide a safe space for you to vocalize your needs. It's highly unlikely that he will react rashly to what you want; instead, he will practice patience and understanding. With Logan, I learned that communication with your partner about how you're feeling (no matter how complex those emotions may be) is key. Without honesty early on, a connection is impossible. Logan was kind and communicative before hitting the road. But fame can change you, and not necessarily for the better.

I, on the other hand, experienced my own transformation. With a fresh outlook on love and a more self-assured persona in pursuing romance, I was ready to reenter the dating scene. Logan's tool kit may have been lacking in courage, but that very quality is what he ignited in me. I finally trusted my heart to lead the way in constructing the connection I deserved. Life's too short. It was my turn to make the first moves. ♥

# Chapter 11

# The Showmance Turned No-mance

I WAS NEVER ASKED TO prom. As a little girl, I romanticized the evening, ripping out pages of prom dresses from *Seventeen* to save for when the time was right. My school prom never worked out, but a stint on a reality show provided a chance for redemption. I shouldn't have gotten my hopes up—the evening ended in hours of tears shed behind closed doors.

Let's rewind to grade school. Prom was our only dance, and since middle school, I scouted the classroom to see which boy could take me when we were older. Unfortunately, as the evening approached, my options were limited. I used to blame it on my reputation. I'm talking about the twelve cupcake books I co-wrote with my mom when I was eight, which my entire grade was privy to (school newsletters made it impossible to ignore). Girls in my grade saw me as a "mommy's girl" unable to break free of my mom's influence. They worried that every time we hung out, she would tag along. Guys, on the other hand, were more focused on the cupcakes. "Hey, cupcake girl!" one kid shouted across the common room in sixth grade. "Are you going to put me in your next book?" As he playfully punched a friend's arm, I could tell he was dared to ask me. Was I that much of an outlier among my peers, that people had to *dare* their friends to talk to me?

I squeezed my way into several groups and conversations that took place. But I always knew I was different. My peers were focused on social gatherings and homecoming games while I was already planning my future. I spent my Saturday nights in high school attending fashion shows and movie premieres with my publicist while others hosted "ragers" at their apartments. I was never invited to them. The one time I did go to someone's grade-wide party (my invitation was a last-minute addition), I felt like a stranger among my peers. I walked into a weed-infused haze. Red cups were scattered across the dining room table, vape pens were passed around like candy, and a couple was having sex in the bedroom down the hall. Someone handed me a drink, and I anxiously fiddled with the cup. When no one was looking, I spilled the alcohol in the sink and held onto an empty cup, so I looked like I belonged. But I didn't. I never did.

In high school, I sat alone at the lunch table and spent free periods in the library, but I never felt sorry for myself. I knew who I was, and I preferred spending time getting homework done over trying to fit in. When junior prom rolled around, it was no surprise I faded into the background. Since I avoided hanging out with those who teased me behind my back, I didn't know guys in my grade particularly well. I figured they still saw me as the "cupcake girl" and didn't take me seriously. In their eyes, bringing me to prom was like asking out that eight-year-old author. Still, it hurt to see the dozens of "promposals" take place outside the school. There were extravagant posters, personalized sushi deliveries, and serenades. I applauded from a distance. Sure, I could ask a guy out myself, attend solo, or go with a group of friends (not that I had many). It wasn't worth it, though. I knew I would be spending the night on my phone in the corner of the venue. A date with Netflix sounded much better.

When I graduated from high school, I felt uneasy about not attending the prom. COVID-19 made our principal cancel senior prom, but the sting of missing out on junior prom lingered. Even as I found my friends in college, a group of people who finally shared similar interests and supported my goals, I secretly hoped that a school dance was still in the cards.

An opportunity to attend prom presented itself again but not where I expected. I participated in a reality show where I was living with fellow social media influencers. About halfway through the experience, they hosted an on-camera prom for the series' competitors. Initially, I was thrilled. I flirted with one of the guys (let's call him Cole) on Instagram prior to the show, so I imagined we would attend as a couple. Not only was I going to get my prom redemption, but it was going to be broadcasted on a global scale. I envisioned the guys I went to high school with watching the show with regret over not taking me.

Blinded by the prospect of getting a prom redo, I didn't consider that this was an unusual situation. I was living in a house with *influencers*, not high-school students. Every man was for himself—we were competing for a grand prize, not a boyfriend or girlfriend. However, I was so immersed in the experience, I thought that maybe, just maybe, I could find myself a guy.

The day that prom was announced, invitations were scattered throughout the house we were staying in. I didn't notice until the early afternoon when I found an open envelope sitting near the television. I read the details about the evening and frowned. Where was my invite? I was a part of the show, so naturally, I was invited. But I wasn't coupled up with anyone, so ensuring my attendance was an afterthought.

It was like I was in high school all over again, and that was a painful memory I wasn't prepared to relive. I thought I was done witnessing "promposals," but not even influencer life could provide an escape. One guy descended a staircase with a poster while serenading a girl to a song by her favorite artist. Another worked for hours on a poster highlighting his girl's favorite foods. I was jealous. I sat back and watched other guys ask girls to prom while I crossed my fingers behind my back, praying that I was worthy. I sat alone in my room, staring at the ceiling as I heard laughs and cheers coming from outside. It made me feel unlovable.

## Double-Tap This:

### THE JEALOUSY COMPLEX

If you're the only one not coupled up among your friends, you know just how much it sucks. It's awkward, embarrassing, and often anxiety-inducing. You may wonder why you're the odd one out—are your friends sexier? More confident and flirtatious? Seeing your girls with significant others is not an easy spot to be in.

I've been at dinners where friends have whipped out sex-themed card games, or brunches where people bragged about their body counts. I smiled and laughed at their stories, but deep down, I was painfully insecure. I felt inexperienced. But I couldn't tell them that—I was too ashamed to own that I was the youngest of the group.

I get jealous very easily, especially when it comes to my friends' love lives. What I've realized is that jealousy is a healthy emotion as long as you own it. There's no shame in being jealous. In fact, the emotion only reveals what you desire. My jealousy towards my friends showed me what I crave: a healthy, loving relationship.

Those dinner conversations about sex may be awkward, but I've come to expect them, and as you mature, so should you. Instead of agonizing about what you don't have, listen and allow yourself to fantasize about what could be. There's no need to compare yourself to your friends. Everyone is on their own path. You may even learn a thing or two from their stories—call it beginner's advantage. Be grateful they're sharing experiences. With knowledge of their mistakes and successes, you're more ahead of the game than you think.

Once I got myself together, I took a deep breath and tuned out all the noise. *There's no need to be upset*, I tried to convince myself. *Your confidence shouldn't be defined by how a guy sees you.* Yet

I still wondered why Cole hadn't asked me to the prom. We were the only two without dates. Behind the scenes, it was suggested that I "prompose" to him myself, even though it made me uncomfortable.

I decided to be a good sport and support my friend in his "promposal." I walked outside to help with his poster yet found someone else was already holding the markers: Cole. My insecurities came rushing back. "The poster looks good!" I said, forcing myself to stay positive. "She's going to love it." Cole was too busy helping his friend with finishing touches to even look up at me. "Um, Cole, when you're done with that, can I talk to you for a second?" I asked. "Sure!" he said. It didn't seem like he knew what I wanted to talk about, and frankly, neither did I. I just needed to know what was going through his head, and I wanted him to know how I was feeling too. We would take it from there.

We started circling the perimeter of the house. "How do you feel about this whole prom thing tonight?" I asked, twirling the hem of my t-shirt. The sun was shining down brightly, and I squinted to see his reaction. "I never had my senior prom," he said. "I'm just here to have a good time. I'm here for the vibes." He also missed out on his high-school dance, so surely he would understand where I was coming from. We took a seat on the stairs in front of the house. Vocalizing your feelings is scary, especially face to face. In this case, I decided to be upfront.

"I knew about this whole prom thing since the very beginning. I was nervous about it because I was kind of going to ask you," I confessed, surprising myself with how forward I was. At that point, I was ready to run back inside and crawl under my covers. I figured girls aren't supposed to ask guys. This wasn't how it was supposed to go. He raised an eyebrow. "You were going to ask me? Where's your 'promposal,' dude?" he said. "Where's *your* 'promposal?'" I shot back. He shrugged. "I didn't make one because I thought I was going with Squish," he replied, referring to another cast member's stuffed animal. It seemed like I was the second, inferior option. Was he joking? Was a Squishmallow really my competition?

"Are you open to taking someone? I was secretly hoping you would ask me," I revealed. He looked down at his scuffed Nike sneakers. "I don't care. I'd be down," he said. "We could go together, but all of us are still going to be vibing anyway. I could go with Squish, or I could go with you. It's still going to be fun either way." He relegated me to the status of a plush toy. I buried my head in my hands. "Ugh, this is scary!" I exclaimed, thinking out loud. I couldn't bring myself to look at him. I had an outgoing personality, but something about his presence made me retreat into myself. "Why is it scary? It's a prom in a house with ten people. It's literally going to be so much fun," he reassured me. "So do you want to be my prom date?" I asked. "Let's do it!" he shrugged, extending his arms for a hug. I was in the friend zone, but part of me still had a crush. I put a lot of pressure on the prom to be special. Cameras were on us at all times, but a part of me hoped that Cole had a heart and would make it an evening to remember. He did—but not for good reason.

After my unofficial "promposal," Cole and I went opposite ways in the house. I placed my focus on getting ready. One of the producers helped me curl my hair. I slipped into a pink strapless mini dress then spent an hour meticulously perfecting my makeup. At around 7 p.m., someone knocked on my door. It was Cole, all dressed up. "Ready to go?" he said. He didn't even acknowledge my outfit or hairstyle. It was as if he were picking me up to go to the grocery store. Still, I played along, grabbing my phone and shutting the door behind me.

We stood arm in arm in the hallway waiting to enter the prom. His actions felt forced, though, as we stood there in silence. "Looking sharp," I said, finally breaking the tension. "Thank you, you look nice too," he replied. Nice? What was that supposed to mean? I straightened out my dress.

I didn't have too much time to decipher his words. Soon enough, we were the first duo entering the living room, which was completely transformed for the prom. A disco ball hung from the ceiling, and fairy lights dangled from the walls and staircase. Gold balloons were scattered across the floor, and Cole and I bounced one back and forth before other couples started entering. As soon as the other guys arrived, Cole ditched me to talk to them.

One guy pulled his girl aside to have a romantic talk with her, and another couple filmed videos together. I was hoping Cole would come talk to me, but he was occupied. He tried on different glow sticks and continued to kick balloons around. At one point, he grabbed my phone and took selfies of himself—without me. I practically begged him to take prom photos together like the rest of the cast. He was too busy socializing with his friends (notably, another girl who already had a date) to care. If only he knew how much those photos meant to me—they would capture the memory of my first-ever prom. "Come on, let's go take cheesy prom pics!" I urged him, poking his shoulder. We stood awkwardly in front of a curtain dripping in fairy lights, the last couple in the house to take photos. I directed Cole to face sideways and put his arms around my waist for a traditional posed snapshot. I tried to stay close to him, inserting myself into conversations and making small talk. He was my date, and the fact that he was ignoring me was strange and upsetting. "Has he said anything about me?" I whispered to a friend, putting a finger over my microphone so that it didn't capture the dialogue. "Nah, he says he's just here for the vibes," he replied.

When it was time for the slow dance, my heart pounded in anticipation. Cole took a seat next to me on the couch, and I wondered if he was going to offer his hand and take me to the dance floor. Instead, he sipped his drink, and someone else wedged between us as we watched other people sway from side to side. The rejection was painful, and I scrolled through TikTok to distract myself.

When I finally looked up from my phone, I noticed that Cole was halfway across the floor and headed for his bedroom. "Alright, I'm in for the night. Goodnight, everyone!" he said, not even looking me in the eye. He disappeared into his room only an hour into the prom. Considering his actions throughout the rest of the evening, this wasn't a surprise. I didn't flinch, but inside, I was hurting. This was supposed to be my perfect prom. All I wanted was to feel special, and Cole made me feel unworthy. I wanted to escape, to engage in a disappearing act of my own. After such an awful high-school experience, I thought this time would be different. I was wrong.

I soon headed back to my room, holding back tears. The camera had embarrassed me enough that day. I didn't want my crying to be captured as well. I hid how I was feeling, even after I spotted Cole walking around in his PJs soon after he left. "Hey," one of my guy friends stopped me on the way back to my room. "You looked stunning tonight. Seriously, the best dressed," he insisted. I smiled and pulled him into a hug. "Thank you. That means more than you know," I said.

When I was in my room, I ripped the GoPros off the wall so that no cameras were rolling. Once I knew I was in private, I broke down. I laid on my bed in my prom dress, curled up into a ball. I felt small and insignificant. I told myself it was my fault Cole didn't want me. I convinced myself that *I* was the one to blame. He must have left the prom because there was something wrong with *me*. It felt like I was a pity date. Cole most likely agreed to go with me because I was targeted by other cast members during the week. In his own words, I had the "shit end of the stick" in the house. Perhaps some part of him was empathetic and didn't want me to be alone on prom night. But the reality was I was alone and in tears while everyone else was all smiles on the dance floor.

I avoided Cole the following day—looking at him was a painful reminder that I was alone in the house, with no boyfriend (or any friend, for that matter) to have my back. However, an evening activity excited me. The group was playing Truth or Dare with a twist: if we didn't answer a question or perform a dare, we had to eat a jalapeño pepper dipped in hot sauce. I watched with envy as one couple locked lips for the first time, patiently awaiting my turn. Finally, a cast member faced me: "I dare you to kiss someone in this room on the lips." I pretended I didn't know who I wanted to kiss, spinning around blindly as if I were randomly selecting. Then, I pointed at Cole. I figured there was no way he would make me eat the pepper. He looked around anxiously and combed a hand through his hair. "So I have to choose the jalapeño or Carrie?" he laughed. It was humiliating—his words made me feel disgusting, as if having to kiss me was a punishment. In fact, I later found out that in his confessional video, he said he "couldn't and won't" kiss me. Was a peck *that* big of a deal to him?

He never verbally turned me down, but after a few moments of awkward silence, someone handed me the pepper. I took a bite, literally tasting the sting of Cole's rejection, and ran to the fridge to grab a drink. "You can't drink anything after! That's against the rules!" someone shouted. I didn't care. At that point, I was only looking out for myself. I walked around holding a cup of almond milk to my lips for hours so they'd stop burning. I only lowered the drink when Cole walked by. "Thanks a lot," I said. He could have given me a quick kiss, just so we could avoid eating the pepper. Even that was too much for him. He pulled me in for a hug. "Sorry!" he laughed, never explaining why he declined.

The next evening, I gave Cole one last go. The group was watching a horror movie on the couch, and it seemed like the perfect opportunity to cuddle. Couples had their arms draped around each other, and I took a seat next to Cole at the edge of the couch. "It's freezing!" I exclaimed, hoping that he would share his blanket with me. "Oh, let me grab some extra blankets from the closet for everyone!" he said, jumping up from the couch. I rolled my eyes—he didn't get the memo. Once he brought me a blanket, I closed my eyes on the couch and leaned my head in his direction. I pretended to fall asleep when really, I was waiting to see if Cole would put his arm around me and make a move. He never did. In fact, he disappeared not even a quarter of the way into the movie to go to bed.

After one too many hours of tears, I had an epiphany: it's a lot of pressure to be on a reality show, and on top of that, I was forcing myself to find a guy. I was so focused on scoring myself a prom date, I never even considered what it would be like to strut confidently into the dance stag. Self-confidence is one of the most attractive traits you can have. On the show, I learned how to be assertive and stand up for myself—who would have ever thought *I* would be asking a guy to prom?

I allowed myself to be disappointed about that night— feeling all the feels is *okay* but not for too long. Trying to woo Cole while socializing with everyone in the house was draining. I stayed in touch with my emotions and knew when to space myself from my peers (three-hour naps during my breaks were a savior). It was also crucial to separate the emotion from my self-worth. Cole didn't deserve the power to make me feel unworthy. There's always going to be someone hotter or prettier than you—the girl with bigger breasts, a cheekier butt, or a larger-than-life personality. People like her seem to always get the guy. But regardless of what they—or you—look like, remember one thing: if he doesn't see your beauty, that's on him. You're doing you, and if he doesn't embrace that, then *sayonara*.

I didn't necessarily do anything wrong for Cole and I not to work out. Maybe I just wasn't his type. You can't control another person's feelings. Hundreds of hate comments on the episodes reiterated his rejection: "Girl, he just doesn't like you. Why are you going after someone who's uninterested? It's sad." What would be "sad" is liking him yet never coming forward. I go after what I want, and I'm not ashamed of my courage.

My openness and honesty got me in trouble on the show. Although I always led with the truth, I was a target and got caught up in a lot of drama. Associating yourself with me was risky if you wanted to win, which was likely why Cole kept our conversations quick and minimal. I also later learned that his friends encouraged him not to get into a relationship—show-mances can turn "messy" pretty quickly. Despite his disinterest, I led with my heart. To me, the show was more than just a means to a monetary prize. I wish he recognized that.

## Swipe Left:

### DON'T BELIEVE THE ROMANCE ON REALITY TV

Reality shows are *not* reality. Trust me—there's a lot going on behind the scenes that isn't shown.

I learned this the hard way. Going into the series I was on, I dished about how excited I was to join the cast. "Maybe I'll even meet a cute boy!" I said. I was encouraged to go for it and not to hold back. Little did I know, reality TV is poised to bring out the most extreme version of your personality. I was persuaded to pursue romance to the point where I looked needy and desperate.

As a fan of dating shows, I assumed any reality TV series held the potential to find romance. The cast spent all day in each other's company, so I was hopeful I'd make a connection. I was shocked by how difficult it was to tell what was real and what wasn't. I would be having a conversation with a guy and then, out of nowhere, someone would en-ter the room to cause drama. I couldn't trust anyone, and you shouldn't necessarily trust what you see on TV either.

Reality TV romance is rarely real. The connection is established in an unnatural scenario, so it only makes sense that the "relationship" is inauthentic too. It's impossible to be the truest version of yourself when cameras are in your face—it's awkward, intrusive, and uncomfortable. Thus, when two people are trying to form a relationship on a show, the way the couple acts on screen isn't necessarily how they act behind it. All I wanted was a genuine connection with someone—reality TV makes that virtually impossible.

A few days after our prom, I hid in the bathroom and had a FaceTime dance party with Jordan to Rihanna's "Bitch Better Have My Money." I flailed my arms, shook my hips, and lip-synced the lyrics as if I were screaming them. I was dressed in a sweatsuit, not a mini dress. It was a dance-off with my bestie, not a slow dance with a boyfriend. But I was confident, happier, and far freer than I was with Cole.

I can now say that prom is overrated. My favorite rom-coms convinced me otherwise for a while, but that was then. We're in the 21st century—we don't need a giant "promposal" poster to let us know how special we are. ♥

# Chapter 12

# The Dating App Disaster(s)

I KISSED A GUY WITH a fly on his tooth. Not intentionally, of course. After we made out, he smiled, and there it was—a tiny fruit fly squished on his front tooth. Needless to say, the dating app that brought us together lied—we were not a match.

I've always despised dating apps. Something about forming a connection with a stranger you meet online seemed scary— what if I was being catfished? I also knew that dating apps had a reputation for being hookup-centric. In signing up for one, I was asking for trouble. But isn't that how you spice up your life?

I was eighteen, the youngest eligible age to sign up, when I joined my first dating app. Now that I was "legal," a whole new category of men was made available to me. I could now date guys in their twenties. The smallest age range I could select was between eighteen and twenty-four (quite intimidating for a dating app novice). Was I really ready to date a twenty-four-year-old? I always wondered if going out with a mature male would secure me a long-term relationship. But a twenty-four-year-old is at a completely different stage of life than an eighteen-year-old. Not everyone is going to be okay with the age gap.

I added my favorite selfies to my profile, along with two full-body shots. I wrote a short bio about my passions and filled out three superlatives (i.e., how I won't shut up about how I ran the NYC Marathon). Swiping through men was addicting. It was like a video game that could occupy my attention for hours. I got instant gratification from seeing people who "hearted" my photo and called me beautiful—it gave me an ego boost. That said, I avoided messaging guys all day long because I didn't want it to seem like I had no life. I turned off my dating app notifications so I wouldn't be tempted and limited myself to checking once or twice a day.

## Learn the Lingo:
### KITTENFISHING

People online are not necessarily as they seem. *Kittenfishing* refers to how one may lie about small details of their appearance or lifestyle on the internet. Someone may increase their height or age, enhance their job description, or use old photos of themselves to win you over. This is separate from *catfishing*—where one pretends to be an entirely different person—but still concerning. Watch out for highly-edited profile photos or inconsistencies in your conversations with a potential partner. Make sure you're equally as truthful: if you don't present the most authentic version of yourself online, you can't expect others to do the same.

When I did open the app, I noticed that I made several matches (one of them, ironically, was a high-school ex, whom I quickly unmatched with). I always waited for the man to make the first move, so I knew for sure that he was interested (although nothing says you can't slide in first). How was I supposed to navigate all the messages? Do I talk to multiple different guys? Go on several dates? What if I caught feelings for multiple people? How would I know if I made the right choice or if I was letting go of a good thing? I was overwhelmed. I felt like I was the

Bachelorette. I found it difficult keeping track of all the men—where they were from, where they worked. Admittedly, I often got people confused and had to ask again. I didn't want to limit my options to one guy, especially if I never met him, but I also didn't want to feel like a player.

Luckily, the guys made it easy for me to filter through them. Some whom I talked to were extremely forward—and not in a good way. I spent an hour on the phone with someone who was interested in me. After the call, he texted to set up an in-person plan. "Let's hang this weekend," he said. I asked him what he wanted to do and was taken aback by his reply: "It's more like what I want to do to you." Why did he stay on the phone with me for so long if he wasn't interested in a meaningful connection? Did he want to win me over that badly? The guy unfollowed me on Instagram as soon as he realized he wasn't going to get what he wanted (most likely sex).

I flirted with another guy on Snapchat for hours, only to find out he was in a three-year relationship, his girlfriend just cheated on him, and they hadn't talked about it yet. The worst part: he wasn't even planning to tell me. I saw it for myself when I followed him on Instagram, and his feed was filled with couples' photos. It seemed like he was lining me up to be his rebound.

I was knocking out potential suitors like bowling pins, one by one, day by day. I was tired of getting my hopes up only to become disappointed several times a week. I felt like I was constantly holding my breath then letting it go. Talking to multiple guys at once was exhausting, not to mention a major time commitment. I had to carve time aside every evening to answer guys' messages. I got burnout if I went on several dates over a week, but I worried that if I skipped one, I'd miss out on a promising connection. Sometimes, I just needed a break. A solo Netflix night on the couch is not pathetic—it's paramount. Self-care takes priority—I needed to learn how to say "no" to a guy when needed.

## Swipe Left:

**THE STRANGEST DATING APP PICK-UP LINES I'VE RECEIVED**

My mom always told me to assume the guy is an asshole unless proven otherwise. These men showed their true colors from the start.

- "I know it sounds cocky, but I don't need college."
- "Congrats for matching with me."
- "I have it better lifestyle-wise than most people my age."
- "Does your social media define you? People with big followings make it a point to show off their profiles."
- "How does this sound: you, me, and the best belated Chanukah ever?"
- "Vibe check: is a hot dog a sandwich?"
- "I'd chokeslam my grandma if you let me take you out on a date."
- "Let's nap together. I want to know how you nap."
- "Date night idea: coming to your place, ordering in, getting drunk, watching a movie, and hooking up."
- "I always thought people in the fashion industry were bitchy and corrupt and I want to know more about that drama."
- "Let's meet at 9:30, St. Mark's Place. We can get some boba?"
- "Come over let's watch a movie and order fire food."
- Someone copied and pasted the lyrics to "Barbie Girl."

## Learn the Lingo:
### DATING BURNOUT

There is such a thing as serial daters: people who go on as many first dates as possible for the adrenaline rush. *Burnout* can occur after a series of unsuccessful dates. The abundance of affection reverses, which enhances feelings of rejection and failure. It's ironic how mass dating can make you feel lonelier than ever. In this situation, do something that brings you joy independent of another person. Take a cycling class, treat yourself to a spa day, or visit a neighborhood coffee spot you've been eager to try. Avoid spots where you may be tempted to seek out a man.

There's a lot of pressure on dating apps to make things work—you're expected to date, after all. You can't have a normal conversation without the thought of going out looming over your heads. You also can't keep to online chatting for too long because he may get bored and move on. I like to have a text exchange to get a feel for the person before deciding if I want to meet him IRL. It's suspicious if he jumps into making plans without having asked anything about you. It makes me feel as if I'm just another girl he's taking out. I've learned you should both put in effort to become acquainted with each other. You don't want to be the one posing all the questions.

That said, I don't make myself too available or open up too fast. I don't look at his Snapchat, double-text, or respond right away if I'm not dating the person. It makes it seem like I'm anxiously awaiting his message. You want to keep him on his toes. Match the tone of his texts—if he's using lots of exclamation points to express his enthusiasm, I do the same. If he's writing short messages in all lowercase letters, I don't give him more than he's giving me. Your emojis can demonstrate how you're feeling. I use white hearts over red hearts and smiley faces over kissy faces.

I generally don't like games, but in getting to know someone on an app, it helps to play hard to get. I sometimes act like I'm disinterested when I'm really not. It's a risk because he may lose interest, or it'll make him want you even more. My trick is to send single-word texts like "haha," although it may seem passive aggressive if used too much. Guys will pick up on the vague text and hopefully become more intrigued to learn about you. If I have to text someone multiple times for them to respond, I stop chasing. You don't chase—you attract. It's best not to message someone more than they message you. I'm also cautious of texting too late at night—it can be interpreted as a booty call. The first few weeks of talking to someone set the stage, so it's important not to give off the wrong impression. I keep things friendly and casual in the beginning ("where are you from," "what's your favorite movie," and so forth).

I didn't realize until I joined the dating app that some guys know how to text "hot." One person asked me out on a "cuddling" date after sending a mere "hello" (he didn't waste any time). Another said, "It's freezing outside...but damn, you're hot." A guy who texts that way knows what he's doing—he most likely just wants a hookup. It's suspicious for someone to be so aggressively flirtatious through the phone when you hardly know them.

Case in point: the first guy I met on the app was named Aaron, and he'd call me "sweetness" and "babes" before we even met. The nicknames were very belittling. I love someone who isn't afraid to flirt, but Aaron was over the top to the point where I was skeptical. He referred to me as "my b," even though we had talked over the phone. He was possessive, and that worried me. Even more off-putting was that in person, he acted the exact opposite.

We met at a local coffee shop. I prefer coffee in the daytime over dinner or drinks for the first date. It's more casual and puts less pressure on your time together. Plus, you can leave if you're not feeling it without being stuck at a dinner table. In my experience, a lot of guys who insist on drinks in the evening (especially sans prior small talk) are only interested in a hookup. A horny guy is often too impatient to go on a date with no physical interaction. With Aaron, that certainly wasn't a concern. Unlike his text messages, he was extremely quiet and reserved. There would be awkward silences every now and then, and I sipped my water to fill the gaps. He wasn't fun to talk to. He sat with perfect posture and only seemed interested in serious conversations about work and school. Besides his lack of humor, he anxiously checked his watch to see what time he had to be back at his office. He was a lawyer, and most conversations were centered around his job. In fact, he told me that "if I ever need a lawyer," I could reach out to him. The question was inappropriate—we were on a date, not at a business meeting. I felt like I had to speak more formally in front of him to get on his level. I was outside of myself and eager to jump back into my own skin.

Aaron walked me to school after lunch, and we ended the afternoon with a hug goodbye. You'd expect me to be disappointed by the outcome of the date, but I was just confused. Where was the man behind the screen sending me flirtatious texts every day? Twenty-somethings don't tend to video chat, so there was no way I could've assumed his true personality beforehand. Besides, his antique Android made it impossible to FaceTime before we met. I should've listened to my intuition and assumed the green text bubbles were a red flag from the start.

Surprisingly, Aaron continued to flirt. I was going in for ambulatory surgery that week, and he offered to bring "soup" or a "hug" if needed. Kind words quickly turned creepy. He offered to wake me at 7 a.m. before heading to the hospital and instructed me to leave a key under the mat. It all seemed too serious, too fast, but I tried my best to hold onto hope.

I continued casually texting Aaron, and he gradually laid off the flirting. On Thanksgiving weekend, he attended a friend's engagement party. He cut ties with me as soon as he returned. "I want to see you again, but I'm not sure I see us progressing relationship-wise," he texted. When I received the message, I was in my journalism class at school, and I rushed out of the classroom to catch my breath. I stood in the hallway and stared at my reflection in the window as I cried. I had zero emotional attachment to Aaron. I probably would've called things off if he hadn't. I was upset because my first dating app experience was a failure, and I figured that if it didn't work this time, it never would. The second Aaron was done with me, I wanted to be done with dating apps. Rejection isn't fun. It was important for me to cry it out and acknowledge my disappointment and frustration before moving forward.

Once I mustered the mental strength, I was able to reflect on why Aaron wanted to end things. It was not a coincidence that his text was sent after he returned from an engagement party. Aaron was twenty-three—he was still young, but his friends were starting to get married. Perhaps he was looking for a wife, and I wasn't moving fast enough for him. I'm usually the one moving *too* fast. The second I slowed down, it was too slow for him. According to my past, establishing a label quickly never ends well. It puts a lot of pressure on the relationship and makes it feel rushed, so you don't really get to know each other first. I had the right idea in questioning Aaron's love-bombing language. He most likely was being affectionate over text to draw me closer to him. I was proud of myself for not trusting him too soon.

While Aaron may have wanted a life partner, Matt was the exact opposite. Our connection was promising at first. I decided to take him to a complimentary influencer dinner downtown (big mistake—the guy should always pay on the first date to demonstrate he values your company). "Carrie!" he shouted from across the South Street Seaport. He pulled me in for a hug, and I instantly caught a whiff of his strong cologne. It was the holiday season, so the restaurant was "Winter Wonderland" themed. We entered through a tunnel strung with Christmas lights, revealing rows of heated glass cabins on the other side overlooking the East River. Several Christmas trees decorated the space as well as a large movie screen playing holiday films. "This place is so cool!" Matt exclaimed as the host walked us to our cabin. The lights decorated the entire restaurant, illuminating the space as if the sun was still shining.

"This place is so cool," Matt said again. He must have complimented the restaurant six or seven times before saying he'd stop. "I should keep a tally or something," I laughed. I assumed it was nervous energy. I was usually the anxious one, but the fact that Matt assumed that role made me feel more comfortable. If he was nervous around me, then there was no need to be nervous around him. Nonetheless, this was only my second in-person dating app interaction. I had my reservations. "I don't really use dating apps, so this is all new to me," I said. He claimed it was new to him too and promised he was genuine.

Matt drank *a lot* at dinner, even though I didn't. He mixed alcohol: a Montauk Pale Ale, an Old Fashioned, and another cocktail. I wasn't used to having a guy drink so much in front of me, and it threw me off. I had to repeatedly "cheers" him with my water. With each drink, Matt grew more confident and let his guard down. He told me how much he loves to go out. "You do a little bit of this, a little bit of that," he said while raising the roof. His impromptu dancing was goofy, but I didn't mind. It was kind of cute.

After dinner, Matt and I walked down Wall Street under the stars. We approached a large sculpture with a circular cutout in the center. I ran inside the artwork to examine it. "There's an echo in here! Come and see!" I shouted. Matt stepped inside, towering above me at his 6'2" stature. Once we locked eyes, he leaned down for a kiss. No cars were in sight, and Matt's kisses were slow and gentle. I forgot that I had just met him for the first time. He took my hand. We stepped out of the sculpture and into a deeper connection.

We shared a taxi to bring us back uptown. He anxiously tapped his foot and adjusted his grip several times as we held hands. "Sit still," I laughed, placing a hand on his thigh. As the driver sped up the highway, Matt and I cuddled. I even began to fall asleep in his arms. He wasn't solely focused on a hookup, which was refreshing. "You think you're so smooth," I joked every time he snuck a kiss. Every so often, we sat in silence. I listened closely to the wind, accented by the sound of his beating heart. "What's your favorite restaurant in New York?" he asked randomly, breaking the silence. "Hmm…" I said, glancing over his shoulder and out the window. He kissed up my neck while I considered the question, which threw me off. "I forgot what I was going to say," I giggled.

"Let's stop here!" Matt suddenly directed the driver. We were nowhere near our final destination, but Matt spotted his favorite bar and wanted to stop inside. "You know, I had my first kiss in the back of an Uber," I said as we shut the door to the car. "You don't want to know what I've done in the back of Ubers. That's more of a third-date conversation," Matt laughed. I wasn't sure whether to feel embarrassed for being one-upped or excited because he indicated a third date.

He wanted to sit at the bar with me, but I turned him down. It was getting late, and this was only our first date. I aimed to leave him wanting more. Instead, we walked to 82nd Street and 2nd Avenue, so we could reminisce. It was a nostalgic block for both of us. Although he was older, we both hung out at BurgerFi, 16 Handles, and Pinkberry during our middle school years. I went to BurgerFi every night in seventh grade, praying that a cute boy would take a seat next to me. I was an insecure seventh grader hoping for a hookup. Now, I was an adult confidently strolling hand in hand with a potential boyfriend. I was proud of how far I had come.

When I got home, I was floating. I'm always in a good mood after a successful date. "Now, you wait and see if he texts you," my dad said as I skipped into my bedroom. Matt messaged me less than a half hour after our kiss goodbye. "I had fun! Let's meet up again soon," he typed. However, his idea for a second date wasn't what I anticipated. A few days later, he texted me in the evening that he wanted me to come to his birthday party. I asked where and when, expecting an 8 p.m. start time at a restaurant. He instructed me to come to his home address at two in the morning. Suddenly, I was skeptical about Matt. I worried all he wanted was sex. I wanted to date him—not his penis. So many people on dating apps are solely interested in sleeping with their matches. I thought he was different. Where have all the good guys gone?

Matt wasn't great at making plans. I was always the first to reach out. I spent a lot of time overthinking about waiting to text him or why he wasn't texting me. I considered the worst-case scenario (that he wasn't interested anymore) if he took more than twenty-four hours to reply. A watched pot never boils—and our text chain was no different. I sensed Matt was pulling back because he'd leave me on open on Snapchat. Ignoring someone's photo or message is like giving you a virtual middle finger. He would snap me at random times, and I worried that when he wasn't texting me, he was on other dates.

To win him over, I told white lies. When he asked what I was up to over the weekend, I pretended to have clubbing plans when in reality, I was laying on my couch watching TV. I thought mentioning clubbing would make me seem "cool" or mature, but it just made me feel guilty. Pretending to like partying made our situation more stressful than it already was. You shouldn't have to lie to please a guy. Don't be someone you're not to satisfy your date. They should accept you for you and bring out the best, most authentic version of yourself. They should challenge—not change—you.

Matt ghosted me for an entire month. I figured he found a better option. Being ghosted never feels good—it's humiliating. I felt like a loser. Was I too young for him? Was my lifestyle too different? I kept contemplating what I did wrong. A quote from *One Tree Hill* ran through my mind: "People always leave." Another guy was gone and so was my self-confidence.

After days of reflection (and several Peloton workouts to boost endorphins), I came to a simple-yet-reassuring realization. There are bigger and badder things in the world to worry about—boys are not the worst it gets. If I could make it through a forty-five-minute Tabata class, I could regain confidence in the dating scene. I realized that my thinking may have been flawed in recalling that *One Tree Hill* quote. After all, people can't leave if they were never there for you to begin with.

I thought I would never speak to Matt again—until he reached back out via text. He only made plans when it was convenient for him, a month after our first date. He requested dinner at nine, which was suspiciously late for a meal. I was nervous he would ask me to go back to his apartment afterward, and I thought it was too soon. I figured he only reached out to me as a second choice to whoever he was seeing during the time he ghosted me. So I ghosted him right back. To my surprise, he started spamming me with texts to try to make plans. I felt smothered. A guy should fight for your attention, but you shouldn't feel pressured to see or text him all the time.

After Matt's one-month silence and hint at a hookup-only hang out, I wasn't interested anymore. Not to mention, I was starting to date someone else at the time. But I didn't know how to let him go. Do I block him? Call him to explain? Send him a text telling the truth? Having the strength to get rid of whatever or whoever isn't serving you is scary—but I knew it was for the best. I ultimately decided to stop texting Matt. He got the hint and did not take it well. He unfollowed me on Instagram and Snapchat and sent a nasty text: "Pretty rude just for the record idc but u should know it doesn't go unnoticed." He couldn't stand rejection; his ego was hurt. I sent a polite message back that I was seeing someone else, even though my current dating life was really none of his business. He never replied, but he refollowed and readded me on all social media.

At this point, I was convinced I had bad karma on dating apps—which brings me back to "fly guy," aka Gavin. My family and friends referred to him as "Elton John," since he offered to buy us tickets to a concert for the first date. The gesture was a bit extravagant, so I politely declined. Alternatively, I suggested breakfast at Chelsea Market one Sunday morning.

The night before, Gavin and I texted back and forth for an hour. I took this as a positive sign. We had a silly, pointless conversation; he didn't take life too seriously. We sent our favorite emojis back and forth, and I even pretended I had a date with Justin Bieber after ours. "I can tell you have a great sense of humor," he typed. I've never been afraid to make my date laugh—you should be able to joke around without worrying about him judging you. I didn't have to think too much or filter myself before sending a message to Gavin. Our conversation flowed naturally—it didn't feel forced. A consistent text chain over the course of an hour or so can mimic the bounce of an in-person interaction. I like a guy who is engaging and writes messages other than just "hey" or "what's good." He shouldn't take days to answer texts. He should hold a conversation—and not just when he's making plans to see you in person. He should make an effort to ask about your day.

That said, a guy who overly texts before you're dating is questionable. He may be super into you or weirdly obsessed. Most of the time, it's the latter. Looking back, I should've picked up on Gavin's string of emojis as overenthusiastic. Since I was texting him at night, I was tired and naïve, so I played along. Besides the emojis, ironically, Gavin was very formal in the way he texted. His messages were written with perfect grammar and punctuation, and each one addressed me by my first name ("How was your day, Carrie?"). I assumed he was trying to impress me, but his tone threw me off.

Gavin was eager to please in person as well. He agreed with everything I said and kept complimenting my outfit. Although texting Gavin was effortless, it wasn't as easy to converse in real life. He was pretty awkward. "Do you know what you want to order?" he asked several times while we were in line at a café, as if we had nothing else to talk about. I noticed him nervously fiddling with the pocket of his jeans or glancing off to the side to avoid eye contact. When we sat down to eat, Gavin admitted that the dating app wasn't the first place he saw me. "I saw a sponsored teeth whitening video on Instagram and knew you looked familiar," he said. "Clean teeth are very important to me. A girl can't have yellow or crooked teeth. Your teeth look great." I was slightly uncomfortable with the dental assessment, but I let it slide.

# Swipe Left:

← **BOYS TO BEWARE OF ON THE APPS (AND IN GENERAL TBH)**

- Someone who lives in a different state or country. I met someone on a dating app who lived in Delaware. Why waste time messaging someone I would rarely see? I'm all for being friends, but we met on a dating app. Chances are he just wants a hookup buddy when he vacations in New York.
- Someone who makes you schlep to see him. Don't travel more than twenty to thirty minutes to get to a first date. One guy wanted me to take thirty-mile (not minute…mile!) car ride. Another offered to take me to a Red Hot Chili Peppers concert…in Philly.
- Someone who is unresponsive via text. A guy confirmed with me just thirty minutes before our dinner, so I had to scramble to get ready. You should have been on his schedule, not a last-minute afterthought.
- Someone who forgets your name. If a guy is into you, the least he can do is remember your name. It's even worse if he calls you someone else.
- Someone who kisses up to you too much. Flattery is nice, but sending compliments every text is excessive. Watch out for someone who agrees with everything you say as well—it's as if he doesn't have a mind of his own. He's not necessarily being truthful and may just be trying to please you.
- Someone who tries too hard to relate to you. It's obvious when a person lies about sharing similar interests, so you seem more compatible. You shouldn't try too hard to relate either. One time, I was video chatting with a guy and saw he had a *Star Wars* poster in the background. I pretended I had a *Star Wars* poster under my bed, but when I had no proof, it was clear I wasn't being truthful. He ghosted me after that.
- Someone who uses old photos on his dating app profile. Some photos may be years old—for example, a now-adult who includes a photo in a tux at his high-school prom. Guys use their best pictures on dating apps. It's not full-on catfishing, but beware: he may not be as cute or put-together in person as his profile photo.
- Someone who's obviously lying. One guy asked if I liked to write children's books but pretended he hadn't Googled me. If he's lying early on, he's definitely going to hide things in the future.
- Someone who only texts you late at night. In the evening, men may be bored, lonely, and horny. He could be texting you when he's in bed and craving

a sexual connection. On the other hand, he could be out drinking with his friends and mustered the liquid courage to message you. In either scenario, texts sent past midnight are never a good sign.

- Someone who answers his texts within seconds every time—and expects you to do the same. A guy who always responds right away is too attached, especially if you're just starting to date. One guy used to point out every time I left his Snapchats on open. We'd never even met, and he pressured me to answer every message as soon as I read it. Leaving someone on open doesn't necessarily mean I don't like him—I could just be busy and waiting to respond until later.

- Someone who is too clingy. If the person is desperate to hold onto you before you're even dating (texting too much, double or triple-messaging, "selling" you the idea of an extravagant first date), let him go. The same goes for you: don't be needy. If he's not interested—thank you, next.

- Someone who only reaches out when it's convenient for them. Your time is sacred. Avoid those who ghost you for several weeks or months. Clearly, they aren't interested in putting in effort to see you. A guy ghosted me and messaged two months later, "Sorry, my phone died. How have you been?" I never knew a phone could stay dead for so long. Another person messaged me five months after we stopped talking to invite me to his fraternity formal via DM. He probably copied and pasted that message to several girls to see which one would be down. I guess his original plus one canceled.

- Someone who never initiates plans. If you're always the one asking when he's free, you're trying much harder to make things work than he is.

- Someone who flakes out at the last minute or is running very late to a first date. It's not fair to you or your schedule. Clearly, you're not important enough for him to make time for you. If he doesn't put you first now, he never will.

- Someone who avoids conversation. I prefer texting someone instead of Snapchat because it forces you to actually communicate. Most older guys don't even use Snapchat. It's immature when he only sends selfies of himself instead of getting to know you. Sending photos in return is a waste of time.

After breakfast, we considered where to go next. "Wherever you want, Carrie," he said. I suggested the flea market, and Gavin made a sharp turn towards the shopping area. "Sure, Carrie." As we browsed the booths, Gavin insisted on buying me everything I was eyeing. He purchased body butter, smiley-face bracelets, and even an accessory I was going to buy for my mom. "I hope she likes it," he said. Wasn't it a bit too early to impress my parents?

Afterwards, we strolled along Pier 57. Gavin was still antsy. He would stutter and keep a foot's distance away from me. "Let's sit down," I said, hoping it would put him at ease. I noticed he had dry hands, so I rubbed in the body butter he bought me. "How should I pay you?" he asked. I laughed. "That's for you to decide." Once I was done massaging his hand with the lotion, I made another joke. "Where's my tip?" I said as I put away the product. There was a brief silence as he contemplated his next move. "How about a kiss instead?" he proposed. Although I wasn't physically attracted to him, I realized that I may have been asking for it by offering a physical connection. I agreed to kiss him, but he hesitated before leaning in. "One second, I have to spit out my gum. Do you have a napkin?" he said, scanning the area for a garbage can. His words made me cringe—way to ruin the moment. "I kiss with gum all the time. You're fine," I insisted. Gavin wouldn't give in. "I don't want you to choke on it," he maintained. I folded over and started laughing. "This is so weird," I said. He tried his best to keep the moment alive. "No, it's great!"

Gavin finally spit his gum into a receipt and kissed me. The make out was anything but affectionate. He leaned in with his tongue out and swirled it inside my mouth. His hands were awkwardly placed: he rubbed my back in circles, and the stroking was out of sync with the rhythm of the kiss. There was no sexual tension—it was like I was getting a poor back rub while being slobbered. He rarely let me come up for air.

We sat with our arms around each other, staring out at the water. Neither of us knew what to say. Gavin was starting to bug me...literally. When I looked up at him, he flashed a smile—a fly was sitting right on his front tooth. I screamed. We were just shopping at a flea market—little did I know a flea would end up in his mouth. He had just been preaching the importance of clean teeth, and ironically, a dead insect was on his smile. I picked the fly off for him. My kiss probably killed the bug—the thought of that made me want to throw up.

Thankfully, I had an excuse to get up and leave. I had an event afterwards, and I was going to be late. "You don't have to go. You can be late to your event," he said. I shook my head. "Uh, no I can't." I gathered my backpack and shopping bag. I tried so hard to like the guy, but I just wasn't into him. I knew it was best not to force things if I wasn't feeling it. With Gavin, there was no chase. He was too easy, and that was part of the problem. I'm both annoyed by and attracted to someone who plays hard to get—but that's the fun of it. Uncertainty builds tension so that when you're positive you two like each other, the moment is more exciting. My kiss with Gavin was anticlimactic.

I wasn't sure how to let him down gently. I felt terrible telling him I wasn't interested in a second date. We discussed in person how we don't like when people take too long to text. Now, I was the one waiting all day to message him because I didn't know how to call things off. I waited until right before I went to bed at 12:30 a.m. to thank him for the gifts he bought me. I never told him why I wasn't interested anymore, but I assumed he understood. He asked me how my event was, and when I didn't respond, he never followed up. Gavin and I had a good start, but my experience just goes to show that people online don't necessarily act how they act in person.

After several failed dates, I considered deleting the app. Are all dating apps just inherently hopeless? A virtual path to someone's bed? Or is there hope for real love and relationships found online? Gavin aside, it seems like most guys on dating apps just want to get in girls' pants. A voice in the back of my head always worries that a guy just wants my body. Thankfully, I've become an expert at spotting red flags. Being picky isn't a bad thing—it's essential. I depend heavily on instinct to indicate who isn't a good fit. At this stage in my life, when dating, listening to my gut has never been more important.

I go on dates with low expectations. That way, when someone disappoints me, it's easier to let them go. When someone excites me, it's a pleasant surprise. I got ghosted a lot on dating apps, even after giving guys my number. But I tried not to take it too personally. You don't need to impress anyone. Be yourself, and the right guy will gravitate towards that.

I haven't sworn off dating apps, but I don't depend on them. It's difficult to build trust with a complete stranger online. It takes a lot of focus and energy to filter out the boys with bad intentions. Not to mention, spontaneity is often sacrificed in a dating app setup. When you click with someone organically in person, you don't know what's going to happen—there's excitement in the unknown. I find the feeling of "living on the edge" to be missing during my dating app experiences. With the apps, you know exactly what you're in for because you signed up to scout out a boyfriend. Personally, I think forming a spontaneous connection in a social setting is more exciting.

I'd rather meet someone naturally, but we're living in a digital world. The reality is many people meet each other online these days. You very well may find someone you like and whose relationship needs match your own on an app. Just remember to keep your guard up, be cautious, and take things slowly—the last thing you want is a "fly guy" of your own. ♥

# Chapter 13

# The Workaholic

I FOUND ONE GEM ON a dating app—he lasted for a little while at least. Wyatt was five years older, and he made it clear he wasn't just interested in a hookup. Instead of asking me out to dinner or inviting me over to his apartment right away, we started off with coffee.

I met him at a café on a cold winter morning in the city. Naturally, I was late. When I got there, he was already waiting inside on a high-top chair. We got the cookie-cutter questions out of the way: where we went to college, if we have any pets, and why we like New York. The conversation flowed easily as I learned more about his education and interests. He was a music geek and very knowledgeable about the entertainment industry. It made it easy to discuss my social media career with him; he asked all the right questions. I felt unusually comfortable around him. My heart wasn't pounding, and I didn't feel a need to put any pressure on the date. But I wasn't sold on him. There were no sparks, and our time together was fairly short.

I found one glimmer of hope as we wrapped up. "I like your earmuffs," he said, touching the faux fur around my ears. "I like your sunglasses," I replied. "Can I try them on?" We traded accessories: he sported the pink earmuffs while I wore his glasses. "They look good on you," he said. With that flirtatious remark, I decided to give him another shot.

# Double-Tap This:

**FIRST DATE TIPS**

- Keep your expectations low so that you may be pleasantly surprised. If it doesn't work out, he just wasn't the right person for you.
- Maintain good hygiene. Take a shower beforehand and apply your favorite body spray or perfume. If the person you're meeting is sweaty or smelly, move on. One guy I met had ear wax sticking out of his ear, and another had spinach wedged between his two front teeth.
- Do your research. If you know he likes fantasy football, go into the date with a few points of conversation to support his interests (i.e., which teams won NFL games over the weekend).
- Be punctual. Arriving five to ten minutes late isn't a crime, but you should respect his time (and he should respect yours as well).
- Don't do anything too serious. No candlelit dinners or picnics under the stars. A simple brunch or coffee date will suffice.
- Don't order anything too messy. No spaghetti with sauce or sloppy burgers. Keep it classy. The last thing you want is to stain your outfit or have food all over your mouth.
- Make sure you're talking an equal amount. He should make an effort to understand you and your passions and vice versa. For example, when I told one guy I was a writer, he expressed interest by asking to read some of my articles. (Bonus points if he remembers small details you told him and brings them up later!)
- Try your best to relax. Don't put too much pressure on yourself. Guys will pick up on nervous energy. Just sit back and let your personality shine.
- If he suggests a date close to his home, consider that a red flag. It's smart not to rush things by going to his place too soon. You don't know him well yet, and you want to make sure you trust him before spending time together in private.
- Avoid staying out late. Time flies when you're having fun—but make it home before the clock strikes midnight, Cinderella. You should leave him wanting more of you.
- Guys like it when you're mean to them. It sounds counterintuitive, I know. A little bit of banter can actually be a turn-on—as long as it's not *too* mean. Acceptable: "I'm going to kick your butt at bowling." Not acceptable: "Be a man."
- A kiss goodbye is okay—but don't go too far physically. You want him to respect you first and foremost.
- Don't have him drop you off in front of your home afterwards. For safety reasons, you shouldn't show him where you live right away. Worst case scenario, he's a stalker and won't respect your boundaries.

For our next date, Wyatt suggested we go to the movies. I picked *The Batman*—the film is nearly three hours, and I knew it would maximize our time. When we sat down in the theater, I started to get nervous. Embarrassingly, I must've gotten up three or four times to use the bathroom while waiting for the movie to start. "Nervous energy," I said, hoping he would appreciate the honesty. Luckily, he laughed.

We sat with our hands in our laps at first with an armrest between us. "You smell good," he said suddenly. "Yes!" I blurted out, embarrassed by my excitement. I sprayed on my favorite perfume—Sol de Janeiro Brazilian Crush Cheirosa 62 Perfume Mist—in hopes that he'd like it. He placed his hand on top of mine and began to caress it. After a few minutes, I rested my head on his shoulder. I could feel his eyes on me. My gaze shifted away from the screen. Our eyes met, and moments after, our lips.

Seated in the back of the movie theater, it felt like we were the only ones there. It was just our second date, but when he kissed me, I felt safe. I could sense his intentions were pure. I giggled between kisses and gently stroked his facial hair. "I'm not usually into beards, but I don't mind the scruff," I said transparently. "I'll shave it for you eventually," he claimed, subtly alluding to the future.

"What are you thinking about?" I said as he glanced off. He looked back at me. "I'm thinking about how much I wish we were in my apartment right now," he replied. I was caught off guard. Perhaps all he wanted was to get me in his bed. "Let's take it slow," I maintained. "I don't want to mess things up by going too quickly." He kissed my forehead. "We can take it as slow as you want."

While I waited for my Uber after the movie, I placed my arms on his shoulders. "I'm as tall as you!" I laughed. In my boots, I reached his height at 5'6". "Hey!" he joked, playfully pulling me into a hug. I could sense insecurity in his eyes—he seemed to genuinely care about what I thought of him. I assured him there was no need to worry. "It's alright. Short guy, big actions," I teased. We transitioned into talking about music; his favorite artists were Pink Floyd and AC/DC. "We should go to a rock concert!" I exclaimed. He took my hand and sandwiched it between his two palms. "The artist I want to take you to isn't performing until May, but I promise I'll take you then," he said. May was four months away—I saw his comment as another indirect reference to being together in the future.

The next time I saw him, we met in the early evening at a café for trivia night. We shared a DIY plate of s'mores as well as Butterbeer (non-alcoholic, Harry Potter style). "Do you want to take a picture of the s'mores?" he asked, aware it was a good social media opportunity. I shot a Boomerang roasting a marshmallow, then flipped my phone to show him. "Do you want me to tag you?" I asked. I was hesitant, since we weren't officially dating. But a tag is just a tag, right? Wyatt said he didn't mind, so I inserted his username in small font.

The waiter passed out trivia cards as we assembled our s'mores. The melted marshmallow got all over my fingers, and I accidentally dropped my graham cracker on the floor. As I buried my head in my hands, the marshmallow on my fingers transferred to my cheek. Wyatt reached across the table to wipe it off, then licked his finger. I burst into laughter. "You have the cutest laugh," he smiled. As I nibbled on a chocolate square, Wyatt suddenly asked if my parents knew I was out on a date. "Yes, of course. I'm a big girl," I said. He knew I was nineteen, but his question made me feel like I was on a permissive playdate. He stroked my knee under the table as we spoke, which kept me grounded.

Our knowledge, even combined, was limited during trivia. We gave up and decided to head out. His birthday was that weekend, so I insisted on paying for our drink and dessert. Besides, he picked up the bill the previous two times (and every time that followed). Before we left, he walked me to the bathroom. Wyatt informed me afterwards of a comment a woman in line made while I was inside: "You know, you can go in with her." I wished he had—we wouldn't have used the bathroom for its typical purposes. A little privacy would've been nice.

After dinner, we walked hand in hand in the freezing cold. We wrapped our arms around each other, and at one point, I decided to make a move. I find that a bold personality is not only appreciated, but it's also considered attractive. I reached down and flirtatiously pinched Wyatt's butt. "Gotcha," I joked, quickly removing my hand. "I see you making moves," he laughed.

We sat on a park bench and continued to learn more about each other—and not just our favorite colors or movies. We talked about our most embarrassing dates, past relationships, and heartbreaks. From what he revealed to me, it was clear he had major trust issues, which I hoped wouldn't affect our relationship in the future.

Our final stop that evening was an ice cream shop. We didn't order any treats, but we admired the door lined with ice cream cartons. "Let's take a picture, so we can remember this," he said, turning on his selfie camera. Before I could even register, he pulled me in close and snapped a photo kissing me on the cheek. I'm usually the one urging my friends to take pictures for memories. Wyatt suggested it before the thought even crossed my mind.

On our fourth date, I went to his apartment for the first time. He knew I lived with my mom and dad; he moved out of his parents' home just one year prior. Visiting his independent space first made the most sense. I was comfortable because I knew it wasn't going to be the last time I saw him. It wasn't just going to be a hookup followed by a forever *au revoir*. He reserved dinner across the street from his place, so I knew what was to come. "Do you want to walk around? Or we could hang out in my apartment for a bit?" he suggested after we finished our sushi date.

"You think you're so smooth," I laughed. "Yeah, it's cold. Let's see your apartment."

The first thing I noticed in his home was all the Jewish touches: a mezuzah, challah, and a rabbi rubber duck in the bathroom. I wasn't surprised—I did find him on a Jewish dating app. Besides the subtle nods to his religion, his space was covered in music memorabilia. A guitar decked out in stickers hung next to his desk, each decoration holding a special meaning or memory. Albums resided in frames or on shelves in front of a record player. "Can I pick something to play?" I asked, kneeling on the ground to rummage through his collection. I chose a Queen album. Wyatt sat beside me and gently guided my hand in teaching me to use the turntable. As the music started to play, I turned to kiss him.

We moved to the couch, and he positioned himself on top of me. Every step of the way, he made sure he had my consent to move forward. In my eyes, he defined what it means to have a guy's respect. He kissed me slowly, paying attention to my body to see what was reciprocated and what wasn't. "Want to take this into the bedroom?" he asked after a while. With my permission, he scooped me up, and my legs instinctively wrapped around him. His hands worked their way up my back, over my chest, and through my hair. As his lips trailed from my neck to my shoulder, I caught a chill. My legs tightened around his waist. I could feel his heart rate quickening. He threw me down on the bed. It was pitch dark outside, and the lights were turned off throughout the apartment. He traced his fingers down my stomach. The sexual tension was palpable. However, I didn't want to give too much of myself too soon. I teased him instead. "Oops," I said, fiddling with my bra strap but not slipping it down. At one point, we just laid beside each other. "So...what exactly are you looking for?" I asked. I had a hunch he was interested in a serious commitment (his previous relationship lasted several years), but I didn't want to make any assumptions. "I'm looking for a meaningful connection," he confirmed. I reciprocated that I was searching for the same.

At around 11:30 p.m., I wrapped things up. It was his birthday in a half hour, and I wasn't sure if he wanted me there at midnight. I headed to the bathroom one last time before leaving, where I was greeted by a surprise. "Oh, my God!" I screamed, racing into the living room. "There's a huge cockroach!" Wyatt ran inside with a broom. "Don't worry, I'll kill it," he said. The insect disappeared, and I stood a few feet behind Wyatt, suggesting where it could've gone. "Check behind the trash can," I said. My suspicion was correct. Wyatt slapped the ground repeatedly with the broom until the roach was dead. Seeing him take charge was incredibly attractive.

Once he washed his hands, he found me in the kitchen and pulled me into a hug. "I'm so sorry. That's never happened before," he said. I rubbed his bare back and rested my head in the space between his cheek and shoulder—it fit perfectly. "Guess I'm never coming back. I'll just escape out the window," I teased, glancing outside. The record was still playing, and one of my favorite Queen songs came on, "We Are the Champions." "I love this song!" I exclaimed, still in his arms. I started singing along, and he harmonized as we swayed from side to side. I'd never sung with someone I dated before—hearing our voices, feeling his arms wrapped around me was profound.

He walked me to my Uber, parked a block away from his apartment. "When am I going to see you again?" I asked. I suggested Monday but quickly regretted it. I didn't realize it was Valentine's Day. I figured it would be a lot of pressure to go out on a date then, but Wyatt insisted it was fine. I went home, texted him "happy birthday," and went to bed elated. The chemistry I once questioned now existed in full force. Forget the cockroach—I couldn't wait to go back to his apartment.

We never wound up going out on Valentine's Day. Wyatt celebrated his birthday with friends over the weekend, and he said he had work to do on Monday. I assumed he just felt uncomfortable planning a Valentine's Day date with me so soon—it made sense. Nonetheless, several special dates followed. We went out at least once a week. One evening, we walked around the Deutsche Bank Center, where we bought glow-in-the-dark star stickers to decorate his bedroom ceiling with. Afterwards, we snuck into the movie theater from our first date and made TikToks in an empty screening room.

# Double-Tap This:

### DATE NIGHT IDEAS

Dating is enhanced by the adventures you have with your significant other. With someone by your side, you can see your hometown in a new light. Seize the opportunity to be a tourist in your own city and embrace experiences you've never tried. If you're stumped on date night ideas, explore some of the options below to upgrade your relationship.

- Go art gallery hopping. Bet on how much one of the pieces costs—loser buys dessert.
- Experiment in the kitchen. One of my favorite dishes to make is DIY fondue: melt chocolate chips (an aphrodisiac) in a bowl and dip strawberries.
- Go window shopping. No need to actually make a purchase—rank some of your favorite pieces through the glass.
- Chill in a coffee shop. Sometimes, they have trivia or karaoke nights.
- Do a seasonal athletic activity. Try ice skating or tennis; even if you're inexperienced, your date may be able to show you the ropes.
- Go bowling. A little healthy competition never hurt anyone.
- Take a long walk in the park.
- Visit tourist attractions.
- Buy tickets to a local fair or carnival.
- Explore a museum.
- Ride bikes or rent electric scooters.
- Do dinner and a movie—cliché but fun.

Another night, I took him bowling. We had a private room decked out in LED lights with food, drinks, and a personal stereo. I leaned against the bowling ball return system while he took a swing. "Go ahead. Not distracting you at all," I teased. I was in the lead at first, so I decided to help him. "Here, let me show you," I said, stepping behind Wyatt. I first mimicked the motion with my arm, then took his hand to guide him. I lost my groove, and he won by a landslide. I guess I was the one distracted in the end.

That evening, I sat in his lap on a chair at an outdoor café in Midtown. "I need to ask you something," I started. We had been going out for at least a month, and I wanted to know where he stood. "Are we exclusive?" I asked. I was afraid to bring it up because I worried about driving him away. The last thing I wanted was to jump into a relationship too fast or pressure Wyatt to make things official before he was ready. I didn't want to be territorial over him.

"I'm not ready to be boyfriend and girlfriend, but I'm not seeing other people," he explained. "I don't know what label that gives us." I translated his words: it seemed like we were exclusive, but he wasn't ready to verbalize it. "What do you tell your friends?" I asked. He shrugged. "I tell them we're dating." He never gave me a clear answer as to if he saw us progressing. Nothing changed. We forgot that conversation even happened—at least he did.

I invited him over for breakfast at my apartment one day when my parents were out of state visiting my grandparents. I was supposed to join them, but I ditched so I could see Wyatt. My parents were only gone for a few hours, but I fibbed that they were away for the weekend so Wyatt would feel more comfortable coming over. He'd also see that I was capable of living in an apartment on my own. I was always concerned he'd hate that I was so much younger than him. In fact, before he arrived,

I removed several family pictures. I didn't want him to feel like my parents were "staring" from a frame if we sat on the couch.

I opened the door in sweatpants and a sweatshirt, the most casual he had ever seen me. "I literally just woke up. I'm not even wearing any makeup," I said. That morning, I sensed that something about my cooking made him uncomfortable. "Are you sure you want to cook?" he said. "I can pick up something and bring it over. I don't want to waste your parents' food in the fridge." I insisted that I didn't mind, so I made scrambled eggs for the two of us. When we were done eating, Wyatt got up to check his phone. I placed my hands on his shoulders as he was glancing down and leaned in to kiss him. "It's good to see you," he said. "I know, I missed you!" I exclaimed. He never reciprocated the statement, but I quickly brushed it off. Words of affirmation weren't his forte.

The physical connection, however, was strong. He once again picked me up and carried me to the couch. He tripped on my dog's wee-wee pad in the process, nearly dropping me. My dog followed close behind us as we laid down. I picked her up and let her lick my face. "You jealous?" I teased. He suggested we shut the blinds, so no one could witness us fooling around. As soon as we hit the cushions, I gently lifted up his shirt. "Oh, you want me to take this off?" he said sarcastically. I took his tee and threw it on the coffee table. "Nice shot!" he said. I was afraid that the morning wouldn't set the scene for an intense make out, but I was wrong. We picked up right where we left off that evening at his apartment.

However, he checked his phone every few minutes, nervous about missing a meeting he needed to run off to. I knew Wyatt was busy with work, and I supported him by applauding his career accomplishments. But it started to become a problem when it frequently interfered with our time together. Exhibit A: he abruptly ended our date mid-make out, so he'd be on time for his appointment.

A week later, we spent a lazy, rainy Sunday at his apartment. He usually kissed me hello, but this time, I got a hug. I slipped my shoes off and sat at the edge of the couch. "It's good to see you," he said, planting a peck as he hovered over me. Those words seemed to be his only way of showing verbal affection. "I'm falling back on the couch," I retorted. Wyatt stayed silent while I let myself fall—physically and metaphorically. I scrolled through Netflix on his TV and selected a comedy for us to watch. We cuddled on his small sofa, but I couldn't get comfortable. It was too difficult to lay on him while simultaneously watching the screen, so eventually, I just dozed off on his chest. The sound of thunderstorms outside woke me. "Look how badly it's raining!" I said, getting up to look at the window. He came up from behind to kiss me, but we had a time limit once again. Wyatt running off to work commitments was starting to become a pattern.

I was leaving for vacation the next day, and I maintained that I would stay loyal while on my trip. "This TikTok guy asked me to collab on thirst trap videos while I'm there, but I turned him down," I said. Wyatt shrugged. "I mean, if it's for work, I get it. Some people just might be jealous." I smiled. "And by someone you mean…" "Me," he said, finishing my sentence.

The day after, I flew to Miami. At first, Wyatt was responsive via text. But as my vacation progressed, he started to pull away. He was working so much that he could never find time to answer my messages. I found myself increasingly nervous as he laid off texting—was he busy, or was he just ignoring me? Every time I got a text, I was paranoid. What if he leaves? What if he doesn't like me anymore? I accepted my fear and stopped making assumptions. Sometimes, it's good to be nervous—it means you care.

I was lucky if I received one message from him every day. When he texted me back, I considered making myself unavailable to even the playing field. Ultimately, I decided not to play around. I usually responded right away. It pained me sometimes because I didn't want to seem like I was sitting by my phone waiting for him to message back (I was). Guys like girls who are mysterious. I always like the guy to be the last to text, so he's hanging on my every word, anticipating my reply. But being attentive and expressing interest in someone you're dating is the mature thing to do.

I wondered if Wyatt wasn't replying because he was seeing someone else. Frankly, with his work schedule, he had no time to be a player. It seemed like he didn't have time for me or a relationship in general. I wanted to be someone he was actively trying to see. I set time aside during the week just in case a slot in his schedule opened for me. I was eager to see him more, but it felt like I was always pursuing him to suggest a date and time. I was tired of chasing—I wanted to be chased.

There are two types of career guys: workaholics and those who hardly work. My time in Florida illuminated just how much of a workaholic Wyatt was. Whenever I asked him for plans, he told me he was going to be at the office late. I wanted to be more to him than just an escape from his job. I liked that he was comfortable with me, but I didn't just want to be someone he reached out to when he got a break, someone who gave him a release. I wanted to mean more.

As he started to wean off of texting, his lack of flirtation became clear. I'm a very flirtatious person, and he was not. When I was affectionate, he didn't reciprocate. He seemed to view our connection as more casual than I did. His inability to express his feelings made me want to retreat. How was I supposed to know what was going on inside his head? When we first started dating, I said I wanted him to make "big actions." Now, I realize I should've clarified what I meant: someone who goes out of his way to make himself known, someone who makes me feel special. All I felt around Wyatt, and when I was away from him, was nervous and on edge. He was living in my head. I was preoccupied with fear that he was going to leave me.

We were about two months into dating at this point. I had no idea where Wyatt was at and if he saw us further developing our relationship. After I asked him if we were exclusive, I didn't bring it up again. He made it clear he didn't want to put a label on us just yet. From my perspective, I wanted to ensure he was loyal and only had eyes for me before giving more of myself in the bedroom. I wanted the boyfriend/girlfriend label because I would have felt more comfortable trusting him knowing he was committed to me. I was afraid of moving forward sexually too quickly. It seemed like he wasn't looking to commit, and I worried he would get frustrated and leave if I didn't give him anything. Most significantly, I contemplated if I should I wait until I'm in a committed relationship to have sex. Wyatt wasn't pressuring me, but I found it increasingly difficult to restrain myself. There's no handbook on how much of yourself to give and when.

Wyatt wasn't even my boyfriend, but he held such power over my emotions. Why couldn't I let go and put less pressure on our relationship? Why was I incapable of having fun and just dating him? Dating seemed fruitless if our feelings were pushed aside. I wanted to vocalize that I was ready to call him my boyfriend, but I was scared that getting serious would make me seem clingy and drive him away. He confirmed he wasn't dating anyone else at the moment, but he never officially rendered us "exclusive." How did I know he wouldn't be seeing anyone in a week? I told myself that if he didn't want a relationship, he wouldn't have gone on so many dates with me. But I needed some reassurance from him. It's hard to progress if both parties don't open up. I wondered why we couldn't just be open about our feelings without fear. Communication is key in a relationship. If revealing your feelings scares him off, it just means he wasn't the right one, and he'll leave the picture before you get hurt.

On the way to family dinner one evening, I barked at my parents for calling Wyatt my boyfriend. It reminded me of the type of relationship I wanted but didn't have—and that hurt. My dad, in particular, sensed my anxiety. "If you date someone, there are two potential outcomes," he explained as we walked the dog after dinner. "You either break up or get married. The chance this will be the guy you marry is very slim. It'll end eventually anyways." His reasoning sounded pessimistic, but he was right. I had to stay grounded and stop romanticizing my relationship.

Wyatt had said he was looking for a meaningful connection. I wondered if that was still true. He was stopping himself from falling by closing his heart off to me. We're emotional beings, and it's natural to trust others in seeking love. I wanted to trust that Wyatt had pure intentions and still wanted to build on our connection. In reality, I just wasn't sure. I liked Wyatt, and I wanted to fight for him, fight for us. I tried to make sense of his feelings, but only he knew his heart. I wasn't sure when or if I'd ever become his girlfriend. I held on for as long as I could.

My texts with Wyatt made it difficult to keep the faith. I told him I missed him, and all I got in response was, "Ikr, it's been a while now!" His words reminded me of a phrase my dad told my mom to avoid commitment when they were first dating: "We're light and fluffy like popcorn." Although in my case, trying to keep up the connection with Wyatt felt more like trudging through mud.

After two and a half weeks apart, we finally made dinner plans. Wyatt had three hours before he had to rush off to an appointment in Brooklyn. "I don't want to be a burden to your work schedule," I said, suddenly feeling guilty about him having to squeeze me in. "No, I definitely don't feel like you're a burden!" he replied. "I also hate to make other people feel so scheduled around my craziness, so I'm sorry about that. It's just been a crazy stretch for me right now." The situation wasn't ideal, but I hoped the time we had together would bring clarity about where he was at in our relationship.

I was nervous to see him. We didn't talk every day. It felt like the first date all over again. I wondered if we were going to kiss each other hello like normal. He hopped on the wrong train to meet me, subtracting an hour from our already-minimal time. But I was determined to make the most of our evening together. He picked me up at my apartment, and I gave him a flirtatious finger wave as I approached him. He greeted me with a kiss, and we laughed all the way to the restaurant as he recounted his travel disaster. When we got to the restaurant, I was stopped by a group of girls who were familiar with my TikTok. I chatted and took photos with them before introducing Wyatt. "Sorry, I meant to introduce…this is Wyatt," I said, unsure of how to label him. He was grinning ear to ear when the girls walked away, as if he were proud to be by my side.

As dinner progressed, I could sense something was off. Wyatt ate across from me, despite the fact that the waitress encouraged us to sit side by side in the booth. "That's a thing, you know," she said. There were awkward silences, and he kept looking at his work emails. Checking his notifications while we were together was nothing new—now, I was hyper aware of it. I mentioned how summer was approaching, and it was almost Hamptons season. "You have to come visit me!" I exclaimed. He didn't seem too enthusiastic. "Yeah, I wouldn't have any problem getting out there, I just don't know how I'd get back," he said. I mentioned the Hampton Jitney, but he was unfamiliar with (and frankly, uninterested in) the bus service. I told him I saw advertisements for the concert we discussed on date two in hopes that he'd perk up. He took a slow sip of his drink. "I don't know if I'm free that day," he said. It was upsetting to say the least. This was something we had looked forward to since we first started dating. "You promised," was all I managed to utter.

I ate shrimp salad, and he ordered heart-shaped lobster ravioli—the irony was obvious, at least to me. On my way to the bathroom, I handed the waitress my credit card to discretely pay for the meal. It felt like Wyatt was slipping away, and I was making my final plea. "You're a lucky guy," the waitress later said, delivering us a complimentary tiramisu. "I promise I didn't order this," I laughed as she put the plate on our table. I shifted in my seat, anxiously waiting for him to address why we hadn't seen each other in so long. "Do they know you here?" he asked me instead. I shook my head. "Do you come here a lot?" he continued. It appeared that both of us had lots of questions for each other. Wyatt requested the bill. "You owe this girl another special thank you for paying for dinner," the waitress said. His eyes widened. "You didn't have to do that," he said. I smiled. "I wanted to."

After dinner, I took his arm and proposed we walk to a park. "Aren't you cold?" he asked. I shrugged. "I guess it comes with the territory of wearing a cute outfit." Wyatt walked a few feet in front of me and turned around so he could take in the look: a leather dress with a tie waist and booties. "Your outfit is fly," he said. He checked his phone once again to see how much time he had before he needed to leave. "I don't want to interfere with your work," I admitted, reiterating what I texted him a few days prior. "You're not," he insisted. I looked down at my bare legs, covered in goosebumps. "I don't want to be just a work break to you."

From there, everything unraveled quickly. I sensed Wyatt's energy shift and suggested we sit on a nearby park bench. After two and a half weeks of pulling back on texts, he finally told me how he was feeling. "I don't think I'm ready for a relationship," he explained. "I love hanging out with you, though, and I want to keep seeing you in whatever capacity, whether that's casually dating you or as a friend." The word "love" stuck out, as I wondered what it would sound like if it came out of his mouth in a different context.

Was this a breakup? We weren't in a committed relation-ship, so could I even call it that? Clearly, we were moving too fast for him, and he couldn't keep up. Wyatt wanted to maintain our connection but only on a casual level. "I mean, we can still stay friends," he said. I kept my hand on his thigh as we were speaking but wondered if I should remove it. "Is that what you want? To be friends?" I asked, feeling tears start to form at the corners of my eyes. "How you want us to proceed is up to you," he replied.

"I'm asking you straight up. Can you see me as your girlfriend in the future? I'm not talking about in a month or two— I'm saying in the long-term. I want to make sure our connection is progressing, and we're not stuck in the same spot." I asked every clarifying question, leaving no uncertainties that I would agonize over later. "I can't see myself being the boyfriend you want me to be in the foreseeable future. I'm just too busy with work," he explained. "You're a bit younger, and you should live your life without having to wait around for me. It's unfair to hold you back." I wanted Wyatt, but he wanted out. I was willing to wait for him to be ready for a relationship. I was willing to try to make things work, to grow together. He gave up on us.

"I'm independent. I'm not a needy girl," I said, hoping that he'd come around. "I understand you're busy." I could be patient with him as he figured out how to budget his time better. He didn't even want to try. "We're both busy people," he replied, staying true to his initial argument. "You're better at managing your time than me."

I thought I wanted a serious committment, but Wyatt made me reassess. I really liked him, so I considered meeting him where he was at and just casually dating. Maybe doing so would take some of the pressure off? I wouldn't need to hold my breath waiting for his texts, and I could see him while also seeing other people. On some level, though, the thought of dating multiple people at once made me feel sleazy.

"I don't know what to do. I only have eyes for you right now," I said. He no longer desired a meaningful connection, and I wondered what changed. "I wanted a girlfriend at first," he started. "But the past few weeks proved that work is my priority right now." I was confused. He said previously that he would be jealous if I collaborated with male TikTokers in Miami—but now, he was not looking to gatekeep? He wasn't a bad guy, but it was a bit of a bait and switch. I was led on, and that was unfair.

Wyatt's declaration that he was not ready for a relationship hurt because I saw potential for us. I longed to be his girlfriend. "I want so badly to be mad at you right now, but I just can't," I said. I sought to reclaim control over the situation by being angry with him—but it was impossible. I buried my head in his chest as he rubbed my back. I hated how desperate I looked clinging to him. Even as he was crushing my heart, I still felt as comfortable in his embrace as I always did.

"Here," Wyatt said, offering his arm for me to hold as we started walking down the sidewalk. "Thank you for understanding and being so open. I was nervous to talk to you." I clutched his hand as we rushed to make the stoplight. "It's me. You never have to be nervous to talk to me," I assured him. Still, I wondered: was he thinking about how he was going to hurt me the whole dinner? I knew Wyatt wasn't himself, and my intuition was correct. I told him how much I wanted to talk to him too and how confused I was over the past few weeks. "I'm sorry. I feel like I disrespected you by ghosting," he said. "I know I went two or three days without texting you." He was right—I was left in the dark, wondering where he was and how he was feeling. "Yeah, you're probably the worst texter ever," I rolled my eyes.

Wyatt apologized for "dropping the bomb," and I assured him that he didn't. Sure, I previously believed I was going to become his girlfriend. But after Florida, I knew a difficult conversation was coming and was grateful for the clarity. I was glad he spoke up before I was strung along further towards something that wasn't an option on his end: a formal relationship. If I stepped outside of myself, I'd observe that I was in good spirits. I was hiding my pain and disappointment. Even though I anticipated our chat, it still hurt. We went on over ten dates, so naturally, I was attached. "Where do we go from here?" I asked. I wanted to make sure I had the story straight. "We can be whatever you want us to be," he said. But we couldn't be what I wanted us to be: boyfriend and girlfriend. He gave me a choice between friends or friends with benefits.

## Swipe Left:

### WHAT IF I LIKE HIM MORE THAN HE LIKES ME?

You had a great first few dates—but he keeps flaking on your next plan. You tell him how handsome he looks—but he never compliments you in return. Although you shouldn't seek validation in the eyes of your companion, if you're giving more to the relationship than he is, take a pause.

You shouldn't have to fight for his attention—he should put in the work as well. If you're always the first to confess your feelings, or you're constantly initiating plans, the effort is one-sided. If he's unable to reciprocate, who knows if he ever will? Addressing those concerns as early as possible will prevent future heartbreak.

It hurts to want someone who doesn't want you back. Don't fight to make him stay if you sense he's not feeling it. If he wants to go, let him go. No need to force the connection if it's clear his heart isn't in it. Moving on will eliminate any pressure to make him like you. If he's really into you, he'll make it known without you having to beg.

To avoid an indecisive match, search for someone whose personality syncs with yours—think of it like filling in a missing puzzle piece. The conversation should be easy and effortless. If you two really have a connection, you never run out of things to talk about (extra credit if he makes you laugh). You deserve to feel chosen. Someone should look you in the eye and tell you with absolute certainty that he wants to be with you.

Once we reached my apartment, we said goodbye as usual. He pulled me in for our last kiss of the night. Something inside me knew it would be our last forever. I wrapped my arms around him, and he held me in an embrace for a whole minute. Wyatt left the ball in my court, and I had no idea what to do. I'm usually someone who makes decisions in the moment, but I had a lot to think about. I thought his clarification would relieve my anxiety, yet it left me even more stressed and conflicted. When I got home from my date, I sat in solitude and processed my emotions. I self-criticized for being dramatic. Wyatt and I weren't in a committed relationship, but I was broken. I felt my heart physically sinking in my chest.

I headed to the bathroom to shower, and the scent of mouth rinse over the sink triggered me. It was the one I used before every date with him. As I walked into my bedroom, I glanced over at my leather dress taunting me from the closet. I couldn't use the perfume I sprayed on to see Wyatt without thinking of him (it's crazy how a scent can take you back in time). I wore the boots I sported on our date the evening after, but all I could think about was how he walked all over my heart. Every couple I passed on the street reminded me of what could've been. For days, I couldn't escape my emotions. There were so many things I set out to do with Wyatt that we never got around to. We were going to visit the Planetarium. We planned to scale a skyscraper at Hudson Yards. There was so much more of the city to explore together. All of our future plans suddenly became fantasies.

I began to regret opening my heart to him. He knew so much about me. Was I supposed to just reteach everything to the next guy? Not to mention, I swooned over him and showed pictures of us to all my friends. I didn't know how to explain to everyone that our connection would never amount to anything. I could have continued hanging out with Wyatt, but with the reality that he didn't see me as I saw him. That he didn't see *us* in the same way I did. I remembered the *Legally Blonde* scene in which Warner dumps Elle. Like Elle, I was emotionally invested in a relationship and blindsided by a guy who wasn't on the same page. Wyatt and I didn't exactly have the "what are we" talk my friends warned me about. It was more of a "what are we not" conversation. In his mind, we were not boyfriend and girlfriend. A casual fling was all I'd ever be to him. It took time to realize that our descent had nothing to do with me. He really was busy with work. He may have also been hung up on his past relationship and not ready to move into another serious connection.

If it weren't Wyatt, it would've been easy to dump him, to say I didn't deserve to be treated as a mere body in a bed. But he was special to me, so I was reluctant to call things off. My strong feelings for him complicated everything. At first, I thought I could handle keeping things casual. I cared about Wyatt. I wanted to keep kissing him, to remain in his arms. My friend Sonya gave me a wake-up call. I was confident in my ability to casually date when she asked me a simple question: "Carrie, what are you doing?" I began to sob. I realized that I was losing myself by trying to keep Wyatt in my life. Forcing myself to believe in a casual fling was just a desperate attempt to hold onto him. I'd always secretly hope he'd ask me to be his girlfriend, and he was never going to give me what I wanted. He'd never become the loyal boyfriend I wished he would be.

It was time to take my power back. I came to a sudden, difficult conclusion: I had to make a decision for myself. It would hurt too much to date him knowing he didn't see me as anything more than a friend with benefits. Every time I kissed him, I would be reminded of a painful reality: he would continue to use me as a hookup while I waited for him to see me as a girlfriend. In his eyes, the kiss would be meaningless—he would feel nothing. Continuing to spend time with him would force me to feel the sting of rejection over and over again. I didn't deserve to feel that way every time I was around him. If we kept hooking up, my feelings would continue to grow. A part of me would always want something more than just a casual connection. I couldn't pretend I didn't feel anything for Wyatt because I did. My feelings were there, and they were valid. They weren't just going to go away. Letting go of him isn't what I wanted, but what I needed to do. I had to be truthful to myself and my feelings. It hurt a lot, but sometimes, doing what's best for you can be painful.

I waited a few days to tell him my decision on a phone call. I was emotionally exhausted. "Every time I'm with you, I would be lying to myself in saying I don't feel anything," I explained. "Just like saying you don't want a relationship is what you had to do for you, this is what I have to do for me." He was apologetic. "The last thing I wanted to do was hurt you," he said. We agreed to stay friends and keep each other updated on our lives. "I like you as a person, and if you ever want to grab a bite, I'd be down!" he asserted. "Or if that's too weird for you, I understand." Perhaps I would be interested down the road, but at that moment, I was still processing. He was more confident about staying friendly than I was. It was odd to consider hanging out with him as a friend when my feelings were still strong. The call was under ten minutes long. He thanked me once again for being "so cool about everything" before we wrapped up the conversation. "Bye, Carrie," he said. Hearing Wyatt say my name still made me feel close to him.

It took a while to recover from our sudden distance. In the immediate aftermath of the breakup, I did a lot of writing to help myself make sense of it all. Writing about Wyatt fictionalized him. I didn't realize that I was detaching myself from living through the narrative. By turning a person into mere paper, reality seemed less real, therefore less difficult to deal with. The second I stopped writing, the breakup became tangible, and all my emotions came rushing.

The same month I called it quits with Wyatt, my friend got herself a boyfriend, just two weeks after she started dating the guy. While I was agonizing over the label in my own relationship, it came easily to her. I told her I was happy for her (and I was), but her happiness was tearing me apart inside. I was jealous. What did I do wrong? To make myself feel better, I tried to convince myself that their relationship would never work. I knew it wasn't fair to resent her. I wanted to be a supportive friend. But it hurt to hear her talk about her man, especially since I had just broken up with mine. The reality was—as she dished about her relationship—I had never felt more alone. I depended on Wyatt to hold me and make me feel special, and now that responsibility was left to me. I wasn't used to having to live off my own supply of love. I relied on him for validation when I felt most insecure. That validation actually needed to come from within.

I still allowed myself to miss him. Memories raced back. Every time I saw his Instagram story, it hit me that I wasn't seeing him anymore. His name kept popping up in Siri's suggestions list to text. I also saw an article reporting that the place where we went on our s'mores date was closing. I forwarded him the link. "Aw, we should grab s'mores there before they close!" he replied. I couldn't do it. If we were to go out, a repeat of our s'mores evening would never just be "friendly."

It was unfair that he waited after two months of dating to tell me he didn't want a relationship. He claimed that he loved being with me, but he didn't want to assume the responsibility of commitment. He was scared to settle. He didn't necessarily waste my time—I loved being with him as well. He wasted the exertion of my heart. Wyatt may not have told me what I wanted to hear, but at least I got closure. I knew I made a smart decision. Seeing him without the potential for a relationship was too difficult to handle.

I want a partner who prioritizes me and doesn't see squeezing me into his schedule as a chore. I want someone who chooses me—and not just when it's convenient for him. At my age, finding someone like that is rare. Perhaps I never really liked Wyatt—I liked the idea of him being the "perfect" boyfriend— that is, before he shattered my expectations. I've learned that there is no perfect partner or relationship—nor do *you* need to be perfect. If I tempered my expectations from the start, I would have guarded my heart. Instead, I convinced myself that Wyatt was going to be my boyfriend and that I just had to wait while he figured out the right time to make us official.

Love will come when you least expect it. It's not something that needs to be forced. If you're persuading your partner to stay committed (for instance, my final plea by paying our dinner bill), he's not worth your time. This truth is frustrating, disappointing, and downright painful—trust me, I know. Love takes a lot of patience. Let the person come to you. Love will manifest when you sit back and let the universe do its work. Wyatt never actually allowed me to fall in love with him, which buffered a bit of the pain when we stopped seeing each other. His lack of affection made it difficult to see myself falling.

After Wyatt and I called things off, I wondered if he was relieved he didn't have to text me every day anymore. I figured he felt less distracted from work now that I was gone. I started swiping through a dating app a week later in an attempt to boost my confidence, but it felt like I was moving on too soon. "What if I never find my person?" I cried to my mom. "You will," she assured me. "You have too big a heart not to." ♥

# Chapter 14

# The Journey to Self-Love

*Trigger warning: self-harm/anxiety/OCD*

OVER QUARANTINE, I WATCHED A ton of rom-coms. Seeing Kat and Patrick fall for each other in *10 Things I Hate About You* and Lara Jean and Peter beat the odds in *To All the Boys: Always and Forever* gave me hope when life as we knew it came to a screeching halt. I have faith in finding a picture-perfect romance, even when things are dull, and hope seems lost. Throughout the pandemic, my life was frozen and fractured. I had no choice but to look inwards. Self-love had to be enough—but that was easier said than done.

In October 2020, I stared blankly at the ceiling of my bedroom. My heart leaped out of my chest, beating out of control as it struggled to find its way back home. My mind raced in circles. It seemed impossible to find peace as intrusive thoughts entered my brain. It felt like there were two voices in my head: one telling me to believe things would get better and the other saying there was no way out. After a brief second of hope, a single tear streamed down my cheek. My body went numb, and I once again found myself staring at the ceiling.

On the outside, I may seem like the girl who has it all: a loving family, a group of loyal friends, a strong career, and millions of fans on social media. A conversation with my neighbor about my eighteenth birthday present reverberates. She asked my mom, "What to buy for the girl who has everything?" I began to question her words. I'm very fortunate for the opportunities I've been given, but without inner happiness, my luck means nothing.

At the beginning of 2020, I was on cloud nine. I lived in Los Angeles for a month, attended New York Fashion Week, and kissed a boy I was crushing on. But then the pandemic hit. For a while, I was coping surprisingly well. I made the temporary move from NYC to the Hamptons, and I was enjoying the alone time to write, film videos, and work on my fitness regimen. However, in August, something inside of me turned for the worse, and it was a sensation relatively difficult to explain. I was sitting on the couch with my nightly cup of cereal when suddenly, I couldn't catch my breath. It made no sense: I was watching an '80s rom-com with my mom…what could possibly be wrong? I asked my dad to take me for a COVID-19 test—it was negative. That's when my mom offered the idea that it may just be anxiety.

To me, anxiety was just another word for stress. I considered the butterfly sensation I feel when I'm cramming for a final exam or walking the red carpet at an event. I wasn't taught about mental health in school, so I struggled to understand what anxiety really meant. It felt completely different from pre-quiz jitters. My breathing was shallow, and I struggled to find my footing because I felt faint. The anxiety began as solely physical symptoms. I'd wake up feeling fragile, my hands trembling underneath the covers. One time, I was so shaky in the morning that my breakfast fell out of my hand. An afternoon run helped me regain control over my body. I never knew anxiety could manifest itself mentally as well—until an unexpected revelation from a friend at a farmer's market. She had been struggling with anxiety and depression to the point where she cut herself. I wanted to be there to offer support. But when I caught a glimpse of the scars on her wrist, the world froze. I wondered, "Is this what happens to people with anxiety?"

From that evening on, I had occasional bursts of intrusive thoughts. My brain would place terrifying messages in my mind that would force me to question myself: If she has anxiety, and I have anxiety, what makes us different? Am I going to wind up hurting myself too? It wasn't until winter break that these thoughts became more of a preoccupation. I obsessed over them, questioning why they were there, if they were real, and why they wouldn't go away. I felt numb. The fear of what I was capable of penetrated through me. It was as if I had an illness I couldn't shake. Although I wasn't physically sick, it felt like my brain was infected and in need of healing. None of it made sense: I have a wonderful life filled with people I love who love me back. I didn't want to hurt myself, so why would my brain obsess?

The confusion was frustrating. A constant track ran in my mind where I tried to rationalize my way out of the situation. When I was most afraid, I retreated to an escape thought: "Life is great. Your family and friends love you." But my thoughts felt so real—logic wasn't enough to satiate my OCD. Most days, it felt like there was a hole inside my head that I couldn't crawl out of. Friends and family tried to talk to me, but it was as if I weren't really there. My surroundings were blurry. I was stuck inside my brain, detached from the world around me. I did whatever I could to make myself feel more "alive." I created dozens of TikTok drafts, took up cooking and board games, and watched more Marvel movies than I could count. Nothing was completely effective. I felt like a robot, methodically going about my day. I forced myself to move forward. Some days, just existing had to be enough.

I was uncomfortable being alone with my thoughts, so I attached to my family, who continually reassured me that everything would be okay. I cuddled with my mom in bed and cried into my dad's shoulder every day. "My brain is loud," I'd say to describe the intensity of my anxiety. I expressed how my mind felt like it was "on fire." No matter how much my parents reassured me, nothing stuck. Telling me things would get better was like filling a cup with a hole in it. I couldn't find faith—there was only fear.

I attempted to seek joy, love life, and stop beating myself up over my intrusive thoughts. I made myself live in the moment, no matter how difficult it was to do so. I had a few brief bursts of pleasure: a shopping spree, a sledding adventure, or an evening at the Met Museum with my best friend. I tried my best to find courage even when nothing inside my head made sense. But each experience was followed by an overwhelming wash of emotions. I suddenly remembered all the anxiety I faced, as if my brain were making sure I didn't forget it was there. It was like I forgot how to be happy.

Sometimes, it felt like I didn't know who I was anymore. I looked back at images of me from the past, skipping the line at Disney World and scooping up free makeup samples at Beautycon, and I didn't recognize myself. I've always had poor memory, so as the pandemic progressed, I started to feel detached from the past. Anxiety and intrusive thoughts became my new normal, and that was not the life I wanted to be living. I wanted to be exploring the world, embarking on a search for true love and discovering my path—all with my mind clear and at peace. More than anything, I wanted to return to my pre-pandemic self: the girl who fell in love, traveled the country, and filmed a scripted TV series in Hollywood, all in just a few short months. The eighteen-year-old adult body I was living in felt strange and unfamiliar. I was searching for a glimmer of hope, a sign, or a reminder that I was still the same girl I was the year before.

Because of the stigma surrounding mental health, it was hard to bring myself to ask for help. But once I started therapy, I began to understand what I was experiencing. I was diagnosed with generalized anxiety and obsessive-compulsive disorder (OCD), and all the pieces fell into place. When I was eight years old, I practiced physical compulsions: everything needed to be even on my right and left sides, or my brain wouldn't be at peace. The habit faded over time, and I never put much thought into what it meant. Ten years later, my OCD resurfaced in a new manner, and I had to face my demons. My therapist told me that the disorder places unwanted thoughts in my brain. OCD is not just physical compulsions—think excessive cleaning, washing your hands repeatedly, or organizing your kitchen. My OCD was obsessing over disturbing thoughts. I practiced mental compulsions by telling myself why the scary words and images I envisioned didn't pertain to me. It was like there was a piece of gum stuck to the back of my head that I couldn't pull out. I was attached to my compulsions and struggled to escape from them.

Learning more about OCD gave me a sense of comfort. It helped me realize there was nothing wrong with me. I wasn't the only one feeling this way, even though it often felt like it. My therapist taught me several coping mechanisms. First, she explained that I needed to separate thought from feeling in my brain. The intrusive thought existed independently of my fear and sadness. Visualization is also key. She encouraged me to imagine walking my thoughts to a chair sitting at the back of my brain, or to watch them floating away on a cloud. Fighting the anxiety just made me feel more trapped. I needed to let my thoughts flow freely because that's all they were—thoughts. The more attention I gave them, the stickier they'd be.

My mental health was tested several times during the pandemic. One day, I received thousands of hate messages in response to a TikTok questioning my character. I'd been bullied before, so hearing people call me a "clown" was nothing. But I never dealt with that type of mass negativity while trying to work through my anxiety. I received death threats on Instagram, with young children and even mothers typing out "die, die, die," in my DMs. Sure, I could zoom out and see how vicious their words were, but my OCD made me preoccupied by them. My eyes were glued to the phone, as I considered if the strangers' words held any truth. I was scared, silenced, saddened, and constantly submerged in my thoughts.

Anxiety is a series of peaks and valleys. One day, I'll have just a few moments with my intrusive thoughts. The next, I'll be distracted and unfocused every hour, internally shouting at my anxiety to "go away." The turning point in my battle against anxiety was realizing that it wasn't going to go away. It never will. Now that I've faced my fears head on, there's no forgetting what I've gone through. The difference is now I have the tools to tackle my anxiety when it arises. Some days will be better than others, but I now know that joy is still possible. My happiness may have been temporarily lost, but it was never destroyed.

Anxiety and self-love go hand in hand. After working to understand OCD, I've emerged a stronger, wiser, more compassionate person. I now prioritize personal growth and mental health above all else. I've proven my power to myself (by writing this book!), and I listen to my heart when I need to take a breather. Only you can control your emotions. Sure, my parents and therapist were a great rallying squad, but I needed to be my own cheerleader. I've come a long way since that day I sat shaking on my bed. At first, I wasn't able to vocalize what I was experiencing or even say the frightening words flooding my brain aloud. I thought I was alone in my struggles, but I now realize that everyone is going through something. We don't need to admit we're struggling to be heard.

I'm still a work in progress. Intrusive thoughts pop up occasionally, and physical compulsions linger as well. I'll obsess over emails and DMs to make sure I didn't miss anything, and I'll spend hours deleting every single piece of B-roll from my phone once it's edited. OCD is something I'm just going to have to live with. I'm still developing coping skills, but I've grown a lot. I'm proud of how far I've come.

You may be wondering why I'm choosing to end this book by talking about myself, not boys. It may sound corny, but loving others is not possible unless you love yourself. All those months in quarantine, I prayed that the sixteen-year-old hopeless romantic was still inside of me. But that sixteen-year-old is in the past. That sixteen-year-old depended on a boy to make her feel special when in reality, the ability was inside her all along. Self-love is essential. It means something different to everyone, but to me, it ties in closely with my anxiety journey. Self-love means practicing patience and empathy with myself. It means believing in my inner strength yet showing myself grace if I need to let out a good cry. Most importantly, it means embracing my flaws with my whole heart instead of with hatred. My anxiety made me hate myself and my life. I didn't know how to get myself out of bed in the morning. I didn't want to. The sun was shining, but all I saw was the darkness of my thoughts. I looked at the sky and prayed for motivation. I was looking outwards for help when I really should have been looking inwards. The second I acknowledged my anxiety and took active steps to understand it, I began to see my life in a positive, more empowering light. I began to fight for myself.

Now that I've battled anxiety head on, I have a greater capacity to love. I started holding my own hand when I was hurting, not relying on others for validation. I learned how to go through my emotions, not push them away. I was honest with myself about my OCD, so I can be transparent about my needs in a relationship. Life isn't perfect, and that includes dating—it isn't fair to set such a high standard. Most importantly, if I were insecure in my own skin, it would be impossible to understand and accept love from others. Once I became stronger, I found that self-love was the key to loving someone else. I'm always skeptical when a guy calls me beautiful. Is he being truthful or just telling me what I want to hear, so he can get something from me? Answering that question starts with believing you're beautiful. Look in the mirror and say it—scream it. The way you talk to yourself is so important. If you don't see your own beauty, then how will anyone else?

I've gotten increasingly confident in dating guys—and that's because I know myself and my worth. As you begin your own journey to find love, I encourage you to first look within. A confident heart is far more attractive than the boy waiting for you. Believe me—your leading man is out there. Prepare to write your own rom-com. This is your story. Never give up on love. Chase your happy ending—until the credits roll. ♥

# Acknowledgments

THIS BOOK HAS BEEN YEARS in the making, and I couldn't have done it without the love and support of some of the most special people in my life.

First off, Mom and Dad. I am nothing without you. You have always been my biggest cheerleaders, and I am so grateful for your endless support. Thank you for lifting me up, providing a shoulder to cry on, and giving me the wings to fly.

The Berk, Kahn, and Saperstone families—I love you beyond measure. A special shoutout to Gram Bobbi and Uncle Charles: you held me when I was hurting. You helped pick up the pieces when I didn't have the strength to. You both mean the world to me.

I'd also like to thank my five best friends (who will still remain anonymous): J, S, L, S, M...you embody what it means to be amazing friends. You are the kindhearted, supportive besties I always dreamed of having in middle school but never had. I am beyond grateful for you.

Next, I'd like to shout out my superstar cover shoot team. Nigel Barker, you are truly a blessing—thank you for bringing my vision to life. Thank you to my uber-talented glam team—Zoe Davis and Maria Cumella—and male models Harry Cooper, Marc Plaskett, Jeremiah Onyango, Grant Sower and Trystan Edwards. To Daniela Hritcu: I am so grateful for your creativity and dedication to designing the book.

To my book agent, Katherine Latshaw, and the editors and publishers at Post Hill Press, Debra Englander, Ashlyn Inman,

Heather King, Anthony Ziccardi, and Sara Stickney. Thank you for believing in me from the very beginning. This book wouldn't have been possible without you. Also, thank you to my hard-working PR team: Emi Battaglia, Rosanne Romanello, and Mindie Barnett.

Lastly, to all of you. Thank you for reading. In my worst moments, I held onto faith that *My Real-Life Rom-Com* would one day find its way into the homes of thousands. I turned my pain into art because I hoped my words could possibly inspire others. What started off as a passion project is now my solo debut book. Someone pinch me—it feels like I'm living a fever dream right now. All I can say is thank you.

## About the Author

TWENTY-YEAR-OLD **CARRIE BERK** ALREADY HAS a life's worth of accomplishments under her belt. It's no wonder *Bella Magazine* declared her "an ambitious and dedicated boss babe," and *The Wall Street Journal* dubbed her "a community-minded young creator."

She is a verified content creator across several social media channels including TikTok (3.9M+ followers; 117M+ likes), Instagram (950K+ followers), Snapchat (105K+followers), YouTube (100K+ followers) and Pinterest (227K+ followers; 10M monthly views), with a monthly engagement of more than 100M.

A journalism major in college, Carrie is currently a reporter/contributing writer for HuffPost, Newsweek.com, The Daily Dot, The *New York Post*, and others, on topics ranging from beauty and style to celebrity and sports. She has served as an on-camera correspondent for *TigerBeat* and *Girls' Life*, covering red carpet arrivals and interviewing celebs at the Radio Disney Music Awards, New York Fashion Week, and the Teen Choice Awards. She has contributed to *Seventeen Magazine* and *Girls' Life's* print and digital channels.

She has acted on two Brat TV series, *Stage Fright* (as Karina) and *Crown Lake* (as the voice of Heather).

She is a bestselling children's book author with twenty-one books to her credit. She penned her first book, *Peace, Love and Cupcakes*, in 2012. *The Cupcake Club* series went on to publish twelve books (selling 300,000+ copies worldwide), and became an award-winning Off-Broadway show and featured selection in 2017's New York Musical Festival. Her second book, *Fashion Academy*, stems from her passion for fashion. The six-book series also became an Off-Broadway production at Vital Theatre and is currently licensed worldwide by Concord Music Publishing.

Finally *Ask Emma* (a three-book series for Bonnier) was based on Carrie's firsthand experience as a teen blogger and her dedication to being a role model for positive posting. She is a dedicated anti-bullying activist and an advocate for mental health awareness, especially for teens and women.

An avid runner, she ran the New York City Marathon in November, 2022.